D0551028

Rough Guide Credits

Text editors: Jennifer Dempsey, Orla Duane & Peter Shapiro
Series editor: Mark Ellingham
Typesetting: Helen Ostick

Publishing Information

This first edition published June 1999 by
Rough Guides Ltd, 62–70 Shorts Gardens, London, WC2H 9AB

Distributed by the Penguin Group:

Penguin Books Ltd, 27 Wrights Lane, London W8 5TZ
Penguin Books USA Inc., 375 Hudson Street, New York 10014, USA
Penguin Books Australia Ltd, 487 Maroondah Highway,
PO Box 257, Ringwood, Victoria 3134, Australia
Penguin Books Canada Ltd, 10 Alcorn Avenue,
Toronto, Ontario, Canada M4V 1E4
Penguin Books (NZ) Ltd, 182–190 Wairau Road,
Auckland 10, New Zealand

Typeset in Bembo and Helvetica to an original design by Henry Iles.
Printed in Spain by Graphy Cems.

Pictures on pp. 49, 97, 105, 108, 143, 199, 236,
240, 250, 299 & 368 © **Alexis Maryon**
Pictures on pp. 9, 63, 70, 157, 182, 196, 230, 356, 359 & 379 © **Tina Paul**
Pictures on pp. 2, 22, 35, 166, 177, 270 & 305 © **Ronnie Randall**

A catalogue record for this book is available from the British Library.
ISBN 1-85828-432-5

House

THE ROUGH GUIDE

by Sean Bidder

with pictures by

Alexis Maryon, Tina Paul and Ronnie Randall

with additional contributions by

Andrew Burgess, Jim Byers, Johnny Davis
Louise Gray, Ben Harrington, Dan Harrington,
Barnaby Harsent, Pete Lawrence Tamara Palmer,
Peter Shapiro, Chris Sodring, Iain Watt, Kieran Wyatt

Contents

Introduction

From its roots in Chicago and New York clubs, House triggered the biggest musical revolution in the UK since punk, and subsequently spawned a welter of electronic genres that have altered the face of modern music and popular culture. *The Rough Guide to House* traces the route that this propulsive strain of dance music has taken, while pointing towards the elements that may shape its future direction. Presented in an encyclopedic format, *The Rough Guide to House* covers both the innovators and crucial exponents of House – whether they be producers, DJs, bands or record labels.

So what exactly is House? Originally (some would argue it still is) a mutation of disco, House can be widely defined as electronic music with a rhythm set in a 4/4 tempo. While this definition neatly distinguishes House from the abstractions of Techno and the breakbeat foundations of Trip-Hop and drum 'n' bass, it fails to acknowledge the genre's most compelling attribute: its fundamental ability to inspire by bonding emotive, synthesised melodies to locked rhythms. It's this marriage of melody and groove which has formed perhaps the most exciting dancefloor proposition since the birth of disco itself.

House music's roots reside in the hedonistic gay club scene of mid-'70s New York. Manhattan-based DJs such as Walter Gibbons and Larry Levan provided the initial platform for disco to mutate into House by extending and recreating singles from disco labels like Salsoul, Prelude and West End to construct repetitive, hypnotic mantras built to fire up the dancers at clubs like The Paradise Garage (the club which would give House's R&B-soaked cousin its name, garage).

But House music was truly developed in Chicago, initially as a result of Brooklyn-born DJ Frankie Knuckles' residency at the city's Warehouse club in 1977. Like the DJs in New York, he began to alter the raw material of the music he spun at the club by adding pre-pro-grammed drum rhythms from his Roland 909 to the mix to keep the groove constant, thus forming the blueprint for the 4/4 tempo of House, whose name derived from that of his club.

By the early to mid-'80s elemental cuts by Knuckles' disciples, Jamie Principle and Jesse Saunders, began to distinguish themselves from disco with a sound characterised by its raw synthesised energy and simple, skeletal drum patterns. By the mid-'80s Knuckles and another deck virtuoso, DJ Ron Hardy, had influenced a core of talent-ed young kids who seized upon the relatively cheap and easy-to-mas-ter range of synthesizers, samplers and drum machines to create their own sonic inventions. Marshall Jefferson, Larry Heard, Adonis, DJ Pierre and Steve "Silk" Hurley created the blueprint for Acid House and Deep House with singles released by Chicago's two main inde-pendent labels, Trax and DJ International.

Mainstream America was never likely to accept music born from black, gay disco, though, and it was a youth culture bored to death by the materialist aesthetic of the Thatcher era in Britain which catal-ysed the Acid House explosion. Oh yeah, there was also a little some-thing called Ecstasy, but club music and drug consumption have almost always gone hand-in-hand. Pioneered in the UK by DJs such as Paul Oakenfold, Danny Rampling and Mike Pickering, British tech-nicians like A Guy Called Gerald, Baby Ford and Bang The Party emerged to stamp their own style on the genre and irreversibly set in motion House music's domination of British dancefloors. It's a combi-nation of all these factors that led to House's mainstream acceptance and subsequent diversification.

But this is only an outline of the music's history. There's no room here to detail the further importance of New York and Chicago, of Ibiza, Manchester, London, Italy and Paris, of the countless other producers/DJs whose contributions have been pivotal. Instead, that's all broken down into individual entries and detailed inside, providing a comprehensive, but by no means detached, guide to House music.

Thanks goes first to all the writers who pencilled entries for *The Rough Guide to House* and to those who imparted information, photographs and time. A special thanks to the following: Vince Lawrence, Ashley Beedle, Joe Clausell, Dimitri From Paris, Little Louie Vega, Kenny "Dope" Gonzalez, Glenn Underground, Crispin J. Glover, Dave Lee, Omid Nourizadeh, Charles Webster, Sally Jones and Steve Rodgers, Harvey, Kevin McKay, Abacus, Rob at Guidance, Billie and Dave at Nuphonic, JBO, Karen at Twisted, Rob at Pagan, Francesco at Irma, Isabel at Deconstruction, Simon and Richard at Reverb, Jennifer Dempsey, Nicky B, Miss K, Jo Lee, Chris Sodring, Jim Waite, Ben Harrington and Ted Cockle.

Sean Bidder

A Guy Called Gerald

Y ou couldn't possibly have written a better script for the story behind the defining vinyl moment in British Acid House. It's 1988, and Moss Side-born McDonald's worker Gerald Simpson, inspired by avant-garde fusionists Teo Macero, Holger Czukay and Detroit's Derrick May, produces his debut solo studio outing – the **Voodoo Ray** EP – on a simple sampler, a 303 bass synth and a rudimentary drum machine.

With its unmistakable Arabic wail and hypnotic stabbing groove the track immediately became a firm favourite with influential DJ Mike Pickering at the Hacienda. After dominating clubland in England for nearly twelve months since its initial pressing, Voodoo Ray soared to #12 in the UK charts, and the reserved technical genius from Manchester found himself hailed as the figurehead of British House music.

Simpson's musical career had begun in the early '80s, as a DJ, spinning electro and hip-hop around local youth clubs in Hulme. Later, he started jamming with friends Nicky Lovett (MC Tunes) and the Ruthless Rap Assassins, re-creating rap and early Chicago House tracks.

But despite the success of "Voodoo Ray" (the phrase sampled from a comedy record by Peter Cook), from almost day one Simpson's creative abilities were to be matched by a pattern of commercial exploitation which would eventually alter the course of his musical career. Simpson claims he sold the rights to "Voodoo Ray" to buy a second-hand drum machine for £200, and subsequently made no money at all from the single's sales. Quickly rushed back into the studio by Liverpool indie Rham Records to replicate the pattern across an album **Hot Lemonade** (1989) – the result of Simpson's being – suffered from under-production.

Undeterred, Simpson emerged as a central figure in the nascent "Madchester" dance scene, working with 808 State on their finest moment, "Pacific State" (1989), and remixing the Stone Roses' "Fool's Gold" (1989).

With "Voodoo Ray" pirated on both sides of the Atlantic (Voodoo Dolls' "Women Beat Their Men" in the US and EZE & Boy Wonders "Dexterous" in the UK), A Guy Called Gerald was signed to CBS. The next single, "Automanikk" (1989), was an uncompromising piece of complex minimalism and the ensuing album of the same name had little impact with an audience not yet ready for his futuristic, dark sounds.

After a year spent travelling the world and recording with his heroes Derrick May and Joe Smooth, Simpson returned geared up to record a second album for Sony. But **High Life Low Profile** (1990/91) didn't see the light of day and Simpson (turned on by the breakbeat/early Hardcore mechanics of New York duo Musto & Bones) had already decided to reach back to the basics of drum programming, subsequently releasing the landmark drum 'n' bass albums **28 Gun Bad Boy** (1992) and 1995's **Black Secret Technology**.

At the same time Simpson kept recording groovy garage and sparse dubs – like the well-received "Song For Everyman" and "When You Took My Life" (both 1994) – as Ricky Rouge. As the majors finally caught up with House music as a force to be reckoned with, "Voodoo Ray" was re-released in 1996. Credited only to the new singer, the unknown Lisa May, and accompanied by a host of remixes that did little to touch the original, the new release mysteriously omitted Simpson's name – he later reasoned this was due to the fact that his career had been so cursed after the success of "Voodoo Ray" first time around.

Ⓞ **"Voodoo Ray"**   Rham Records, 1988

The definitive British Acid House track. Available on **Classic House Volume 1** (Mastercuts, 1995) where it stands as the only UK-produced 12" alongside classics by Marshall Jefferson, Kevin Saunderson and Jamie Principle.

A Man Called Adam

Sally Rodgers and Steve Jones – A Man Called Adam – have been recording together since 1988 in a career that has seen them ever-evolving musically: growing from Acid Jazz disciples to the driving force behind one of UK House's most respected labels, Other Records. Their genre-defying take on dance music has consistently aimed to develop new sounds and intrigue their listeners; consequently for many they remain as vital now as they were when they first appeared on the club scene over ten years ago.

The two first met after Steve made a guest appearance with Sally's first band, Expresso Seven, a Latin jazz collective who were signed to CBS. After minimal success the band slimmed down to Sally and percussionist Paul Daley (later of Leftfield fame), changed their name to A Man Called Adam, and recruited Steve on a permanent basis. Although CBS offered them another deal on a jazz-based label, they turned the invitation down, instead opting to sign with the Acid Jazz label run by Gilles Peterson and Eddie Pillar, whose clubs they frequently played at.

In stark contrast to the majority of their label mates, AMCA's early releases reflected the changing nature of the late '80s club scene. Their first single, "APB" (1988), mixed percussive Latin jazz with wired samples, producing a vibrant sound. But the arrival of House music's urgent dancefloor aesthetic had become fully evident by the time of 1989's "Earthly Powers/Techno Powers" and "Amoeba/Musica De Amor" singles. Some fans have even heralded these cuts as the beginnings of jazz-House, but perhaps no one artist can lay claim to such an obvious fusion of styles.

They struck a note with Big Life Records regardless, and AMCA's first single for their new home was the moment their sound "all locked together", according to the group. A truly stunning song with an ambient wave-crashing intro driven into motion by a gorgeous piano refrain and Sally Rogers' searing vocals, "Barefoot In The Head" was destined for anthemic status. This became a reality after a live Ibiza performance as part of a Flying Records tour (filmed as a documentary shown on Channel 4, *A Short Film About Chilling*). The island's influence is still evident in both the group's music and their open-minded attitude.

Following several well-received EPs – including 1991's mood-altering **Chronic-Psionic Interface** EP – Paul Daley split to form Leftfield, and the band began recording their debut set. With the pressure on for chart success, endless rounds of post-production retakes resulted in the ultimately disappointing **The Apple** (1991).

Having struggled to find an understanding home for their range of jazz-House and ultra-chilled Down Tempo reflections, after a period of disillusionment Rodgers and Jones regrouped to form Other Records in 1993. At a time when the club scene was dominated by either the increasingly hard progressive House or trance, AMCA were doing what they always have done best; their own thing. Retaining their disco/jazz-funk sensibilities and Rodgers' reflective lyricism, Other's first releases, "I Am The Way" and "Love Come Down" (both 1993), sounded positively fresh compared to the laborious percussive sound of "progressive House".

After a year spent recording further singles as AMCA and Beach-flea, Sally and Steve began to play a significant role in shaping the future direction for a selection of London-based producers. While 1994 bore their second album, Beachflea's **What's That Smell?**, the pair had begun mix-swapping and collaborating with US innovators Ron Trent, Chez Damier and Ralphi Rosario and recruiting fresh talents like DJ D alongside the honed expertise of Chris Coco's Coco, Steel & Lovebomb collective. As Other Records grew apace, so did the London-centric disco/jazz-House scene they'd supported and played a role in developing. Reflecting this, in 1995 and 1996 the label showcased its emerging and established talents with the compilations **Planet Jazz 1 & 2**, whilst also compiling Heavenly Records' lauded compilation of largely unheard production teams including The Idjut Boys', **High In A Basement** (1996). The duo also collaborated with Black Market Records stalwart Roberto Mello to produce the excellent **Fear Of Flying** (1996).

By the time AMCA's **Duende** (1998) appeared, Other Records had released ten albums of dance music. Ranging in moods from the melancholy to the upbeat, the albums' diversity takes in Deep House ("Automatic/Sexomatic") and laid-back soul ("Would-

A Man Called Adam Duende

n't She") alongside what can only be described as Balearic ("Estelle" and "Easter Song").

⊙ **"Barefoot In The Head"**   Big Life Records,1990

One of 1990's best singles and the one which helped define the term Balearic.

◐ **Duende**   Other Records, 1998

Wonderful collection of Ibiza sunsets, oceanic deepness and simple soul. Spanning AMCA's output since 1993, this is an essential purchase.

Abacus

Austin Bascom (aka Abacus) has come to the attention of many a Deep House follower over the past five years with his combination of sleek, jazz-infused melodies and oceanic Techno. Originally brought up in London, Bascom moved to Toronto as a teenager, becoming submerged in the American dance scene during the late '80s; excited by the clubs playing a diverse fusion of disco, early House, jazz-funk and dub. Later in Detroit, Abacus began to produce his own material on some basic equipment. Anthony Pearson (Chez Damier) heard the results and was so impressed he licensed the EP to his Prescription imprint.

This first release was **The Relics** EP (1994). With its deep, hypnotic rhythms and soft, mesmerising keys it made for an amazing debut, with an uncompromising experimental edge that disregarded the trends of that year. A similar track appeared on the **Foot Therapy** EP (1995) containing the same blend of Deep House subtleties and busy Techno-influenced rhythms. In the same year, the **Brazilian Love Dance** EP (1995) highlighted Abacus's impressive and varied talent.

Since 1996 the majority of Abacus's music has appeared on the Chicago imprint Guidance. Sometimes using pseudonyms such as Charly Brown and A:xus, his consistent quality control has continued to impress; most notably, with the jazz-tinged **Earthly Pleasures** EP on the 83 West label, **The Abacus** EP on Derrick May's Fragile label and the rough Chi-town rhythms featured on the **Analog Trax 1** and 2 EPs. 1997's heavenly "When I Fall In Love" (from the **Analog Trax 2** EP) was a respectful cover of the Cole Porter standard featuring simple, swinging beats, classic distorted synth stabs and the enigmatic voice of Esthero's Bratticus. Its popularity led to a high-exposure release on the UK Incredible label a year later, featuring a number of varied mixes.

With an album's worth of new material due for release on Guidance, of "very musical, very Techno-based House music", and plans to take his music live, Abacus has become one of the most exciting new producers in underground dance music.

◑ Hi Fidelity House: Imprint One   Guidance, 1997

This compilation contains Abacus' emotive "Opinion Rated R", which sequences black radical sentiments over a wall of bass.

Adeva

Adeva by name and a diva by nature, Patricia Daniel exuded her Grace Jones-like aura of fierce attitude and feminine sexuality over the male-dominated world of House music in the late '80s. Born the daughter of a missionary mother and deacon father, Daniel grew up singing in her local New Jersey parish. But her remarkable talent soon marked her out and led to a role as director of the choir and vocal coach. Finding herself banned from local singing contests for winning too often, she progressed onto the burgeoning neighbourhood club scene in the mid-'80s, and hooked up with Mike Cameron of Smack Productions to record "In And Out Of My Life" (1988) for NYC indie Easy Street. Timed to perfection, the 12" was championed by DJ Tony Humphries, who took it upon himself to break it through his influential residency at New Jersey's all-powerful Zanzibar club. With her deep, rich, powerful voice and strong marketable appearance – Adeva is rarely pictured without her shades on – she was signed to Capitol Records in 1988.

The immediate results – "Respect", "Warning" and the excellent, piano-infused "Musical Freedom" (all 1989, all produced by Paul Simpson) – all entered the UK Top 40 (although this wasn't repeated in the

States) and made her the first commercial star in England of the "New Jersey Scene". Her excellent Smack-produced, self-titled debut album ensured an international club following, while Adeva took the show on the road, playing a memorable gig at London's Town And Country Club, and in the process proved that dance artists could sometimes provide the same stage presence as any rock band.

But the transition to a second and musically more varied album didn't work. Despite "Love or Lust" (1991) selling a respectable 200,000 units world-wide, it was a weaker proposition and she was dropped from her major label deal.

Since then, Adeva has rarely been able to find a suitable song-writing home to match either the consistency or the quality of her early releases. Greatest Hits packages appeared as prematurely as 1992 (**Hits**) and 1996 (**Ultimate Adeva**), and even though her next manager Victoria Carlotti-Henry hooked up a deal for Adeva to provide vox for Frankie Knuckles' follow-up to **Beyond The Mix** (1991), **Welcome To The Real World** (1995), this focused on smooth yet too often insipid ballads which failed to capitalise on her expansive vocal range.

1997's **New Direction** once again found her voice spread thinly over ten individual productions from D-Influence, K Klass, Joey Mustaphia and Gary Wilkinson.

⊙ Ultimate Adeva　　　　　　　　　　　　　　EMI, 1996

The best compilation of her early club hits, including "Respect", "Warning" and "It Should've Been Me".

Adonis

What function does a bass-line fulfill? Beyond the idea of some collective genetic memory of a distant tribal heritage, the dominance of bass and beat over melody and harmony is one of the perplexing wonders of the late twentieth century. Place James Brown at the centre, stripping soul to the variable basics of funk, and that constant revolving rumble, as audible in Ornette Coleman's **Free Jazz** (Atlantic) with Scott La Faro and Charlie Haden's heavy-shower soloing as in Dillinja's "Brutal Bass" (Metalheadz), seizes the feeling that these are the most distinctive aural mnemonics of our age. House music has its own central bass-lines: Phuture's Acid caverns; the social ascension of Ce Ce Rodgers' "Someday" and Joe Smooth's "Promised

Land"; Armand Van Helden's revamp of "Spin, Spin Sugar" and the London garage shoals that followed its funky tide. If one line is at the very apex of the bass-line, then it is Adonis' "No Way Back" (1986), that is acknowledged deep underground as one of the tracks that defines "us" as a generation spawned and inter-connected by the rattle of low frequencies.

Adonis Smith was born on the west side of Chicago in the early '60s. In a teenage band, vamping the approach of Earth, Wind & Fire, Adonis picked up the basics of bass, leading to a spell at the American Conservatory of Music in Chicago studying contemporary jazz. Jazz wasn't to be his route and the seminal encounter with Jesse Saunders' "On & On 117" that unites so many Chi-town heads drew him into the furious maze of beats at Ron Hardy's Music Box nights. That is the time "No Way Back" came about. Originally intended as part of a Trax double pack with Marshall Jefferson on the **Virgo** EP, label head Larry Sherman declined the idea, instead agreeing to a release on Jefferson's Other Side Records. The idea fell apart and "No Way Back" came as a solo release, back on Trax. It shifted over 120,000 units, defining the bass for a city. But there was a down side; Jefferson reports that Adonis constantly reminded of that one release, never really took his production work ethic seriously from then on, his new-found status as a local "star" becoming his focus.

However the 1987–1988 Acid House releases "Two the Max", "Cool & Dry", "Tom Tom" and "The Poke" (as The Endless Pokers) all display that memorable sense of bass-as-melody. When NY's Jive Records opened its Chicago office in 1989, Adonis was quickly brought aboard. The relationship never paid off with any great tracks. What remains more cheering is that the reworking of "No Way Back" by the wildfire of Basement Jaxx is a poignant reminder of the importance Adonis' bass-line has exerted upon dance music.

◉ **"No Way Back"**   Trax Records, 1986

Still sounds devastating after all these years. As influential as Phuture's "Acid Tracks". Available on **The House That Trax Built** (Trax/PRD, 1996).

◉ **Mad on Acid Volume One**   Trax Records, 1997

Contains the majority of Adonis' Acid House releases from the period 1987–1988.

Paul "Trouble" Anderson

With influences encompassing thirty years of black music stretching from Fela Kuti's African rhythms to Blaze's soulful house vision, DJ Paul "Trouble" Anderson's incendiary Saturday night mix-shows on London's Kiss FM have proved to be more than just the lifeblood of the capital's garage scene over the past ten years, they've been inspirational in the emergence of a legion of like-minded British producers.

A key figure on London's dance music scene since the mid-'70s, Anderson's considerable dexterity behind the decks helped make funk clubs like Crackers and Spats legendary. In the mid-'80s he brought his unique blend of disco, hip-hop and rare-groove to the burgeoning warehouse scene with his Trouble Funk sound system. Later, he became a regular fixture in the nascent rave scene, DJing at the seminal Sunrise and Back To The Future parties.

Unlike many of his contemporaries' though, Anderson hasn't really made the successful transition into the studio that he threatened to do with early productions of The Style Council's "High On Hope" and Leroy Burgess' "Barely Breaking Even". Despite remixing Nomad's 1991 British #2 single "Devotion" and Junior Reid's Jamaican #1 "One Blood", Anderson has only turned his hand to a small selection of remixes since including Blaze, The Pet Shop Boys, The Blow Monkeys, Soul II Soul, Thelma Houston and Byron Stingley.

While critics may point out that he hasn't really broken down any musical barriers since the late '80s and has continued to simply push the "pure" vocal and soul-inflected garage sound in preference to more radical trends, both his radio show and weekly Camden club night – The Loft – have played their part in enabling British producers like Phil Asher to move the music forward.

◉ Trouble On The Dancefloor   x: treme, 1998

Double-mix CD which perfectly sums up Trouble's DJing scope. While one contains a selection of his disco-era favourites, the other is an energised back-to-back garage blend featuring his mix of Byron Stingley's "Get Up".

Phil Asher

Since emerging from the shadows of his mentor, DJ Noel Watson, DJ/producer Phil Asher has been an instrumental figure in producing British 'soulful' House.

Having first DJd at Noel and Maurice Watson's seminal London club Delirium (one of the first venues to play House music in the UK), Asher's

studio career began with a number of remixes, including Adonte's
"Dreams" for Peter Harris' Kickin' imprint: the start of a relationship
which would later find Asher as the lone British producer on Harris' high-
profile garage label, Slip 'N' Slide. But the first track to gain any widespread club appeal was recorded for Tomato Records. Pascal Bongo
Massive's "Pere Conchon" (1991) – a huge percussion vs disco track –
became a favourite of both Danny Rampling and NYC's Junior Vasquez,
as it neatly captured the ruling tribal vibe of hedonistic dancefloors and
was subsequently licensed to Tribal America. Tomato also bore Asher's
punctuated **Ruff Disco** EP (as Nature Boy) and, though it folded soon
after, the "underground" success of such releases helped pave the way
for like-minded London record labels Nuphonic, U-Star and Other later
on in the '90s. At the same time, Asher's 12" release on Guerilla
Records, "Dub House Disco"(1992), captured that label's aesthetic and
became a major influence on many of the UK's new producers.

Asher's musical influences – Tito Puente, Stevie Wonder, Curtis
Mayfield, Ray Baretto, hip-hop, New York House – began to embellish
his more clearly jazz-inflected sound as he recorded well-rated singles
for Junior Boys Own, Strictly4Groovers and Basement 282. But he
really caught the buzz of the dancefloor again at his home from home,
Slip 'N' Slide. 1996's "Mama" – sampling heavily from The Intruders'
disco-era classic "I'll Always Be Your Mama" – fermented the beginnings of a blossoming relationship with studio engineer/keyboardist
"Duke" Luke McCarthy. Recording under the moniker Blak N Spanish,
the duo's 1996 tribute to Paul "Trouble" Anderson's weekly Loft
club, "Jazz Powa" – although far from radical – established Asher's
credentials as one of London's most accomplished mixing-desk technicians.

Since then, the duo have foregrounded their retro stylings on
releases such as 1997's Stan Getz-like "Peaks & Plateaus", the elec-

tro-disco grooves of "Whatever/Je Me Souviens" and 1998's mid-tempo chugging "A New Song/Here Come One" (as Electric Soul). A sure-fire sign of success, Asher and McCarthy have also become an in-demand remix duo, broadening out their blueprint across 12"s stretching from Bah Samba's piano-driven "Reach Inside" to the Brazilian rhythms of Smoke City's "Aguas De Marco – Joga Bossa".

⊙ **Restless Soul: "Mama"** Slip 'N' Slide,1996

The Intruders cut up in a '90s disco stylee.

◐ **Blak N Spanish: "Jazz Powa"** Slip 'N' Slide,1996

A fittingly uplifting jazz-House tribute to DJ Paul "Trouble" Anderson.

Azuli Records

One of the oldest UK independent dance labels on the block, Azuli Records have charted the path of British melodic House and garage more consistently than anyone else in the '90s, and provided a much-needed initial breeding ground for producers Booker T, Mount Rushmore (Chocolate Fudge) and Sensory Elements.

Based in the upstairs offices of Soho's Black Market record shop, Azuli's first batch of releases made an immediate impact, partly due to the fact that they came bedecked with New York telephone numbers and shrink-wrapped to give the impression of being imports. It was a clever marketing ploy which distinguished the label as "another great US imprint" to add to the roster. Azuli's first release, Chocolate Fudge's "In A Fantasy" (1991), set the precedent with its crisp, clean production and raw disco samples, and sounded like it could have been conceived in NYC rather than London. The trio of Baby Sean, Miles Morgan and Larry Dundas pushed the formula further with "What U Want" and "Locomotion" (1992) before becoming one of the hottest UK remix teams of the mid '90s as Mount Rushmore – later returning to Azuli with 1994's "Vibe That's Flowing" and 1996's "Fixation" cuts. Things reached a disco frenzy with the sample-ridden "Sensory Elements Volume 1" (1992), whose producers – Black Market shop workers Robert Mello and Zaki D – continued with a series of five excellent **Disco Elements** EPs from 1992 to 1997, welding snippets of West End, Prelude and even The Clash before releasing **Fear Of Flying** (1997) for Other Records.

London-born DJ/producer Booker T rose to notoriety with his sin-

gles as Underground Mass before hitting the payroll with a stream of big bucks remixes, collected together on his 1998 album **Booker – The Prize Collection**. West London collective KCC, which comprised ex-Bang The Party member Keith Franklyn alongside Colin McBean and Cisco Ferrera, also produced slices of home-grown garage "Groove Thing" and "Heaven" (1992–93).

Ironically, as a label that's always tried to showcase British talent, New York's mysterious Romanthony has been Azuli's most impressive and original asset. Picked up on one of Picconi's many early

Stateside trips in 1991, Romanthony debuted with "Now You Want Me" – a raw, bass-driven vocal track with cutting guitar that would set the standards for future releases by the enigmatic producer, culminating in the breathtaking **Romanworld** (1997).

Other American producers, remixers and vocalists including Lenny Fontana and Michael Paternostro (Tension), Satoshi Tomiee (Black Shells), Basement Boys (Jasper Street Company), Michael Watford and Frankie Knuckles also propelled the imprint into commercial and critical success, most effectively with single releases such as Andrea Mendez' UK Top 40 hit "Bring Me Love", Debbie Pender's "Movin On", Indo's "R U Sleeping" and Tension's glorious "It's A Place Called Heaven". Azuli's savvy in picking up a smattering of commercially viable Stateside House tracks was proved again in 1998, when David Morales' piano-charged summer club anthem "Needin' You" crashed into the UK club and pop charts.

But ultimately it's for pushing British-based acts that Azuli will be remembered. 1997 and 1998 witnessed a return to the UK underground with a batch of club belters from the new breed of London-centric "speed garage" dons. Hyped-up remixes from Tuff Jam (Spirits Of Life's "Music"), Industry Standard (Thelma Houston's "All Of That"), Dem2Dem (Madie Myles' "I've Been Waiting") and Banana Republic (Pepper Mache's "Into You") may have come at the point when the "underground garage scene" has well and truly gone overground, but it's Azuli who've played a major role in opening up such possibilities.

⊙ The Big Wheels of Azuli 1991–1995 Azuli, 1995

Reasonably complete compilation of the label's finest outings from its inception to the mid-'90s, including Disco Elements' fabulous "Running" and Andrea Mendez' "Bring Me Love" alongside more underground gems like "A Feeling" – Jasper Street Company's inspirational slice of garage.

Baby Ford

Coming first to prominence in the underground in 1988 via "Oochy Koochy (FU Baby Yeh Yeh)", the first of a series of extraordinarily varied and adept recordings, songwriter Peter Ford can be credited with introducing to Britain's early House music a much-needed sense of depth. Essentially an experimental House and Techno project, Baby Ford's output ranged from three-minute tone poems and songs to massive dancefloor instrumentals. Baby Ford has always been a solo act, although in the studio he was often joined by various producers and DJs, including Mark Moore, Colin Faver and Eon (aka Ian B) and singers Amy St Cyr and Claudia Fontaine, plus an early appearance by vocalist Sonique, who was to join S'Express before becoming a successful DJ several years later.

Ford moved to London in 1985; his first London work during 1985–86, the "Bite The Bullet" sessions, produced various songs, including early versions of "Change" and "Chikki Chikki Ahh Ahh", then known under its original name, "Disco Me To Ecstasy" (both would appear on later albums). The ecstasy in question had more to do with Barry White's soul music than drugs, although when the single was finally released, Rhythm King felt that a name-change might be sensible, given public concern over Ecstasy use. The record was banned by Radio 1 for mentioning the "E" word.

"Oochy Koochy", the track which would see Ford launched into the hub of London's Acid House scene, began life in late 1987. Working with a few 707 and 909 drum machine samples and an old Arpaxe synth, his idea was to make a dancefloor record which retained a level of abstraction. Ford used cheap MIDI technology to set up an acid track. The result was an instrumental so bass-heavy that its promo single blew out the speakers at Heaven. Ford was signed to Rhythm King at the insistence of their unofficial A&R man, DJ Mark Moore (whom he knew from clubs like the Mud Club, Opera House, Sacrosanct and Transatlantic). Five hundred copies of "Oochy" were released on promo in 1987; a more manicured version, the Konrad Cadet mix, formed its official release in early 1988. It immediately became a staple record of the new House clubs, reaching #1 in the dance charts, its dark insistence a template for the new music. It was followed by "Chikki Chikki Ah Ah" (1988), a more structured electronic disco pop song which, despite a mainstream radio ban, reached the UK Top 50, followed by a cover of T. Rex's "Children Of The Revolution", also a modest hit.

However, it was two albums, **Fordtrax** (1988) and **"OOO" The World of Baby Ford** (1989), which showed Baby Ford's reluctance to be confined to any format. Containing songs, in addition to slighter, thoughtful offerings such as "Poem For Wigan", an elegy for the old Casino, **Fordtrax** blazed the way for **"OOO"**, as well as subsequent releases. Ford tried out various changes of guest personnel (Sonique featured on the "Beach Bump" single, doing her tracks with a broken leg), but two singles later he started DJing, and in 1991 built the Ifach studio, working with Eon and Mark Broom (of Pure Plastic Records). In 1994, Ifach Records released their first 12", "Dead Eye" by Peter Ford and Eon under the name Ifach 001. Ford now runs three labels: Trelik (since 1995) and Pal SL (since 1996).

With the independent success of these labels on the Techno scene and a DJ career to nuture, Baby Ford went into temporary abeyance, with the artist recording as either Peter Ford or just P.Ford. Peter Ford's latest record is **Birds** (1998), a collaborative album with Berlin producers.

⊙ **Fordtrax**   Rhythm King Records, 1988

Simultaneously abrasive and delicate. Contains "Oochy", "Chikki" and gems such as "New York".

⊙ **"OOO" The World of Baby Ford**   Rhythm King Records, 1990

Songs, some with the big twelve-string guitar sound; released to coincide with live UK dates and a US tour supporting Erasure. Fuses House with **Young Americans**-era Bowie sensibilities.

Balihu

In 1995 two releases appeared on a little-publicised US label called Balihu: the **Look Ma No Drum Machine** and **Aphroasiatechnubian** EPs. Both 12"s contained an array of cut-ups and re-edits based upon rare and forgotten disco tracks from the '70s to early '80s. However, it wasn't until the release of **The Morning Kids** EP in 1996 that the talents of producer Daniel Wang were first noticed in the UK. Tracks such as "In A Golden Haze" and 'Free Lovin'' demonstrated how the music of this era could be appreciated, understood and then used effectively to produce modern dance music. In particular, "Free Lovin'" – sounding like a long-lost Salsoul dub of Double Exposure's "My Love Is Free" – caught the attention of many, and was later released on the British label Monkey Fruit.

Daniel Wang followed up with two further releases, **Chroma Oscura** EP and **The Probe, The Strobe** EP, which confirmed that the imprint was setting a high standard. Days (mis)spent hanging out in various New York-based studios, and a chance meeting with the Masters At Work team gave Wang the invaluable experience he required to experiment with his musical ideas and produce fresh, new sounds.

Early releases contained information-packed sleeves with his selected opinions on the current state of the dance scene, including comments such as: "I began making records out of both frustration and love: Frustration with today's disposable tracks with no musicianship, variation, or originality, and a love for the beautiful sounds of yesterday, which continue to bring us joy."

For many, Daniel Wang has done just that – produced innovative tracks with varied instrumentation, using the exotic live sound of xylophones, bongos and kalimbas, whilst steering clear of aimless jazz noodling. 1997 and 1998 releases such as the Georgio-styled "NYTK 1978 Mix" from his **Cristal Plastique** EP and the slow '80s soft beat of the vocoder-layered **Mood Mylar** EP have cemented his underground notoriety. But while his Balihu label releases have gained cult status on UK shores, the move to more widespread acclaim has already begun with the issue of his **Best of Balihu** (1998) compilation album.

⊙ **Best Of Balihu**   US Oxygen Music Works, 1998

The best place for beginners to check out what all the fuss is about. Features the majority of Wang's disco-charged releases.

Bang The Party

Formed in 1986, on the eve of the first House imports in the UK, BTP brought three Islington boys together in a union which, in one form or another, continued officially until 1997. Lawrence (Kid) Batchelor had spent his teens as a footballer, before being seduced into music. Leslie Lawrence, who was to show his production talents, was a music collector and Keith Franklin worked for British Rail.

The trio were well placed to observe the new developments in London's club scene. Batchelor became a member of Soul II Soul's crew, running Warehouse parties such as 80 Portland Street's monthlies, as well as more official ones on Sunday nights at the Africa Centre and Nor-

man Jay's Shake n' Fingerpop. Bang The Party began to explore ways of fusing their love of soul, disco and reggae to the rhythms of the nascent House scene. In 1987, Batchelor – by now contributing to the pirate Kiss FM station – joined printer Simon Gordon in his four-strong collective to organise Hedonism. One of the first unlicensed Acid House parties, Hedonism only ran for four nights, but it proved, alongside

Shoom, to be an inspirational affair which helped kick off the entire scene. Suitably inspired, BTP went into Harrow Road's Addis Ababa studio to record their first single, "Glad All Over" (1987). Primarily a reggae studio, its owner, Tony Addis, had helped give Soul II Soul their first break, and he also ran his own small independent label, Warriors Dance. The record created an immediate stir: it was spacious in its beat and held together with a masterful tension that would characterise the band's soulful atmospherics. The preparation of the sound was everything: heavy and dubby, it was also decidedly low tech.

But it was their subsequent single, "Release Your Body" (1988), that set London's clubs alight. A magnificently insistent record, it summed up the excitement of the period, with Derrick May's "May-day" mix and Batchelor's "Release The Acid" mix ruling dancefloors. Soon after its release, Franklin left to pursue his own goals, forming SLF and then KCC, with some new partners (currently known as The Advent). Batchelor stepped up his DJing duties, playing at RIP, the legendary late-nighter at Clink Street Studios, and at Confusion, Nicky Holloway's immensely popular Soho-based Sunday night club. High-lights would involve Mr C and E-Mix (who worked with S'Express) rapping over Batchelor's DJing. As the House scene grew, so did demand for Batchelor: he DJd at large raves such as Biology and Sunrise and became one of the first British DJs to do regular Euro-pean gigs. He had residencies at Rimini's important Ethos Mama club and the Club dei Nove Nove in nearby Cattolica. A third single, "Bang Bang You're Mine" (1989), continued BTP's momentum, but later releases – including the debut album **Back To Prison**, SLF's "Show Me What You've Got" and a compilation album, **The Tuffest of the Tuffest**, which featured BTP's "Rubba Dub" and Batchelor's produc-tion of Land Of Plenty's "Check This Mega" – were ensnared by the collapse of their distribution company, Spartan.

Although BTP never officially split up until 1997, their recording career was over. Batchelor still DJs and has recently moved into TV, presenting and writing scripts and music. Lawrence recorded some Deep House-orientated records with his KCL Project on Octopus Records. BTP should be remembered as one of the most important outfits of Britain's '80 dance scene, helping to reposition Deep House within a black British context and a credible alternative to Techno.

⊙ **"Release Your Body"**   Warriors Dance, 1988

With two Mayday mixes on its four-mix format, this was the record that would drive the 5am dancers at RIP to a frenzy. Still perfect after all these years.

⊙ **Back To Prison**   Warriors Dance, 1990

Hit by the closure of their distributors, BTP's only album was lost in the ensuing melee. Contains all the singles, plus a handful of other tracks.

Basement Boys

Formed from the trio of DJ Jay Steinhour, DJ Tommy Davies and record shop worker Teddy Douglas, Basement Boys' *nom de disque* stems from the fact that their first series of singles were recorded in a studio set up in Steinhour's Baltimore basement. Though they've never become DJs of note, and have retained a strangely low profile even amongst dance fans, the Basement Boys have produced a stream of vocal hits for Crystal Waters, Ultra Naté and Mass Order since their long-since-forgotten 1986 debut, an unremarkable cover of Rose Royce's disco standard "Love Don't Live Here Anymore".

The mould was really set with 1988's single "Don't Blame Me", recorded with local singer Andrea Holdclaw under the moniker Sublevel, and cemented with the production of 1989's "It's Over Now",

Ultra Naté's debut and UK chart success. Broken by Tony Humphries both at his Zanzibar club and on his Kiss FM show, "It's Over Now" became a huge garage hit on UK dancefloors and though the Basement Boys' production of Ultra's debut album, **Blue Notes In The Basement** (1991), was unjustifiably ignored by critics, it showcased their considerable ability as vocal House producers with a string of gorgeous melodies and jazzy washes accompanying strong soul-based songs. Two more underground 12"s confirmed their prowess and became instant classics at New Jersey's influential Zanzibar club and NYC's Shelter nightspot: the throbbing "Searchin'" (as 33 1/3 Queen), recorded for the estimable Nu Groove imprint, and "Tonite" (as Those Guys), a glorious slab of sexually charged '90s soul featuring the vocals of Eleanor Mills.

In 1991 their productions hit both club and commercial heights. Crystal Waters' simplistic "Gypsy Woman" reached #2 in the UK with its unforgettable "la dee dee, la dee da" vocal refrain, having had months of summer club and airplay across Europe, while Mass Order's gospel-House paean "Take Me Away" worked its way to success on the back of a bootleg which had flown out of independent record stores on both sides of the Atlantic. With vocalists Mark Valentine and Eugene Hayes echoing memories of the O'Jays with their sumptuous harmonies, the track became the unofficial garage anthem of the year.

Davies split shortly afterward, whilst Douglas and Steinhour produced albums for Crystal Waters and Ultra Naté, subsequently creating the Basement Boys label for more underground dub and vocal projects. As well as their mid-'90s gospel-driven singles as 250lbs Of Blue ("Rejoice" & "Risin' To The Top") for Eightball Records, their own label has borne such garage greats as Jasper Street Company's "A Feelin" in 1995 (introducing the talents of Sean "DJ Spen" Spencer),

1996's Jean-Luc Ponty-sampling "Love, Love, Love" (as Those Guys), 007's "Do You Believe" and Charles Dockins' pumping "The Juice" (as Soul Pie). In 1998 the label released DJ Spen's long-awaited **In A Spensane World**, hitting the dancefloor once again with the Tony Humphries favourite, "Love Changes".

⊙ **Those Guys: "Love, Love, Love"**   Basement Boys,1996

A change in direction for the Basement crew, as they come up trumps with an ultimately uplifting House that samples Jean-Luc Ponty's "Computer Incantations For World Peace" with violin and trumpet lines sequenced over for good measure.

Basement Jaxx

Having met at various parties in Camberwell, it was a succession of Sunday afternoons spent in London's Dingwalls club soaking up DJ Gilles Peterson's eclectic mix of Brazilian bossa-nova and jazz-fusion which inspired Simon Ratcliffe and Felix Buxton (Felix B) to take their passion for House music to the next level.

While Ratcliffe had already dabbled in the studio to produce the commercially successful, piano-happy "On Yer Way" (1993) under the guise of Helicopter, the duo's first collaborative effort a year later was a far more complex and exciting proposition. Released on their own label – Atlantic Jaxx Recordings – the nameless four-track EP juxta-posed the squelching sound of the Roland 303 on the bass-heavy "don't stop it" with super-cool synth washes on "undaground" and "deep in the night", all underpinned by determinedly raw, incisive drum patterns and rough, jacked-up rhythms.

Their second EP expanded on the framework with "deep jackin" and the strung-out "be free", and introduced the vocals of local singer Corrina Joseph on the stunning "I'm Thru With You". What really marked these cuts out from the majority and picked up keen attention from fellow UK producers was both their carnival attitude and the detail with which they'd been constructed: endless fresh sounds thrown into the mix, hyper-percussive drum patterns moulded to distorted frequencies, deconstructed vocal snatches and imaginative melodies; all at a tempo aimed directly at the dancefloor.

But it wasn't until their third release, 1995's **Summer Daze** EP, that the duo's Brazilian/Latin influences really began to shine through. Essentially a reworking of Brazilian artist Airto Moreira's bossa classic "Samba De Flora", "Samba Magic" became an instant favourite with

DJs Little Louie Vega, Ashley Beedle and, of course, Gilles Peterson, and bubbled around for two years as an infectious club anthem before finally gaining a re-release on Richard Branson's V2 label and breaking into the UK charts.

By this stage the duo's hedonistic Brixton-based club nights had reached fever pitch. Promoted to attract "properly pissed party people", Basement Jaxx eschewed the cold glitz of the West End for two sweatboxes in South East London – firstly in a church basement and later relocating to the darkened back room of a pub. Here a mini-scene developed more akin to the abandonment of Ron Hardy's Music Box than to local centres of ultra-commerce like the Ministry Of Sound. Playing a modern mixture of dance music, Basement Jaxx would crank up the intensity of sounds through the night, sometimes peaking with a wall of white noise. With Corrina Joseph and ragga toasters singing live, and the accompaniment of local bongo and conga players, the duo sequenced tracks and vocals alongside hard-hitting drum loops, tweaking EQs and dropping specially edited siren and alarm noises into the mix, to create one of London's best-kept secrets. This same lack of respect for musical purism carried over to vinyl and produced one of the club cuts of 1997, "Fly Life" – an untamed slice of discophonic inner-city paranoia.

Well-received 1996 cuts like the jazz-inflected "Slide Slide" and "Daluma" (now an anthem on the Japanese jazz-funk circuit), the samba-styled "Eu Nao" and the disco and Down Tempo mixes of Corrina Joseph's "Live Your Life With Me" are further testament to their diversity. 1997 bore another UK chart success for Atlantic Jaxx with Italian DJ Claudio Cocolotto's Brazilian re-edit "Belo Horizonti" as The Heartists, while Felix B and Radcliffe followed their acclaimed remixes for Lil Mo' Yin Yang ("Reach") and Kim English ("Nightlife") with a stream of deconstructed reworkings that even made INXS ("Everything") sound credible.

1997 releases on their own label again defied definition, the futuristically dark drum programming of "Raw Sh*t" totally at odds with the vocoder vox and string-laden "City People" on their **Urban Haze** EP. Vocals were also stretched into new territory; Corrina Joseph's "Lonely" a slice of warm breakbeat, "Wish Tonite" a sure-fire disco filler, and lovers' rock man Ronnie Richards' "Missing You" a toastin' cocktail of reggae and tribal beats.

It didn't come as much of a surprise then that 1997's compilation **Atlantic Jaxx – A Collection** appeared in the best-of-year album charts in nearly every dance music magazine.

Yet, despite major label attention and press hype, Basement Jaxx have continued to remain at the forefront of cutting-edge House music. In December 1997, they signed a long-term album deal with XL Records and signalled in the press a move to broaden their ever-burgeoning musical horizons. 1998's twisted "Red Alert/Yo-Yo" 12" again stormed the clubs, while the duo's 1999 debut album stands as one of the most original and exciting dance music long-players yet committed to wax.

⊙ Atlantic Jaxx: A Collection   Atlantic Jaxx, 1997

Essential and reasonably complete compilation of the label's cuts to date. Despite criminally omitting the excellent Corrina Joseph 12"s "I'm Thru With You" and "Wish Tonite", it does include "Samba Magic", "Fly Life", "Daluma", "Lonely" and "Eu Nao".

⊙ Remedy   XL Records, 1999

The future of House music and one of 1999's best dance albums.

Ashley Beedle

Producer, DJ and self-confessed "dead-ass soul boy", Ashley Beedle's eclectic range of productions have had him labelled a renaissance man on more than one occasion since he first rose to notoriety in the early '90's. From his disco revisionist Black Science Orchestra project to his dark, African roots-inspired work as Black Jazz Chronicles, via the melange of beats and breaks integral to The Ballistic Brothers, Beedle has been on a mission to inject black music's rich vein of history with an energising sense of the present and of the future.

Excursions to London's reggae clubs progressed to the all-day soulboy scene in Purley and Kent, leading him to form his mid-'80s sound system allegiance with the Shock Sound System. His first studio production followed – "Boys In Shock" (Jaxx Trax) – with fellow crew members and soon-to-become Acid House evangelists DJs Kid Batchelor (Bang The Party), Mr C (The Shamen) and "Evil" Eddie Richards. But the single made no noticeable impact and Beedle's career proper didn't begin to take off until he found himself working behind the counter at London's Black Market Records, from where he released his first important 12".

Inspired by DJ Norman Jay, Beedle began his homage to the disco era under the guise of Black Science Orchestra, with a string-laden cut-up of The Trammps 1976 classic "Where Were You" (1992) with friends Roberto Mello and John Howard. The single was largely ignored on release in the UK, but was picked up by DJ Frankie Knuckles in New York and subsequently hailed this side of the pond, where Beadle's reputation grew with his similarly veined 1992 follow-up "Strong" (based around Philadelphia International artist Billy Paul's "Only The Strong Survive").

Beedle revealed an impulse for the diverse which would subsequently distinguish him from most of his cohorts, producing the one-off "progressive House" classic "De Niro" with Belfast DJ David Holmes as Disco Evangelists (1992).

A move to Flying Records led to his introduction to DJ/promoter Phil Perry and the launch of Beedle's career as a DJ with a regular stint at Perry's influential Queens Club. Deck duty at Perry's hedonistic Full Circle sessions led him to meet DJs Darren Rock and Darren House (Rocky & Diesel), who shared his enduring passion for both disco and DJ Pierre's trademark "wild pitch" grooves, and the trio began recording a series of

propulsive club monsters as X-Press 2. Characterised by their crowd chants, breakdowns and Pierre-imitative grooves, "Muzik Express", "London Express" and the third in the trilogy "Say What" (1992–93) were immediate club anthems in both the UK and NYC, where they became staple soundtracks at Junior Vasquez' Sound Factory.

But with boredom setting in, the trio began to explore their funk/soul obsessions with a breaks and beats collection of sample heavy cuts as **Eccentric Afros vs The Ballistic Brothers (Volume 1)**, yielding the definitive Ballistics single "Blacker" and paving the path towards the collective's acclaimed roots/disco/funk/jazz/beats follow-up albums **London Hooligan Soul** (1995) and the more dub-inflected **Rude System** (1997), incorporating the talents of friend Dave Hill and keyboard player Ucshi Classen.

Beedle meanwhile had begun his singular obsession with seminal disco DJ Walter Gibbons. The first fruit of his obsession was the well-received East Village Loft Society single "I Wanna Sing Sunshine" (on his own Black Sunshine label), which featured a picture of Gibbons on its cover. However, things reached a disco-era epiphany with the release of Black Science Orchestra's debut album, **Walter's Room** (1996), an album clearly drawn from his Philadephia International, Creed Taylor Inc. and Curtis Mayfield record collection.

As his reputation spiralled on both sides of the Atlantic, Beedle also found time to produce one of 1995's most essential EPs for Roger Sanchez' Narcotic Records, rubbing up the disco-cocktail of "Jumpin At The Factory Bar" with the '70s street hustle of "Pimpology" and the laconic "Sleaze Track". Beedle's first solo project, known as Black Jazz Chronicles, culminated in another album, **Future Ju Ju** (1998). His darkest (and sometimes dullest) work to date, its sonically varied textures take black music beyond a disco or funk-based dance culture through the claustrophobic jazz of John Coltrane to Fela Kuti's African tribal rhythms.

And yet he continues to diversify. Having recorded as part of the Delta House Of Funk band and initated his own (admittedly low key) hip-hop label Sun III, 1997 remix work stretched from The Aloof's "One Night Stand" to MJ Cole's "Sincere" and Cornershop's "Brimful

Of Asha". In Spring 1998, Beedle announced he'd split from the Ballistic Brothers to pursue a solo career, releasing the farewell **Radio** EP (1998) with some great mixes by admirers and friends Masters At Work. Later that year, he released the soulful "Ladyland" (on his Afro Art label) and Techno-slanted "Tribe" (both 1998), under the monikers Black Science Orchestra and Black Jazz Chronicles respectively.

⊙ X-Press 2: "Muzik Xpress" Junior Boys Own, 1993

The first in the trilogy of DJ Pierre-inspired wild-pitch groovers and still the one to get your hands on: anyone for "rave disco"? Available on **Junior Boys Own Collection Volume 1** (JBO, 1994).

⊙ Black Science Orchestra:
The Altered States EP Junior Boys Own, 1995

Unquestionably BSO's finest hour, though **Walter's Room** is also essential listening. An inspired disco/funk homage to the Wood, Brass & Steel classic "Funkanova" on "New Jersey Deep" and a wonderful slice of '90s Philly soul on the flip. Available on **Late Night Sessions** (Ministry Of Sound, 1996)

The Beloved

In 1987 Jon Marsh appeared as a contestant on Channel 4's quiz show *Countdown*. But his creativity extended beyond wordplay. At around the same time he slimmed down his pop band – The Beloved – to just himself and guitarist Steve Waddington and began his career proper.

Though the duo achieved limited cult success with both their indie-chart hit "Forever Dancing" (1987) and subsequent **Where It Is** album, it wasn't until the pair dropped the guitars and replaced them with an electronic rhythm section that The Beloved became of interest to dance fans. Having soaked up the heady mix of MDMA and House at Shoom and Spectrum, sequential releases grafted Marsh's Bernard Summer-like voice and pop sensibilities with House music's raw energy to hit the dancefloor and pop charts head on.

1988's "Acid Love" was the first single to give the game away with accompanying Mike "Hitman" Wilson remixes and the trend continued with "Your Love Takes Me Higher" Juan Atkins re-rub. 1989's "The Sun Rising" provided Acid House with the perfect comedown; the single's hypnotic vocal mantra and fresh ambient melodies immediately marked it out as one of the genre's most affective paeans.

The day-glo pop-fusion of the follow-up "Hello" was fully realised on 1989's **Happiness** album, which drew comparisons with New Order's **Technique**. Its inspired four-to-the-floor re-versioning, **Blissed Out** (1990), sadly went largely unnoticed. This was one of the first remix albums ever commissioned; packed with beautiful, acid-tinged intricate melodies and vocal deconstructions mainly by the duo themselves but with the added bonus of stunning "Sun Rising" remixes from Danny Rampling and Tony Humphries.

Waddington left in 1991 to join Steve Hillage's ambient collective System 7, and was replaced by Jon's wife Helena, whom he had met at a Boys Own party in 1989. The results achieved immediate commercial success: in 1993 "Sweet Harmony" became the band's first UK Top 10 single, and similar success continued with the album **Conscience** (1993). A far more mellow affair, the album didn't really make a mark on the dancefloor and it was left up to US remixers (Johnny Vicious' 1994 mixes of "Rock To The Rhythm Of Love" and Todd Edwards' cut-up dubs of "100 Years From Today") to pull in the club pundits.

X (1996) included more traditional House-orientated songs like "Satellite", "Crystal Wave" and "Release The Pressure", the result of Jon's DJing sessions and frequent trips to New York nightspots such as Junior Vasquez' Sound Factory. But although the songs remained as emotive as ever, as a cutting club influence The Beloved's relevance had dramatically faded since the late '80s. Sensing this, Jon and Helena have since released more minimal, underground instrumental tracks on UK independent labels as Adam & Eve and London Authority.

⊙ **Blissed Out** East West, 1990

Forget the day-glo pop shine of **Happiness**, this is an accomplished four-to-the-floor long-player with stunning mixes of the faves, mostly by the duo themselves.

Black Box

Though they've often been seen as pop-fluff, Daniel "DJ Lelewel" Davoli, Mirko Limoni and Valerio Semplici created House which was both irresistably danceable and irreverent in the late '80s/early '90s. Even if it did include the odd contentious sample or two.

Davoli had been DJing since around 1981, playing a mix of soul and disco at clubs like the Marabou Starlight (he recorded the first ever Italian House record "House Machine" in 1987), but failed to achieve any widespread media notoriety before hooking up with like-minded clarinet teacher Semplici and studio engineer Limoni, who had previously twiddled the knobs for Italian pop star Spagna.

The trio, collectively known as production outfit Groove Groove Melody, first met in 1988, formed Starlight and released the upbeat, sample-heavy club hit "Numero Uno". With its driving, joyous piano hook and crisp, clean disco-inspired rhythm it set the precedent for the collective's transformation into Black Box – with the "live" addition of model/singer Katrine – and the band's subsequent international suc-

cess with their debut single "Ride On Time" in 1989. Sampling huge segments of disco diva Loleatta Holloway, as well as the piano refrain, from Dan Hartman's 1980 Salsoul classic "Love Sensation", "Ride On Time" charted at #1 in the UK within only four weeks of its release (where it held court for six weeks), and formed much of the blueprint for what journalists dubbed "Italo House" – anything from Europe with an obvious, chunky piano hook and a few cheesy vocal samples.

But while Italian producers like Gemolotto, Chico Secchi and Franco Bortoletti and the UK's FPI Project ("Going Back To My Roots" and "Everybody All Over The World") were quick to flood the clubs and charts with a host of similarly styled singles, Black Box found themselves entangled in a bitter legal row with Salsoul in the States, as Ms Holloway publicly appeared on TV in the UK to prove that she, and not Katrine (who mimed for *Top Of The Pops*), sang the original vocal. While M/A/R/R/S may have kick-started the sampling debate with "Pump Up The Volume" two years earlier, Black Box brought it to the fore and both parties benefited from the estimated 800,000 UK sales when a deal was eventually struck.

In the meantime, no impending court case was going to get in the way of potential sales, and the trio kept releasing singles under several pseudonyms, notably "Grand Piano" (1989), under the guise of Mixmaster; while as Black Box – still fronted by the miming Katrine – "I Don't Know Anybody Else" and "Everybody Everybody" followed a similar piano-centric pattern of club to chart progression, culminating in their creative zenith, the excellent **Dreamland** (1990).

1991 saw the boys stepping into discos vaults for inspiration again, re-vamping Earth, Wind & Fire's "Fantasy", but by now they were just another Italian production outfit on the block. With the Italian sound splitting twofold in the early '90s – deeper, jazz-inflected grooves from artists like Shafty and CocoDance (aka Claudio Cocolotto) competing alongside the formulaic Media Records chart-factory spewing machine – not even the trio's growing status as remixers, most notably producing ABC's short-lived comeback single "Say It", could save them and only remix albums followed.

⊙ Dreamland   RCA, 1990

Hardly an essential release for most House heads, but you'll find much of the blueprint for a legion of powerful piano-driven club and chart hits herein. File under "Italo House".

Blaze

Alongside Marshall Jefferson, Larry Heard and Ten City, Blaze have achieved their status as soulful House music's most consistent songwriters, having provided much of the format for the NYC garage sound. From their Ace Beat Records debut "Yearning" to 1997's **Basic Blaze**, their releases have been defined by strong reflective lyrics and their musical roots.

Like many of America's black musicians, the original trio of Kevin Hodge (production), Josh Milan (keyboards/vocals) and Chris Herbert (vocals) met at their local church. Although they were inspired both by their gospel tradition and by DJ Larry Levan's semi-spiritual sets at the Paradise Garage club, the direct call to make music was instigated by Tony Humphries' residency at New Jersey's Zanzibar club; Blaze were just one of the many artists who purposely made records for Tony Humphries to play.

Following their eponymous debut, the trio came to the attention of Chris Urbina's fledgling Quark Recordings, on which they released the singles "What You Gonna Do For Love" (a classic at the Paradise Garage), "If You Should Need A Friend" and "Can't Win For Losing" – powerful, soul-based songs which pretty much still define their style and gave the group a strong club-based following.

Soon they were picked up by Dave Lee's Republic imprint in the UK, where they provided the label with some of its finest moments and a host of garage classics – including Phase II's phenomenal "Reachin", Pacha's "One Kiss" and Cookie's "Choose Me" – as well as work for vocalists Michelle Ayres, Gwen Guthrie, Jocelyn Brown, Adeva, Babyface, Jomanda and Coldcut (for whom they produced 1989's "People Hold On"). In the process Blaze provided something of a textbook for soulful House music with their trademark emotional, piano-based chord structures and soul-infused songs.

In 1990 they finally hit the big time when Timmy Regisford signed them to Motown to release their debut album, **25 Years Later**. An exceptional piece of work which spans House, jazz, R&B and even be-bop, the album and subsequent European tour (backing Bobby Brown) were nonetheless a complete commercial failure. In the fall-out, Chris Herbert left to pursue an as yet non-existent solo career, while Kevin Milan helped Regisford set up the legendary New Jersey Shelter club in 1991.

But while under the Blaze moniker the duo remained fairly quiet, Hodge and Milan set about writing and producing a wealth of well-received material for local talent – including long-time collaborator Cassio Ware's "Baby Love" (1992) and "Fantasy" (1994), saxophonist Hunter Hayes' disco-inflected "Why Can't We Live Together" and Black Rascal's "Blaze Theme Track". They were also behind highly regarded vocal cuts from Alexander Hope ("Never Can Get Away" and "Threshold"), Keisha Jenkins ("Going Thru' The Motions") and Roger Harris ("Keepin My Mind").

Blaze gained their biggest commercial success with 1995's UK top 40 hit, De Lacy's "Hideaway", and followed it up with another winning vocal, courtesy of Amira, "Walk" in 1996 (whose Dreem Teem remixes propelled the song towards the UK charts). But back under their own name, 1996's brooding minimalist "Moonwalk" also showed they had a dark side and, as a reflection of their growing popularity amongst London's nu-House scene, it was licensed to Nuphonic Records.

Basic Blaze (1997) was a splendid return to the fore with its deep-seated sense of Afro-American musicality evident on tracks like the Last Poet's beatnik style "My Beat". In the all too prominent world of fluffy throwaway dancefloor ditties, Blaze's well-crafted bittersweet songs and contemplative lyrics transcended the dancefloor and garnered them long-overdue press attention. Since then Blaze have found themselves more popular than ever in the UK with re-releases of "Lovelee Dae" and Cookie's "The Best Part Of Me" turning heads across the country, while in the USA they've continued to release soul-washed 12"s such as 1998's "Directions" and "Seasons Of Love".

⊙ **25 Years Later**   Motown, 1990

Now regarded as one of the few great House albums ever produced, this entrancing mix of garage, R&B and jazz was nonetheless a complete commercial failure which saw Blaze split and re-define for a few years of relative isolation.

⦿ **Basic Blaze**   Slip 'N' Slide Records, 1997

From the late night vibes of "The Garden" to the boogie licks of "Cult Of Soul" and the softly sung lament "Wishing You Were Here", this is an album packed to the brim with soul.

Bottom Line Records

W ithout ever coming close to the consistency levels of other New York-based House labels like Strictly Rhythm or Nervous, Bottom Line nonetheless made an impression with a series of smooth, dancefloor-orientated melodic 12"s in the early to mid-'90s.

The label was created by Muscovite producer Ed "The Red" Goltsmann and his wife Nancy Kay, who, together with studio technician Nelson Roman, have produced the majority of Bottom Line's discophonic releases (under a variety of guises including Red Follies, Devastating, Groovement, Jazzmen and the self-explanatory Sample Minded). After picking up local attention for tracks – including Intro's

"Under Your Spell" – for the New Jersey-based Vista Sounds label, the duo released the vocal groover "Givin' It 2 U" (as Devastating) with diva Donna Comma. The label's first dancefloor revelation came with Tammy Banks' soul-shuffling "My Life" in 1991, whose skipping keyboards and warm chords drew keen appreciation in NYC clubs like The Shelter. Talented vocalist MJ White also provided Bottom Line with some of its best early singles, most notably with "We Will Survive", "Sweet Love" and "What Is Your Want". Bottom Line's most celebrated release came in 1992; Vivian Lee's "Music Is So Wonderful" struck a chord with DJs stretching from Little Louie Vega to Terry Farley with its epic intro and uplifting lyrics, and was later a sizeable club smash when licensed to London's Slip 'N' Slide records.

Under-rated singles by George Lockett Jnr (as Jerzzey Boy), the masterful Reggie Burrell (with 1993's **Falling In Love Again** EP as B.M.E Project) and the jazz-fuelled talents of Lenny Fontana (Fontasia's **Wildlife** EP and **The Underground Church Mass** EP) established Bottom Line as one of the hottest New York imprints in the early to mid-'90s, as did Devastating's "Wanna Be With U" and Myakka's tropical "Escape From New York" 12"s.

After Ed The Red's (aka Ed Goltsmann and Nelson "Paradise" Roman) **Sun Journey** album, subsequent releases have generally failed to ignite a similar spark amongst DJs. Despite that, 1996's **Bottom Line** EP was well received, with the four tracks ranging from MJ White's garage mover "Open Up Your Heart" to Phoenix's emotive "Chains Of Love".

⊙ Ed The Red: Sun Journey   Bottom Line, 1993

A set of smooth and emotionally charged instrumental and vocal House grooves; includes MJ White's skippy "You Bring Me Joy" and Barbara Dixon's swinging "It's Alright" alongside deep and haunting instrumentals like "Red Sun" and "Love Journey".

Brian Transeau (BT)

Brian Transeau (aka BT) was a musical prodigy and his musical obsessions stayed with him throughout high school (at which time he dabbled on guitar in various hardcore punk bands) and on to the Berkeley College of Music before he dropped out and retreated to Washington DC. It was here he got together with Deep Dish, aka childhood friends Ali "Dubfire" Shirazinia and Sharem Taybebi, and the threesome started creating music together. But it was when BT started making music on his own that he really hit his purple patch as a recording artist.

The three singles that followed, "Embracing The Future", "Loving You More" and "Deeper Sunshine", ripped through dancefloors the world over. The tunes helped usher in a new form of House called "Epic House" that combined the chunky rhythms of "progressive" House with the sweeter, string-laden textures of garage and Ambient. All of a sudden, everyone wanted a piece of BT and to find out about this strange man who lived a neo-spiritual existence in the backwaters of Maryland and recorded guitar tracks in the middle of the woods. BT became infamous for the "breakdowns" in his songs – the middle part of the track where the beats drop out and sweeping strings and pitter-patter snare rolls gradually build up to a crescendo of stereophonic sound before the rhythm kicks back in. The intros and breakdowns in his songs were so long that journalists would quip that clubbers were taking sleeping bags and Thermos flasks onto the dancefloor in preparation.

The album that followed, **IMA** (1995), was a stunning piece of work, a glistening stereophonic odyssey of lushy, dreamy House filled with sweet analogue ambient textures and darkly pulsing bass-lines.

The centrepiece of the album was "Sasha's Voyage Of Ima", a 42-minute mix by the revered British DJ that melted BT's hit singles into a rollercoaster ride of euphoric dancefloor moments and introspective home-listening House. But to top even that was the closing album track, "Divinity", which featured the sort of life-affirming pianos that would (and did) make grown men weep. **IMA** remains to this day one of House music's definitive long-players.

At 1996's Tribal Gathering BT paraded on stage resplendent in wraparound shades, leather T-shirt and snakeskin strides, throwing wild shapes around a grand piano bedecked with a colossal candelabra. A second album, **ESCM**, followed in 1998, illustrating how BT wasn't about to rest on his laurels. With neo-Jungle licks and added breakbeat pressure (plus another hit single, "Flaming June"), it cemented his already considerable reputation. After a quiet departure from Perfecto the same year, BT returned with yet another awesome blend of breakbeats and vocal snippets for the Renaissance label, releasing the 12" "Godspeed" (1999).

◉ IMA   Perfecto, 1995

An epic, grandiose, wilfully self-indulgent but ultimately very beautiful piece of work.

Cajmere/Green Velvet

Curtis A. Jones is House music's most flamboyant, startling personality, and one of its most important entrepreneurs. His work as Cajmere, which has grown into the Green Velvet pseudonym, is unique: slamming but funny, ridiculous but never dumb. As a label head he's founded Cajual and Relief Records, the two most significant nurturers of talent in the '90s.

As a student of chemical engineering at the University of Illinois, Jones was exposed to the fledgling House scene, and after scraping together enough money he managed to get hold of some dirt cheap equipment. His early experiments were unsuccessful, and he went to California's Berkeley University to study for a Master's degree. But House drew him back to Chi-town and he quit Berkeley in 1991, halfway through graduate school.

Jones' first track, "Coffee Pot" (1991), was released on ClubHouse records, a Chicago label owned by Hula and K. Fingers, a debut that immediately established his playful sound, whilst he ventured into production duties with Acid House old boy Lidell Townsend, creator of the electro-acid "I Got A Big Dick", and "This is Acid". That partnership produced "Get With U" (1992) for Mercury Records, and its use of vocals led to his work with Dajae, work which led him into a more public position.

At about the time he was working with Dajae, Cajual Records came into being. The first release on the label, Cajmere's **Underground Goodies Volume 4,** is one of the standouts of his career: salacious, licentious and as simple as House gets, but succeeding through a perfect sense of dynamics in being completely beguiling. The work with Dajae, although more popular ("Brighter Days" (1992) hit #2 in the *Billboard* dance chart), was a slight backward step, the standard lyrics never quite inspiring in the way they should. The collaboration did produce one brilliant piece, the Underground Goodies remix of "U Got Me Up"(1992), which adds a whole new style to jazz-house: Charleston Funk, with Dajae's vocals ripped into a series of squeaks and wails.

Cajual Records has been instrumental in ensuring the continuance of Chicago House as a working, underground form and seeing the careers of Gemini, Paul Johnson, Boo Williams, Glenn Underground and DJ Sneak grow and flourish. The continuing popularity of vocal House saw purely instrumental tunes lose kudos, and it was that which led Cajmere to found Relief Records, the bastion of hard instrumental grooves. It was with the creation of Relief that the Green Velvet persona came about, an ironic take on pumping Techno that has been Jones' most successful work thus far.

He opened Relief with Green Velvet's debut, "Preacher Man" (1993), and as with his opener for Cajual, it's one of the best things on the label. A long sample of an evangelist's rant against "the games that people play" (one word: sex) plays out over a minimal tech-House groove. Following up with "Flash" (1995) and "The Stalker" (1996), it was the **Destination**

THE FUTURE SOUND OF CHICAGO
CAJUAL + RELIEF
MIXED BY CAJMERE & DJ SNEAK
A COMPILATION OF THE BEST 15 TRAX FROM CAJUAL & RELIEF RECORDS

Unknown EP (1997) containing "Answering Machine" and "Land of the Lost" which really cemented Green Velvet in dance music's imagination.

Jones has also hit the world's Techno stages, resplendent in green wig, skin-tight shirt and swimming goggles. Though Cajual was declared bankrupt in 1998, Jones returned as Green Velvet a year later, releasing **Constant Chaos** (1999).

⊙ Future Sound of Chicago   Ministry of Sound, 1995

Sublime compilation of the Cajual/Relief story up to the heady days of '95. Mixed by Cajmere and DJ Sneak, it moves from the deranged abstractions of Gemini to the streamlined and steaming Boo Williams and Markey. Also contains Cajmere's "Horny (Horny Toad remix)" and Green Velvet's "Preacher Man" and "Flash". Completely essential.

⊙ Constant Chaos   Music Man, 1999

Primal, apocalyptic Techno clashes head on with Jones' innate sense of humour and funk.

Benji Candelario

Benji Candelario has been an almost constant figure on the Big Apple scene since releasing a raw batch of sample-heavy tracks as Nitro Deluxe ("Let's Get Brutal") in the early '90s.

In typical Bronx fashion, Candelario's early stylings were moulded by his love of hip-hop and inspired by the legendary DJ Kool Herc. But though he began DJing at the age of fifteen, for the next ten years he combined a career as a banker while contributing to the A&R moves of Aldo Martin's infamous freestyle record label, Cutting. In

1990 he abandoned the day job to concentrate fully on production, subsequently making his mark with both dub and vocal singles released on the aforementioned Cutting, Maxi Records, Groove On Records, Todd Terry's TNT label and London's Release The Pressure, among others.

Working with studio engineer Wayne Rollins, Candelario's most influential release was 1994's "Colour Of My Skin", recorded under the moniker Swing 52. Utilising the glorious vocals of one of House music's most accomplished singers, Arnold Jarvis – who had already sung on the garage classic "Take Some Time Out" (1989) and the Kerri Chandler-produced "Inspiration" (1994) – the plea for racial equality coupled with a fresh organ-driven groove and irresistible piano hook drew comparisons with early Chicago productions like Joe Smooth's "Promised Land" and made it one of the vocal anthems of the year, and a sure-fire hit on dancefloors both in NYC and across England.

Candelario hasn't been able to repeat that success, though vocal cuts like the Swing 52 follow-up, "The Madness Of It All", and the darker-flavoured "It's My Time (It's My Turn)" by Michelle Wilson have been well received. Candelario has also turned out a series of sample-heavy DJ tools and dubs such as his "Killer Filler" series for George Morel's Groove On label, "Traxx For The Head" for TNT, and – best of all – the disco-washed **Central Park** EP for Release The Pressure. As a remixer he's never been overly emphatic, but his re-versionings of House Of Gypsies' "Another Worry", Ruffneck's "Everybody", Todd Terry's "Keep On Jumpin'" and Sabrina Johnston's "Reach Higher" impacted on dancefloors.

In 1998 he returned with his biggest club cut since "Colour Of My Skin" with the twisted disco-charged stylings of "The Rhythm" recorded as New Hippie Movement.

⊙ **Swing 52: "Colour Of My Skin"** Cutting Records, 1994

Arnold Jarvis sings his heart out for racial equality, while Candelario and Rollins combine to provide a killer organ-driven melody and piano hook. Without doubt, one of the garage tunes of the '90s.

Derrick Carter

Derrick Carter may have been born on the West Coast, but Chicago's most popular DJ epitomises a clearly distinguishable Windy City legacy in both his virtuoso deck displays and his stylistically opposed productions. While his spinning skills are more comparable with the raw energy of the legendary DJ Ron Hardy than the smooth blending of Frankie Knuckles, the majority of his studio work has taken its laid-back lead from the deep, tripped-out mind-states of producers like Lil Louis, Larry Heard and Marshall Jefferson. And yet unlike the majority of sour-faced deck technicians, whether he's playing "downtown" or guesting at one of his wildly popular visits to UK clubs like Floppy Disco, Ministry Of Sound and Plastic People, Carter's reputation for getting drunk and boogie-ing down on the dancefloor while being able to send a crowd into states of abandoned delirium has also made him one of House's most charismatic figures.

A professional DJ since the age of 13, when he began spinning at Chicago's Basement club, Carter gained city-wide notoriety for his warehouse parties with friend Spencer Kinsey (aka Gemini). A spell behind the counter at Gramophone Records and Imports Inc (the city's two influential record stores) left him well placed to begin his first club night, Alcazar, from where his DJing reputation spiralled. Since then he's played at the city's Shelter, Foxy's, Crobar and K-Bar, held a residency at San Francisco's Sound Factory, and guested across the world, his energised mix of wild Chicago trax, emotive Techno, booming garage and deep, funk-fuelled rhythms leading Ritchie Hawtin to describe him as "America's last true underground DJ". But whereas some DJs use a rapid cross-fade technique to whip crowds into a frenzy, Carter mixes "live", utilising the volume controls to blend and morph fractured emissions into new soundscapes.

This morphing of sounds is also apparent in his studio work, though the inherent energised funk of his DJing sets is nearly always subdued, often to the point of mind-bending abstraction. Carter's recording career began aged 16 with experimental Techno outfit Symbols And Instruments (with Chicago DJs/producers Chris Nazuka and

Mark Farina), who released the well-regarded single "Moods" for Kevin Saunderson's KMS label. Carter's solo debut was the SRO single "Love Me Right", and he subsequently produced for David Holmes' Exploding Plastic Inevitable label and Mr C's Plink Plonk imprint, though his most acclaimed work has been under the Sound Patrol banner. 1994's hallucinogenic "Tripping Among The Stars" combined analogue drum kicks and raw bass-lines with a wash of slow, hypnotic melodies and a sample of Timothy Leary discussing the merits of acid from his 1966 **Tune In, Turn On, Drop Out** album. While other Sound Patrol releases also garnered attention (most notably the Chaka Khan-sampling "The Music"), Carter's spaced-out 4am formula became fully realised on the excellent **Sweetened – No Lemon** (1995).

As Carter's reputation abroad, especially in the UK, has grown, so has his remix and compilation-mixing work. Early re-versionings for Skylab and Slam have been bettered by his 1997 remix of Chez Damier's stunning "Close" and his stripped-down funk remixes with Chris Nazuka under the pseudonym Red Nail. Having already run the (now defunct) Blue Cucaracha label in Chicago, Carter currently runs the London-based Classic Recordings with DJ Luke Solomon; home to both raise-the-roof anthems by DJ Sneak and Blaze and late-nite moments of experimental deepness, many of which were collected together on 1996's **Seasons** compendium.

◉ The Cosmic Disco   Mixmag/DMC Publishing, 1997

Carter the DJ: chopping up filtered disco and raw minimalist beats from Sneak, Jedi Knights, Nelson Rosado and others into a madcap frenzy. Includes his fired-up mixes of Cajmere's "Only 4 U" and The Innocent's "If You Wanna Help Me Jesus".

Ce Ce Rodgers

Written, produced and arranged by Marshall Jefferson, Ce Ce Rodgers' inspired gospel vision "Someday" (1987) proved that the genre was capable of soulful sophistication and lyrical excellence at a time when some critics still denounced it as mechanical and mindless. Yet the song never achieved its commercial potential, despite subsequently providing the basis for UK hit imitations like Ce Ce Peniston's "Finally" and early Hardcore anthems such as Liquid's "Sweet Harmony" and Urban Shakedown's "Some Justice".

From a musical family, Rodgers' gospel roots were honed on a US tour in the mid-'80s with the Jazz Messengers combo. But it wasn't until he was leading the soul act Ce Ce and Company, performing in New York clubs in his mid-twenties, that he was spotted by Chicago's Marshall Jefferson. Introduced to Atlantic Records, "Someday" was the first, and only significant, fruit of the duo's labours.

With its utopian message it remains the ultimate four-to-the-floor pinned paean to hope and unity alongside Joe Smooth's "Promised Land", the chorus "Someday we'll live as one family in perfect harmony/someday when we all come together we will all be free" perfectly encapsulating much of the music's early optimism as well as its sentimentality. But like Sterling Void's equally astonishing "It's Alright" (1987), the lyrics also proved dance music could extend beyond the dancefloor to political comment with the lines "Someday we'll walk hand in hand/I'll go to South Africa and be called a man".

Combined with its chugging-bass intro, incessant bongo breaks and timeless piano hook, the single made an immediate impact in UK clubs and reached out to a wider, as then uninterested, soul-scene audience, selling over 10,000 copies on import before finally getting a British release as the b-side to the otherwise forgettable follow-up single "Forever". A self-titled album followed on Atlantic Records in 1989, but marked the path back to a more traditionally soulful route and never reached the grandiose heights of Rodgers' debut.

With the exception of the David Morales-mixed "All Join Hands" (1992), subsequent singles have only remained "underground" successes, though productions like the fine "No Love Lost" (1994) and Project MSC's "Superstar" (1998) have still acted to confirm his place as one of House's most accomplished male vocalists.

○ "Someday" Atlantic Records, 1987

Ce Ce's gospel brilliance combines with Marshall Jefferson's heart-wrenching string and piano arrangement to provide House music with one of its greatest soulful vocal anthems. Available on **Classic House Volume 1** (Mastercuts/Beechwood Music, 1994).

Kerri Chandler

While many House producers have struggled to carve out a unique production sound in the midst of well-worn sample chic, Kerri Chandler's supa-fat, bass-heavy grooves have marked him out as one of the genre's most distinctive technicians. Though his prolific output has continually diversified between vocal and dub releases, the sound of Chandler's analogue kick drums has become instantly recognisable on dancefloors stretching from Manhattan to Manchester.

A product of the New Jersey garage explosion led by DJ Tony Humphries, Chandler made his debut with "Drink On Me" (as Teule) in 1990. While drawing his influences from jazz, disco and soul, his minimal and experimental grooves immediately distinguished him from the crowd. His 1992 tribute to Timmy Regisford's legendary night club, "The Shelter" (1992), became a classic on the club's dancefloor and Chandler quickly became one of NYC's most prolific producers, recording a mass of dubby cuts for his own MadHouse label (check Kamar's "I Need You"), Movin' Records ("She's Crazy") and Strictly Rhythm (as KCYC).

After a slew of 12"s, Chandler produced an outright classic in 1993 for Shelter Records with the **Atmosphere** EP. The four-tracker contained the lucid keyboard stabs, rolling sub-heavy bass-lines and crisp kicks of "Track 1", a cut which has clearly influenced a wealth of producers from Chicago's Chris Gray to London's "speed garage" disciples. Chandler followed up with 1993's **Stratosphere** EP (heralding more mad, bass-obsessed instrumentals;1994's **Ionosphere** (which included the gospel-vibed "Glory Be To God"); and 1996's **Trionosphere**, though none came close to capturing the brilliance of his original effort.

As his popularity among UK headz gathered momentum, in the mid-'90s Chandler became a regular fixture on the books of London's Freetown Records, for whom he produced much of his best work. 1995 heralded one of garage's finest hours with the Arnold Jarvis-sung "Inspiration", while 1996's **Hemisphere** album, though largely neglected by the music press, mixed deep dubs ("All Alone") and wonderful sax-inflected grooves ("Simmer Down") with Chandler's unique kick drum patterns.

Although some tracks inevitably fell by the wayside – often as a result of Chandler flooding the market with weekly releases – his **Fingerprintz** EP (1995) and vocal productions of Christopher McCray's "Get It Right", Kristine W's "Feel What You Want", Susan Clark's "Deeper" and Jill Riley's "I Can't Stand It" were well-regarded dancefloor fillers. Chandler has also recorded for King Street Records, mixing one of their best 12"s of 1996 – Carolyn Harding's "Pick It Up" – and releasing his **Kaoz On King Street** album (1997).

Alongside his series of stripped-down **Raw Grooves** EPs for Jeff Craven's Chicago-based Large label, Chandler has expanded on his

minimalist, bass-heavy blueprint, incorporating "live" instruments on his releases for Joe Claussell's Ibadan Records. Taking Latin and jazz influences to the fore, 1997's bossa-styled "Escravos de Jo" was a critically acclaimed masterpiece. Further 12"s, the Billie Holiday-penned "See Line Woman" (as The Songstress), the ultra-percussive "Espirito Du Tempo" and Fela Kuti-inspired "Lagos Jump", have broadened his appeal to include jazz aficionados as well as House freaks.

And yet, it is the title of his 1995 Madhouse Records compilation, **A Basement, A Red Light And A Feeling**, that probably best sums up Chandler's aesthetic. Whether it's deep dubs, vocal floor-fillers or jazz-inflected singles, Chandler's tracks are rarely short of that often elusive quality – raw emotion – that makes them so special for many.

⊙ Kaoz Theory   Harmless, 1998

The full spectrum of Chandler's productions are catered for on this excellent compilation, though serious fans should also check out his Madhouse and Freetown Records LPs. Includes the trend-setting "Atmosphere Track 1", the Arnold Jarvis-sung "Inspiration" and the jazzy lines of "See Line Woman" and "Escravos de Jo", alongside a stack of minimal dubs and vocal cuts.

Chez Damier

Antony Pearson (aka Chez Damier) remains one of House music's most enigmatic characters. Perhaps best known for his work with Ron Trent on Prescription Records in the mid-'90s, Damier has cultivated his mark as a master of "spiritual House" over a number of 12"s since first emerging as a DJ in his native Detroit.

In the late '80s, along with George Baker and Alton "Aphrodisiac" Miller, Damier co-owned The Music Institute, the only club to play House music at the time. Situated in downtown Broadway, this 400-capacity venue (now a clothes shop) was one of the most influential clubs of its time. Techno deity Derrick May played alongside the trio, inspiring young artists such as Carl Craig, Austin "Abacus" Bascom and Stacey Pullen, whom Damier would later collaborate with.

It wasn't long before Damier hooked up with Kevin Saunderson (who was making a name for himself with Inner City) and began recording on his KMS label, forming Power 41 with Mark Kitchen (MK). This relationship gelled most effectively through MK's dub on the flip side of Damier's vocal 12", "Can U Feel It?" and the wonderful "Never Knew Love" (both 1991), whose string-laden tech-House dynamics gained widespread approval on both sides of the Atlantic. The time spent at KMS, where he worked on and co-wrote tracks for Inner City, was instrumental in developing Damier's deep-rooted love of live instrumentation and pure, soulful grooves, marking him out as a distinct technician.

It was around this time that Damier first met Chicago producer Ron Trent. An obvious similarity in ideas and outlook led to the pair working together on a vast quantity of deep and soulful House slates that featured both vocal mixes and more metallic, angular dubs. Though the duo first picked up recognition for their work on KMS, it was when they formed Prescription Records in 1993, and Balance Recordings in 1994, that they hit a creative zenith with single releases like the **Prescription Underground** EP (1993) and **Foot Therapy** EP (1995). The labels also provided a platform for some of the best work by producers including Romanthony, Roy Davis Jr, Abacus, Stacey Pullen and Glenn Underground.

Apart from Prescription, his friendship with British DJ and

Back2Basics resident Ralph Lawson led to the pair recording together under the moniker Chuggles. Alongside the well-rated ambient disco of "Remember Dance", the pair released the single "Thank You" (1995) for the Leeds-based Back2Basics label, a favourite with DJs like Rocky & Diesel, who provided an X-Press 2 remix. Having parted company with Ron Trent in 1996, after a spell of inactivity, Chez returned in 1997 with one of the year's most soulful vocal House 12"s for French label Distance. "Close", an emotive ballad strung out over 12"s of warm analogue washes, was also accompanied by a club-storming Derrick Carter b-side remix.

Damier's reputation is that of a God-fearing, deeply spiritual man whose interviews are littered with references to the soul and spirit. He also talks about music with the same hushed reverence, fuelling his image as a mysterious messenger of spiritual House for his fans.

Antony has been Chez now for fifteen years, but there are indications that this double life could soon be coming to an end. After the eagerly anticipated release of an album for Distance, Chez has said that he intends to become Antony Pearson once again, leaving his alter-ego behind. It will indeed be the end of an important chapter in his life, but the book, it would seem, is far from finished.

◉ The Collected Sounds of
Prescription   Prescription/Slip 'N' Slide, 1996

A good compendium from one of House music's best-loved labels. Includes tracks by Damier and Trent alongside singles from Romanthony, Stacey Pullen and Abacus.

⊙ "Close"   Distance, 1997

For lovers of soul, this is a modern masterpiece.

Chip E

Although as a producer Chip E has never come remotely close to reaching the creative levels attained by his contemporaries, in his short-lived career he produced a small collection of influential singles which helped to define the sound of "jackin'" Chicago House.

Chip Eberhart first made his mark as a teenage DJ, earning his spurs at local warehouse parties while attending Columbia College to study marketing and music theory. A job behind the counter at Chicago's Imports Inc. record store left him well placed to absorb the developments in the city's nightlife, most importantly those taking place on the then predominantly disco-charged dancefloors of Frankie Knuckles' Powerplant and Ron Hardy's Music Box clubs. A breeding ground for local producers and DJs, Imports Inc. acted as a filter between the Windy City radio DJs like the all-important "Hot Mix 5" and the club kids: it was Imports Inc. who sold and built up the vibe around Chicago's first House music 12"– Jesse Saunders' "On & On 117" (1985).

Chip E's first EP, **Jack Tracks** (1985), sold half its initial pressing in the first day, but more importantly it successfully transferred the raw energy of Hardy's dancefloor onto vinyl and formed a bare-bones model for the simply constructed, sample-heavy succession of singles that would make Chip E's name. On the back of the singles success in the city, he was quickly signed to Rocky Jones' DJ International label, from where he released the pre-acid classics "Like This" and the eponymous "Time To Jack", favourites not only in Chicago, but on the dancefloors of Mike Pickering's Hacienda nights in Manchester and Pete Tong and Terry Farley's "The Raid" nights at Tottenham Court Road's YMCA. "Time To Jack" (1985) was also one of the first Chicago House tracks to use a sampler, with its lyrical refrain repeated over and over to devastating effect. Coupled with its adrenalin-charged melodies and fierce kick drums that owed little to the subtlety or smooth stylings of disco, it immediately helped set off a new and lasting trend amongst the batch of emerging Windy City stars.

Chip E's biggest track though was "Godfather Of House" (1985), which sampled its enveloping bass-line from an old Samandi jazz track and was instrumental in the popularity of "jackin'" House on British dancefloors. In the same period Chip E also produced several of DJ International's other artists, most notably Femme Fion ("Jack The House") and The It, whose hypnotic "Donnie" was one of the year's most memorial tracks. But Chip E's own productions soon sank into the realms of commercial pap after the release of 1986's mediocre "If You Only Knew" and, with the exception of the odd DJing date here or there, he's since faded into the realms of mythology.

⊙ **"Godfather Of House /**
Time To Jack / Like This"   DJ International, 1985

Though all these pre-acid singles have savagely dated since their mid-'80s release, Chip E's productions helped to put Chicago's "jackin'" House sound on the global map and remain an essential part of the music's history.

Joaquin "Joe" Claussell

Few producers or labels have attempted to take House music's inherently mechanistic structure and rhythm toward a "live" sound over the past few years. The exception, however, is Joe Claussell, whose ultra-percussive and acoustic trademark has resulted in some of the genre's most beautiful, spine-tingling productions since 1996, released on his Spiritual Life imprint.

Like nearly every other New Yorker who experienced it, Claussell admits it was the Paradise Garage that ultimately proved most influential to his music, but he also took his cue from time spent at NYC's rock-based Mud Club and David Mancuso's Loft, as well as drawing on such influences as jazz, folk and bossa-nova.

Claussell's career proper began in 1989, when, from "behind the counter" at the city's Dancetracks record shop, his choice tune-buying earned the store a reputation second to none and made it a favourite for DJs Little Louie Vega, François Kervorkian and Kerri Chandler, among others. But although over the next few years Claussell dabbled in production – mixing the Shelter club classic "Over" by Instant House (1990) and 95 North's "The Journey" (1993) – it wasn't until he bought Dancetracks with his partner Stefan Prescott and later founded the Spiritual Life imprint that he began to attract attention outside the Big Apple's close-knit House fraternity.

Since the label's inception in 1996 with African Jazz's "Stubborn Problems", Spiritual Life has helped define the "live" House sound, with a cutting selection of well-rated productions ranging from the breezing Haitian folk of Jepthe Guillaume's "The Prayer" to 1997's exceptionally deep and percussive **Fiat Mistura** EP and 1998's jazz-soaked **Directions** EP, utilising and often bringing out the best in like-minded NYC producers including Timmy Regisford, Blaze, Mateo & Matos and Kerri Chandler.

But with the considerable exception of the Claussell-produced Jepthe Guillaume releases – including the well-regarded "Kanpe" and "Lakou-A" – many of Claussell's most compelling singles have emerged on the Brooklyn-based label that he co-runs with owner and ex-East West A&R man Jerome Syndenom – Ibadan Records. The gorgeous 1996 percussive remix of Ten City's "All Loved Out" was one of the best singles of the year, immediately winning attention from the dance music hierarchy, and perhaps remaining Claussell's most emotive release to date. His samba-style "Escravos de Jo", with Kerri Chandler, came in a close second, while 1998's ultra-mellow **Dub Life** EP continued the Ten City revival with a collection of remixes of "Nothing's Changed", "Suspicious", "My Piece Of Heaven" and "All Loved Out". In the interim Claussell began to selectively pick up on the remix roster for other like-minded labels, turn- ing out another trade- mark percussive mix on the classic "Hiroshi's Dub" by T.P.O for Mr Bongo's Disorient Records and a driving ten-minute "Body & Soul" mix of Paul Simpson's "Love & Respect" for Maxi (1997).

Spiritual Life Music

1998's "Come Inside The Loft" and "Agora e Seu Tempo" singles, alongside his continued DJing residency at NYC's Manhattan club Body & Soul, have continued to strengthen Claussell's position of influence. He shows no sign of slowing down either. Jepthe Guillaume's well-regarded **Voyage of Dreams** was released in 1998, followed by the remix of Carlos Sanchez' "Flying High" and Mutabaruka's "Dis Poem" (both 1999).

⊙ Spiritual Life Music   Spiritual Life/Euphonic Records, 1997

Damn near perfect "spiritual" music – one should come free with every pair of headphones. Highlights include Ten City's ethereal "All Loved Out", Claussell's "Escravos de Jo" and Jephte Guillaume' folk-masterpiece "The Prayer" alongside one of Mateo & Matos' best cuts, "Mixed Moods".

Clivilles & Cole

One of the main reasons for dance music's crossover success in the States was C&C Music Factory. In a country where "disco" was still a dirty word, from 1991 to 1995 Robert Clivilles (DJ/production) and David Cole's (keyboards/production) ever-changing collective of singers, rappers and musicians rivalled major-label pop and rock acts for chart position and album sales, winning 28 awards, including a Grammy in 1994 for their contribution to the *Bodyguard* soundtrack. Their thundering, reconstructed 1990 remix of Natalie Cole's "Pink Cadillac" crashed into the Billboard Top 5 and set major-label executives on a previously unthinkable mission to utilise House remixers, while the duo went on to produce and remix for the likes of Whitney Houston, Mariah Carey and Michael Jackson. But despite scaling the grandiose heights of big-budget slick corporatism, with the exception of "A Deeper Love", their most dynamic House cuts were conceived in the years leading up to 1991.

C&C first collaborated in the mid-'80s behind the decks at Bruce Forrest's Times Square disco, Better Days, where Clivilles spun records and deconstructed songs to make his own instrumental edits,

while Tennessee-born piano/church-organ-trained Cole plugged in his electronic keyboard and jammed to the beats, the duo thus effectively creating their own remixes. This inevitably led to production, where Clivilles' ear for a tune, Cole's keyboard wizardry (he'd previously picked up attention for his skills on Arthur Baker's ground-breaking remix of Fleetwood Mac's "Big Love") and a shared appreciation for thundering bass-lines eventually produced one of NYC's first sample-ridden, commercially successful House tracks, the fierce "Do It Properly" (1987). Created as Two Puerto Ricans, A Black Man And A Dominican, with DJ David Morales and editor Chep Nunez, the single was essentially an energized bootleg of Adonis' "No Way Back" with a great synthesised riff and mass of samples thrown over the top. Selling over 100,000 units, it paved the way for C&C's big-budget work with Columbia Records as C&C Music Factory and as remixers to the stars.

But it was in the ensuing period where C&C created many of their under-achieving but most affable productions, taking their trademark sound of corpulent bass-lines, layered percussion and Cole's keyboards to work on Seduction's "Seduction" and "One Mistake", and Sandee's orgasmic "Notice Me" (1989) – perhaps their finest moment.

Combining the same formula with a keen appreciation of the pop ethic, C&C Music Factory was born in 1991. Initially a vehicle for singers Zelma Davis and Martha Wash, and rapper Freedom Williams, the collective debuted with the world-wide hit "Gonna Make U Sweat" (1991). Its jagged rock guitars and anthemic chorus marked what was probably the group's finest hour, before spiralling into the realms of predictability. The album of the same name eventually sold more than six million copies, but things reached a diabolical level with the overtly commercial, sickıy-sweet "Things That Make You Go Hmmm" single in 1992.

Despite the welcome respite of 1992's ultra-positive, gospel-inflected "A Deeper Love", things went from bad to worse with an abysmal cover of U2's "Pride (In The Name Of Love)" and the multi-generic (salsa, reggae, hip-hop) sophomore album **Anything Goes** (1994), which spawned the pop hit "Do You Wanna Get Funky" among forgettable others. By this stage they had become overly corporate and commercial and by the time their **Greatest Hits** album reached the shelves in 1995, their more credible efforts were merely a distant memory.

However, to their credit, C&C Music Factory were one of the first dance acts to get MTV rotation and a world tour following the success of their first album. Often thought the musical genius of the duo, David Cole sadly passed away from spinal meningitis in 1995, aged only 32. His last track, "I Believe In Him" (1995) – recorded with George Morel – remains a poignant reminder of his talents.

⊙ **Clivilles And Cole – Greatest Remixes Vol. 1** Columbia,1992

Wade past the pop fluff and you'll find the duo's finest moments as producers and remixers herein. Includes the early essential classics "Do It Properly" and "Notice Me" (Sandee), the anthemic "A Deeper Love" and their choice '90s remixes of Lisa Lisa & Cult Jam's "Let The Beat Hit 'Em" and Chaka Khan's piano-driven "Clouds".

Coco, Steel And Lovebomb

Inspired by the growing enthusiasm for House music at his Brighton-based "Coco" club, Chris "Coco" Mellor produced his debut EP, **Future Sound Of Europe/ Miracles**, with Marc Woolford. However, it was his follow-up 12", "Feel It", initially produced simply for the club, which caught the attention of many. With the interest in the track escalating, Chris joined Sheffield's Warp Records, and Coco, Steel and Lovebomb's "Feel It / Touch It" (1991) received a full release.

The EP reflected the new surge of inventive music rising out of the UK House scene, which would later be dubbed "progressive House". The metallic tech-funk beats and rumbling bassline of "Feel It" mixed with the deeper African-influenced House of "Touch It" complemented each other to produce an EP with impressive production skills and originality that stood out on British dancefloors. Kid Batchelor's 5am mix gave the record further credibility. Although Mellor and his collaborators struggled to meet the expectations raised by the EP, gems such as a remix of "Touch It" called "Work On The Negative" (1992) proved that he was capable of producing sublime slices of Deep House. 1993's "Work It" became a favourite on Junior Vasquez' Sound Factory dancefloor, while its under-achieving re-versioning as "Dub It" (1994) should have been in the crates of every self-respecting House DJ; perhaps it would've been if not for the fact that it lay tucked away on the b-side to the single "Set Me Free". In 1994 Coco,

Steel and Lovebomb released IT!, collecting together the collective's tougher moments, while illustrating a move towards blissful Ambient soundscapes on tracks like "La Cote Sauvage".

Chris Mellor teamed up with A Man Called Adam's Other Records, and in 1997 he produced a follow-up album, **New World**. A progression from the mellower side of IT!, Mellor's remarkably original version of ambience sounds like Deep House submerged to a beatless collage of intricate melodies, scattered with voices and instruments from around the world. Mellor continues to record for Other Records, releasing his third album, **Sun Set**, in 1998.

⊙ New World   Other, 1997

If you're expecting a regular collection of 4/4 grooves, then forget it. Chris Coco's highly original album weds Ambient melodies to a collection of rhythms that range from beatless to drum 'n' bass.

Cowboy Records

Founded by club entrepreneur/prankster Charlie Chester and Flying Records DJ Dean Thatcher (better known as core founder of sonic experimentalists The Aloof), Cowboy defined much of London's "boys on drugs" messy club culture in the early '90s and provided a base for bands like The Aloof to later make an indent on the national consciousness.

Having set up the UK arm of Italian label Flying Records with an Ibiza-inspired Thatcher remix of Ian Dury And The Blockheads' "Hit Me With Your Rhythm Stick", Chester and Thatcher gained exposure as organisers of the crazed and immensely popular Flying club nights at London's Soho Theatre, where Euro anthems and Housey favourites would accompany impromptu tambourine playing, glammed-up dressing and gurning. Before launching Cowboy, the pair founded the reasonably successful Volante Records with single releases such as Audio Deluxe's Balearic "60 Seconds" and the white-boy soul of Tyrrel Corporation's "The Bottle" and "Going Home" (1992).

Cowboy gained early club success with the similarly styled soul-sters Secret Life (their Stevie Wonder covering debut, "As Always", just missing out on the UK charts) and The Aloof, who debuted with the percussive brilliance of "On A Mission". But the label began to achieve real notoriety and club play for its output of moody, dub-heavy instrumental tracks from scene DJs like Fabi Paras (aka Charas), Phil Perry (aka Faith Department) and Chester himself (aka Perks Of Living Society).

But despite Secret Life's well-regarded debut album, **Sole Vision** (1995), and with the notable exception of The Aloof's rise to the ranks of adulation, that commercial success never really arrived. Despite the fact that Cowboy helped pave the way for other like-minded UK imprints, the label faded from sight in the mid-'90s.

⊙ **Cowboy: The Album**   Cowboy, 1993

Complete early collection of the label's moody instrumentals alongside superior dancefloor fillers like Secret Life's soulful "As Always" and The Aloof's bongo mash-up "On A Mission".

D-Mob

While 1987/88's genre-defining singles like Phuture's "Acid Trax", Bam Bam's "Where's Your Child" and Armando's "Land Of Confusion" may have helped spark the UK's Acid House boom, London's D-Mob provided the scene with one of its most contagious catchphrases (alongside "mental" and "on one") and one of its most ridiculously likeable anthems, "We Call It Acieed" (1989).

D-Mob was the creative vehicle for producer "Dancin" Danny D (Daniel Kojo Poku). Like Manchester's Gerald Simpson, Poku was another ex-McDonald's employee who took up part-time DJing at London nightspots like Gullivers, before moving into club promotions for Loose Ends (for whom he produced his first remix), Total Contrast and Full Force. Though his own productions began with the minor US dance hit "Warrior Groove" (under the guise of Taurus Boys), his commercial vision was rooted in street soul/R&B and he later applied his remixing skills to Adeva, Kid N' Play and Eric B & Rakim amongst others.

D-Mob, though, never really flowered as a major House act and follow-up hits "It Is Time To Get Funky", "Put Your Hands Together" and "That's The Way Of The World" (all 1989) were pretty much standard dancefloor fodder, although "C'mon And Get My Lovin'" introduced vocalist Cathy Dennis and was a joyful throwaway pop-dance tune. Their debut album **A Little Bit Of This, A Little Bit Of That** (1989) never took itself too seriously either. D-Mob returned in 1993, again with Dennis, for the standard garagey belter "Why", followed by "One Day", though they soon faded into obscurity.

⊙ A Little Bit Of This, A Little Bit Of That   ffrr/London Records, 1989

A fairly standard dancefloor selection, which is partly saved by D-Mob's two finest outings – the '89 phrasebook anthem "We Call It Acieed" and the Cathy Dennis-led "C'mon And Get My Lovin".

Daft Punk

"*We wanted to make something for people to listen to in their bedrooms. Maybe if they have homework to do. Or want to relax.*" This self-appraisal of the Daft Punk sound is neat, if not entirely helpful. Daft Punk's music – although initially likened to that of The Chemical Brothers and the late '90s "Big Beat" acts – is actually a splice of disco, funk and hard electro beats more suited to club sound systems than the lounge stereo.

A Parisian-born and -based duo, Thomas Bangalter and Guy-Manuel De Homem Christo have remained friends since meeting at school in 1987. The pair immersed themselves in classically cool pop music (Beach Boys, Scott Walker, Marc Bolan) before forming their first band, Darlin', in 1992. They released a cover of The Beach Boys' "Darlin'". The single was released on British indie band Stereolab's label Duophonic as part of a four-track EP, but was unkindly dismissed by *Melody Maker* as "daft punk". Taking the criticism as beneficial, the band altered musical direction whilst using the same name by which they had been slammed. The new-born Daft Punk released their debut single the following year, a caustic 12" called "New Wave/Alive" (1993) on Scotland's Soma Records, having met representatives of the Glasgow-based Techno label at a rave held in EuroDisney.

In 1994 they released a second 12", "Da Funk/Musique", a regular DJ favourite with The Chemical Brothers, who not only made it an anthem wherever they played, but invited Daft Punk to remix their single "Life Is Sweet". This brush with fame saw them retreat into wearing masks for interviews and photo-shoots; the pair shunned the fame that the track's 1996 re-release, with pre-sales of 70,000 copies,

would bring. That move, immediately resonant of the masked Techno guerrilas of Underground Resistance and of Larry Heard's disdain for the mechanisms of publicity, issued a message that they would resist the crushing blows of temporal popularity that had destroyed their heroes, be they Adonis or the Beach Boys' Brian Wilson.

"Da Funk" (1996) duly crashed into the UK charts, a moment of sublime underground crossover. The sound, as on its infectious follow-up "Around The World", is beautifully incessant, one of pure melody constantly circling rather than the atonalities of the "Acid House" it is clearly modelled on. A deal with Virgin Records led to the release of their critically and commercially successful album **Homework** (1996). Live tours of the UK, France and Belgium proved the two young Frenchmen could stand proudly alongside bands such as Orbital and Underworld as a "live" force to be reckoned with. Never providing any human performance to watch, devoid of Karl Hyde's Rock spectacle, they played solely on dynamic movements and the bond between audience and beat.

While their remix work has been highly selective (featuring I:Cube, Ian Pooley and Gabrielle), Daft Punk have continued to counter their commercial success with a prolific underground 12" output under a variety of guises. Having released a single as Indo Silver Club in 1996, Thomas Bangalter has persisted with his record label Roule, releasing his own dynamic cuts ("Spinal Scratch", "Trax On Da Rocks") as well as those by Roy Davis Jr, Alan Braxe and Romanthony. Guy-Manuel, meantime, has concentrated on his label Cydramoure (home to such fabulous disco cut-ups as Le Knight Club's "Holiday On Ice" and "Mirage"). In 1998 Bangalter (whose father wrote Ottowan's early '80s hit "D.I.S.C.O") achieved even greater chart success, despite his attempts to remain anonymous. The Chaka Khan-sampling "Music Sounds Better With You" by Stardust (co-written with Alan Braxe and featuring the vocals of Benjamin "Diamond" Cohen) became the club anthem of the year and entered the UK charts at #2, and "Gym Tonic" (written for fellow Parisian Bob Sinclar in under an hour) was similarly massive, despite incurring the wrath of Jane Fonda, whom it sampled. Daft Punk, two of the most talented and socially significant musicians of our time, have also paved the commercial path for a whole new wave of French dance acts including Motorbass, Cassius and the above-mentioned Bob Sinclar.

⊙ Homework   Virgin, 1996

A popular history of dance music spun out on analogue technology, FX warps and burning melodies. Spliced with DP's wry sense of humour, **Homework** moulds together underground structures with the most accessibly direct of melodies to make for addictive, essential listening.

⊙ Stardust "Music Sounds Better With You"   Roule, 1998

The best club record of 1998, courtesy of a masked Thomas Bangalter and an ingeniously worked Chaka Khan sample.

Roy Davis Jr

he wild-pitch era – House music's early '90s regeneration as a form which could contain both abstract electronics and the more quantifiable horns and exhortation of 1970s funk – pushed surprisingly few great producers into the underground imagination. If DJ Pierre, already the man who started the Acid sound with Phuture, is the established genius, continually refining his idea of a perfect musical form, then Roy Davis Jr has developed the broadest vision, using the techniques of wild-pitch to create discography that has been logical in its growth, but unusually surprising in its depth.

Amongst the slew of tunes Davis put out in his early days, taking in Acid and wild-pitch and the range between, The Believers' "Who Dares To Believe" (1994) is the one people most remember. Licensed to the Ministry of Sound label in the UK it is an instant crowd-pleaser, all sax and strings, and provokes the most immediate of responses with hands shooting up and smiles spreading over faces. Listen to it on **DJ Dukes' Journey By DJ** (1994), a hard wild-pitch mix revolving around the Power-Large-Strictly Rhythm New York axis, and it's almost a welcome relief, a launch into sounds you recognise and a break away from the near psychosis of Felix Da Housecat and others. And yet, there is a nagging sense of obviousness about it all; where the track fails is in its ignorance of production possibilities, its absence of Davis' best attribute – his ability to merge melody with involved minimalism.

The second period of Davis' career is when that ignorance is redressed. Hooking up with Jay Juniel, a series of projects leaked out that are amongst House music's most beguiling releases. Released in 1996, **The Men From the Nile** EP sees Davis unlock the technical possibilities of wild-pitch in other sonic landscapes. "All Night Jam" is gospel-seduced funk, its double riffs, chant and horn, flit back and forth as the EQs move through dull and bright, distant and close. It's here that Davis diverges from Pierre's template and becomes a distinct artist. Pierre's focus is specific, constantly refining the wild-pitch model; Davis begins to spread through styles, but always it's the production methods of wild-pitch and the specifics of phase and distort he continues to explore.

Looking elsewhere, his tenure with Phuture produced "Inside Out" (1992), a cut which sees Davis and Juniel offering a full demonstration of second-generation House and its new emotional regions.

Releases have always flowed easily, but in 1996 phase three of Davis' career kicked in with a release that only the UK garage boom of 1997 could catalyse. "Gabrielle", originally out on Jeff Craven's Large label, then licensed to XL in 1997, is a massively popular piece that drifts over shop sound systems and from blasting car stereos. But it's a diamond too subtle for simple terms like House or garage, despite the track's easy acceptance by both. The production is desiccated to the point of whispering, Davis' professed lack of interest in rigid 909 patterns producing a jittering beat that leaves the whole closer to Sly Stone's "There's a Riot Goin' On" or Marvin Gaye's "I Want You" – an endorphic soul on the verge of internal collapse, but still emitting waves of inspiration.

Since the release of "Gabrielle", Davis' prolific flow has slowed a little. "The Beautiful Ones", released in early '98, is another wonder – the essence of Deep House in its choice of sounds, but using the production lessons of "Gabrielle" to push its effectiveness further out so the lick glides easier whilst the electronics fizzle like a shock wave. Concentrate on that rather than Davis' lost project with Juniel and Marshall Jefferson. Given money by the Big Beat label in the States, they hired, amongst others, the Chicago Symphony Orchestra to flesh out their grooves. Perhaps it was a great opportunity lost, but more than likely it would have proved once again that dance artists cannot always cope with the scale of fifty musicians in a studio. Nor do they really need to, when the possibilities of complex productions like "Gabrielle" are open to them.

⊙ **The Men From the Nile EP**   Undaground Therapy, 1996

Constantly surprising moment of artistic evolution. "All Night Jam" is a neglected classic. "Just" a b-side, but an exhilarating slice of hedonism.

◉ **"Gabrielle"**   Large Records, 1996

The most famous, the most maltreated. A completely modern piece of drowning soul. Available on his **DJ MIX X Sight/Coldfront**, 1998, alongside eight of his other deeply funky cuts.

Tony De Vit

One of the most popular DJs Britain has produced, Tony De Vit was also one of the most distinctive. Unlike the huge roster of guest DJs who simply spin the latest vinyl releases, De Vit specifically manipulated the trance-inflected "Belgian hoover sound" that was so prominent on London dancefloors like that of the legendary Trade club where he resided, and toned it down in order to transport his vision of "nu-energy" across mainstream dancefloors the world over. In the process, he helped shatter the infiltration of cheesy handbag House into the clubbing meccas of the UK by taking the music in a harder, faster and deeper direction, without ever letting the temperature slip below boiling point.

Tony started off as manager at a Birmingham-based industrial company, which he held for seventeen years. He began spinning disco at Birmingham's gay club The Nightingale. But it seemed Lady Luck was conspiring against him in the '80s; he came second in three DMC Mixing Championship contests – even though he resorted to dressing up as a moustached leather queen to grab attention in 1988 – leading Britain's *Mixmag* to label him "Birmingham's Hard Luck Story".

A 1991 visit to London's long-running, cutting-edge gay House night, Trade, changed all that. Inspired by what he heard he bombarded promoter Lawrence Malice with mix-tapes until he finally secured a slot in 1992. He held a residency there from 1995 until 1998. As his popularity reached new heights he became a regular fixture at the commercial, large-scale nights like Sheffield's Gatecrasher, London's Ministry Of Sound, Derby's Progress and Liverpool's Cream.

As a producer he left a considerable mark on the dance music community. TDV Enterprises started at the beginning of 1995 when De Vit and Trade regular/producer Simon Parkes foregrounded his upbeat, trance-directed nu-energy tracks like "Feel My Love" and "Burning Up", which was subsequently signed by PWL and charted at #25 in the UK. De Vit also had chart success with the 12" "To The Limit".

As remixers, De Vit and Parkes turned their hand to both a breadth of pop stars (Louise, E17, Michelle Gayle) and underground nu-energy productions, operating under the banner of V2. Meanwhile, De Vit's trademark chunky, energised re-versionings of less well-known dance acts like Sandy B ("Make The World Go Around"), 99th Floor Elevators, The Blob and Diddy ("Give Me Love") cut swathes across mainstream UK clubland, many of which were collected together on **Tony De Vit: The Remixes** (1998).

De Vit began his own label, Jump Wax, in 1998. That too achieved reasonable club success with 12"s like "Do What You Do" and "Don't Ever Stop/Bring The Beat Back" before his untimely death from bone marrow failure and bronchial pneumonia on July 2, 1998. But it is as a truly remarkable DJ that Tony De Vit will be remembered; UK clubland paid its respects with a memorial club night at Birmingham's Sundissential, while tribute articles ran across the British dance music press.

⊙ **Tony De Vit: Live In Tokyo**   Global Underground, 1997

This compilation is an especially heady mix of nu-energy and uplifting trance. It also includes two of his own cuts, "Feel My Love" and "Get Loose".

Deconstruction Records

Before Deconstruction became associated with M-People, the label had helped pave the way for mainstream dance music acceptance in the UK with seminal releases by acts including T-Coy, Black Box, Guru Josh, N-Joi and K Klass.

Formed by Keith Blackhurst and Pete Hadfield as a reaction to the burgeoning dance scene in the North of England, Deconstruction debuted with Hot! House's forgettable "Don't Come To Stay", featuring the husky vocals of Heather Small (later singer with M-People). The label followed up with one of the first ever British House tracks, "Carino", courtesy of the Manchester-based collective T-Coy (aka Hacienda DJ Mike Pickering and producer Richie Close), who subsequently recorded eight cuts for the ground-breaking **North** (1988) compilation. Tracks from Sha-Lor ("I'm In Love") and Marina ("Sly One") quickly became club anthems and helped establish the label's UK standing.

Licensing Black Box's "Ride On Time" gave Deconstruction its first #1 UK chart hit and an international profile, while local artists like A Guy Called Gerald, Gina Foster and Annette were brought to a wider audience with the release of **The Further Adventures of The North**. The label also helped usher in the sound of hi-NRG and bounding pianos on **Italia** (1989).

1990 found Deconstruction breaking more new ground: ushering in the proto-rave/nightmare single "Infinity" by media-friendly charlatan Guru Josh and the happy breakbeat machinations of Essex duo N-Joi, whose "Anthem" reached #8 in the charts. The pop success continued in 1991 with hands-in-the-air piano stormers from K Klass ("Rhythm Is A Mystery") and Bassheads ("Is There Anybody Out There") both reaching the UK Top 10. The label's licensing of Felix's "Don't You Want Me" (1992) helped pave the way for commercial trance acts like Robert Miles and Sash in the late '90s.

1993 brought more Top 10 hits with the arrival of Pickering's M-People collective, and with it industry acceptance when the band won the Mercury Music Prize in 1994 for their second album, **Elegant Slumming**.

Since then, the label has continued to bring both chart success and press hype to a roster of studio technicians whose careers developed elsewhere but who under Deconstruction have achieved a widespread profile. Justin Robertson may well have achieved legendary club status before signing his Lionrock collective to the label, but singles like 1998's "Rude Boy Rock" have made him as well known to BBC1 viewers (where it's been used to soundtrack numerous programmes) as Most Excellent attendees. Similarly The Grid were well-established electronic-adventurists, but it took the DeCon chart success of "Swamp Thing" and "Texas Cowboys" to give them a pop persona, as was the case with Sasha and Scot Techno wizard Dave Clarke.

Having won the International Dance Award for best label in 1994 and the DMC/Mixmag Award for Best Major Label in 1995, Deconstruction's ability to bridge the divide between "underground" cool and "commercial" success has continued with the signing of Way Out West and Deep Dish, and the licensing of acts like speed garage gurus The Dreem Teem.

○ Deconstruction Classics   Deconstruction,1995

There's no Deep Dish or Way Out West here, but ample proof of the pivotal role the label played in popularising dance music from 1987 to 1995. From T-Coy's "Carino" to Black Box's "Ride On Time" and Lionrock's "Packet Of Peace", it's pumping dancefloor classics all the way.

Deep Dish

I t was nigh-on impossible to step foot into any House club in 1995 without being bombarded by the subsonic bass, wild percussive frenzy and incessant groove which pleaded *"I need a hide, hide, hide, hideaway/don't make me run away."* Sure, the soaring vocals came courtesy of NYC diva De'Lacy, but the remix which pushed "Hideaway" into clubland's consciousness belonged well and truly to Deep Dish.

The Iranian-born duo of Ali "Dubfire" Shirazinia and Sharam Yayebi first hooked up while DJing at a Washington club in 1991, where Sharam's mix of hi-NRG and House and Dubfire's penchant for hip-hop and indie immediately made for a unique combination. A year down the line, they'd already formed Deep Dish Records and began gaining limited notoriety for their uncompromising agenda of rich, jazz-tinged slates that referenced Larry Heard's subtlety, MAW's drum breaks and the Ambient-Techno vision of Carl Craig (with whom they later worked on Naomi Daniel's "Fire" single).

From Washington DC the pair opened their recording account with as Moods the organ-fired, minimal slab of deepness "A Feeling" (1992), but really began to pick up recognition for their 1993 production of school friend BT's "The Moment Of Truth", quickly followed by BT's "Relativity" and Watergate's stunning "Lonely Winter". These three cuts forged much of their early mark, with their resolutely epic, trance-like, deep but funk-fuelled rhythms.

The formula was applied in equal measure to their early releases on the DDR subsidiary, Yoshitoshi Records. Their dreamy "Submarine" debut and irrepressible "Satori" (1994) immediately stood out on the UK's cooler dancefloors, though the tracks' producers still remained an enigma to most. It was their epic trance-House hybrid "High Frequency" (as Deep Dish presents Quench) which solidified their burgeoning reputation alongside hardened old-timers like Danny Tenaglia and Junior Vasquez, and secured them a lucrative deal with New York's Tribal Re. That relationship yielded a wealth of acclaimed Deep House grooves in the period 1994 to 1995, including the dubby vocals of Prana's "The Dream" and Chocolate City's saxual "Love Songs", alongside Deep Dish's lush mixes like the rambling "Casa De X" and bass-heavy "Up In This House" (as NYDC).

Fresh sounds were again in evidence when Deep Dish hit back in 1996 with "Stay Gold". The track broke new ground with its combination of Techno-laden hi-hats, succulent strings and intense, semi-industrial finale.

Since they listed Led Zeppelin, Pink Floyd, Brian Eno and This Mortal Coil among their favourite bands, 1997's surreal indie-House 12" "Stranded" perhaps shouldn't have come as any real surprise. Nevertheless, 1998's debut album, **Junk Science**, took Deep Dish's propulsive creative ethic to the extremes.

Vocalist Richard Morel (who had provided the vox for "Stranded")

continued the surreal vibe over to "My Only Sin", and Everything But The Girl's Tracy Thorn even chipped in with vocals for a re-versioned "Stay Gold" called "Future Of The Future", while Deep Dish stretched their epic soundscape from its Deep House inception across the dark breakbeat of "Monsoon", the Eno-like ambience of "Morning Wood" and "Persepolis" and the incessant tribal breaks of "Summer's Over". **Junk Science** was a truly ambitious release which stands out as one of the debuts of the '90s.

Ⓞ Penetrate Deeper   Deep Dish Records, 1995

Some of Deep Dish's finest moments from both the DDR and Yoshitoshi labels are featured on this compilation, including "The Dream", "Love Songs" and "Casa De X".

Ⓞ Junk Science   Deconstruction Records, 1998

Assured and eclectic debut which confirms Deep Dish as one of dance music's most exciting and forward-thinking producers. An essential purchase.

John Digweed

One day the young John Digweed was shown the future by a soul fan when he was taken to look at his Technics decks. Through hard labour in the glamorous worlds of gardening and shopwork, he managed to save up and buy his first decks, amp and mixer and a DJ star was in the making.

Digweed did parties, weddings and residences at local clubs. After a brief stay in London, where he saw the talents of Frankie Knuckles at Delirium, he started his own club night at The Crypt in Hastings called Bedrock, before moving on to promoting nights at Hastings Pier. In 1990, he hooked up with rave promoters Storm to put on some of the south coast's biggest dance events.

In the meantime, he sent off his own mix-tapes to promoters, dance labels and magazines. For six months he warmed up for Fabio and Grooverider at Rage. His big break came when he was made joint resident at Renaissance in Mansfield with Sasha in 1994. His style of deep and hard experimental House won him the admiration of many.

The partnership with Sasha blossomed and as DJs both have earned the respect of fans and the industry alike. They have also continued to record under the banner Northern Exposure, producing a mix CD series with which they have toured the globe. The third part of the Northern Exposure series, **A New Beginning** was released by InCredible in 1999.

Digweed's remix work has been steadily growing, working with the likes of M-People, Marco Polo and Sasha. His biggest tune "For What You Dream Of" (1993) as Bedrock (a name he also remixes under) with Nick Muir was included in the *Trainspotting* soundtrack.

Since April 1997, Digweed and Sasha have had a residency at Twilo in New York, a club which has become as much a part of club legend as The Sound Factory. Apart from Northern Exposure, Digweed has mixed sets on two ground-breaking Renaissance CDs, for Journey by DJ, Jackpot and many others. Sales have totalled over 430,000, but he finds it hard to see himself as a celebrity DJ. The best buzz of the night is when his set reaches a crescendo and he confronts a mass of people getting off on his music.

In 1998 he opened his own venue in Brighton called The Beach. His usual eye for detail and knowledge of club culture has ensured that the venue is one of the best in the country. Digweed's love of music and his truly remarkable talent behind the decks have secured his rise to the top of the DJ ladder.

◉ Northern Exposure One Ministry Of Sound, 1996

More mellow than many fans would have expected, this graceful manipulation of Ambient grooves includes offerings from Future Sound Of London, William Orbit and Apollo 440.

◉ Northern Exposure Two Ministry Of Sound, 1997

Lush melodies, epic House and exceptional mixing accompany a collection of little-known tracks from the likes of Gus Gus, Furry Phreaks, Spooky and Fluke. Mesmerising.

Dimitri From Paris

In retrospect it's probably not surprising that Dimitri From Paris's first ever studio production was a club remix for Princess Stephanie of Monaco. Unlike the serious artistes who dominate dance music, Dimitri's Serge Gainsbourg-meets-Studio-54 style has always retained a sense of fun within its deep funk. **His Shibuya Connection** EP (1997) for Disorient Records perfectly summed up his scope: the three tracks stretched from disco cut-ups ("Back In The Daze") through sleazy loungecore electronica ("Love Love Love") to the Inspector-Clouseau-as-chanteuse shenanigans of "Toujours L'Amore". Although Dimitri didn't really garner any widespread notoriety outside Paris until the timely UK re-release of his 1996 **Sacré Bleu** album, he and Laurent

Garnier are the father figures of the mid-'90s French House explosion typified by artists like Daft Punk and Motorbass.

Born in Paris in 1964, Dimitri's musical tastes were somewhat constrict-ed by the dominant monopoly owner-ship of French radio until President Mit-terand came to power in 1981 and a host of pirate radio stations sprang up in the city. Discover-

ing his mentor, disco remixer extraordinaire François Kervorkian, in the mid-'80s, Dimitri started making rough edits of vocal and instrumental mixes at home. Early Tony Humphries mix-tapes and the first-hand experience of witnessing Fab Five Freddy and Afrika Bambaataa DJ in

Paris in 1985 led Dimitri to experiment with longer edits, cut 'n' paste techniques and scratch mixing. Soon afterwards, he sent his ten-minute mixed segue into the CFM radio station and was employed to provide a "remix of the week" where he'd extend a popular track using basic editing and scratching techniques. Within six months, he'd moved on to doing the same thing using studio quality reel-to-reel technology and in 1986 finally got to exert a real degree of influence with his radio show on the more commercially orientated Sky Rock station.

Remix offers came in, and after he'd turned his hand to Princess Stephanie of Monaco's forgettable pop foray, Dimitri fell into a four-year pattern of providing club remixes for throwaway French pop – often alongside engineers Etienne De Crecy and Phillipe Zdar (Motorbass). In 1988, after singles by Bomb The Bass and S'Express had broken the French pop charts, Dimitri became the first DJ to host a House music radio show.

Although his first Italo-House-styled production was completely forgettable, singles such as Groove Council's "You Won't Be Happy" for Canada's Hi-Bias Records proved that the time in the studio had been well spent and an early '90s remix of Björk's "Human Behaviour" became an essential 12" for DJs like David Morales and Little Louie Vega. Unfortunately, all the acclaim mistakenly went to Super DJ Dimitri from Deee-Lite. It was clear a new name would be necessary to stand out from the crowd, hence DJ Dimitri from Paris.

During the next few years, as Dimitri segued hip-hop, Down Tempo cuts and House for in-store tapes and catwalk shows for the likes of designer Jean-Paul Gaultier and Chanel, he set about carving the blueprint for his debut album. When legal wranglings prevented the fashion clients for whom he mixed tapes from playing other artists' recordings, Dimitri slipped into the studio to forge his own edits in a similar fusionist style. Extending his own mix of '70s cop show soundtracks, disco, piano-bar jazz and exotic electronica, he released the **Equisses** EP in 1995 on the Paris-based Yellow label. He continued this formula on **Sacré Bleu**, but it took the briefly fashionable loungecore movement epitomised by groups like Mike Flowers Pops to gain the album a UK audience.

Dimitri's smooth production technique, sense of humour and inherent disco sensibility have since combined to produce such gems as the Dirty Harry-sampling Larry Levan tribute, "Dirty Larry", the Salsoul Orchestra-stealing "Just About Right", "I Want The World To Know" (which sampled Carl Bean's gay disco classic, "Born This Way") and 1998's irreverent remix of Atmosfear's "Motivation".

⊙ Sacré Bleu   East West/Yellow Records, 1997

Mixing up seemingly disparate elements of disco-House, soundtracks, salsa, dub, schmooze and loungecore electronica with a wry sense of humour, **Sacré Bleu** remains essential for music lovers with an open mind.

⊙ Monsieur Dimitri's De-Luxe House Of Funk   Mixmag/DMC Recordings, 1997

Dimitri's rapid-fire DJing sets have proved that good House music doesn't have to be introspective or deep. Gorgeous disco edits, vocal tracks and funk-fired instrumentals mixed to perfection and guaranteed to put a smile on your face. Includes his own exclusive and essential re-workings of Björk's "Isobel", UFO's "Spy's Spice" and Brand New Heavies' "Sometimes".

Of all the sound systems that grew up in the immediate wake of the Acid House explosion, DiY have enjoyed the greatest profile. A collective of DJs who came together via innumerable House parties in their adopted base of Nottingham during 1989, they have been the standard bearers for quality House music ever since. Most significantly, they have done so by straddling the underground-overground divide with ease: facing off the police at warehouse gatherings, throwing endless free parties and lending their support to a myriad of political causes while also hosting a hugely successful club night, Bounce, and running a record label, Strictly4Groovers.

DiY's popularity reached new heights in the summer of 1992 at the gargantuan Castlemorton Common free festival. A week-long disco bender, this spontaneous congregation of 50,000 Techno travellers is now regarded as the apotheosis of the free party movement. Of course, DiY were there, dropping the deepest House in a sea of gabba and hardcore Techno sound systems.

They've also evangelicised their Deep House gospel all over the globe. In 1991 they organised The Big Trip when 43 members of their posse hit San Francisco for a summer-long excursion into chunky House, free love and serious bodily abuse. DiY-style House collectives flourish there to this day, as well as in Dallas, Canada, Australia and much of Europe.

They launched the Strictly4Groovers imprint in 1993 with a four-track EP by Alabama 3. The main purpose of the label was to serve as an outlet for the frequent studio excursions by core DiY DJs such as Digs, Woosh, Simon DK, Emma, Jack and Damian, although artists like Nail, Glasgow's Fresh & Low and Ladbroke Grove's Phil Asher have all had releases on the label. A compilation album, also called **Strictly4Groovers**, was released on Sheffield's Warp label in 1994.

In 1996 they renamed their label DiY Discs, consolidating their reputation with 1998's compilation, **2922 Days of DiY**, a Deep House retrospective with bonus remixes. 1998 also saw the launch of the sister label Di-Versions, an outlet for more downbeat, jazz-tinged sounds, the first release being the **Serve Chilled** collection. DiY also made a successful return to clubland with the establishment of the hugely popular Floppy Disco nights at The Bomb in Nottingham and The 333 in London.

⊙ Strictly4Groovers   Warp, 1994

The essential free party, Deep House collection, complete with the aquatic groove classic "51 Days" by Paper Moon.

⊙ Serve Chilled   Di-Versions, 1998

Phat, blunted and abstract moves that soundtracked DiY's legendary mammoth all-day chill sessions.

DJ International

A long with Trax, DJ International provided the other outlet for the majority of House music produced by nearly all of the Windy City's major players from 1985 to 1990. Owned by entrepreneur/visionary/businessman/producer/DJ Rocky Jones, the label prided itself on the fact that it never released anything in a different musical style. But like Trax, it also has a history littered with tales of artist exploitation and short-sighted management.

In 1986 there were around seventy acts signed to the label, but by 1990 the artist roster was almost non-existent and the city's once flourishing scene was nowhere to be found: Frankie Knuckles had moved back to New York, Farley "Jackmaster" Funk and Marshall Jefferson were spending an increasing amount of time recording and living in London, Steve "Silk" Hurley had moved toward the remix and R&B payroll, while Hip-House – a sub-genre pioneered by Rocky and cohorts Tyree, Fast Eddie and Kool Rock Steady – had been lost in the mire.

In 1985, though, it was a completely different story. Jes Say and Trax Records had set the House ball rolling, but it was DJ International who forged another precedent with its commercially successful vocal-dominated initial output. The label's first release, JM Silk's "Music Is the Key" not only sold over 100,000 copies and made #9 on the US dance charts, but introduced one of House music's greatest producers, Steve "Silk" Hurley, and one of the genre's most capable vocalists, Keith Nunally. Following the duo's "Shadows of Your Love" single and Chip E's awesome sample cuts "Like This", "Time to Jack" and the monumental "Godfather of House", DJ International broke the mould, taking House mainstream with Farley "Jackmaster" Funk's "Love Can't Turn Around" (reaching the UK Top 10 in August, 1986, via a deal with ffrr) and later following it with House music's first #1, Hurley's "Jack Your Body" (1987).

Although the ensuing period witnessed a stream of hopeless one-off attempts to cash in on the big bucks by acts that have fallen by the wayside, 1987 and 1988 saw a host of releases that both extended the parameters of House music and provided the genre with some of its greatest moments to date. 1987 heralded the release of Larry Heard's melancholic "A Path" and "Mystery of Love" with vocalist Robert Owens (as Fingers Inc) and Donnie's remarkable "The It". Frankie Knuckles released his **Ultimate Productions** EP, which included Jamie Principle's "Baby Wants to Ride" and "Only the Strong Survive", while Sterling Void produced the vocal classics "It's Alright" (later covered by the Pet Shop Boys) and "Runaway Girl", as well as their fine debut album **It's Alright**. Joe Smooth emerged from nowhere with one of House music's most effective and lasting paeans to hope and peace, "Promised Land", and the subsequent, less ambitious albums,

Promised Land (1987) and **Rejoice** (1989). Trax producer Marshall Jefferson released the anthemic "Move Your Body", while Hot Mix 5 DJ Kenny "Jammin'" Jason teamed up with Fast Eddie to produce the string-soaring "Can U Dance".

The moulding of hip-hop and House also came courtesy of DJ International, who released such energised gems as "Ain't No Stoppin' Hip House" and Tyree's massive "Turn Up the Bass". Although Acid House had been originally carved out by Trax stalwarts Marshall Jefferson and, most effectively, Phuture, DJ International unleashed such classic 303-infused slates as Adonis' "The Poke", Fast Eddie's "Acid Thunder" and Tyree's "Acid Over" (all 1988).

⊙ **House Sounds Of Chicago Volume One**   DJ International, 1987

Impeccable compilation of the label's pre-Acid classics, including Hurley's "Jack Your Body" and "Music Is the Key", Fingers Inc's "Mystery of Love", Chip E's "Like This", Farley's "Love Can't Turn Around" and Jefferson's "Move Your Body". Good luck finding it.

Boris Dlugosh

Though he has yet to achieve the commercial success of his Peppermint Jam label partner and sometimes co-producer Mousse T, Hamburg's Boris Dlugosh remains Germany's best-loved House DJ. Graduating from teenage years spent playing the drums, he has been resident at Hamburg's Front club for the past ten years, bringing his blend of US-style dubs and vocal cuts to countrymen more used to soaking up the aggressive Techno stylings of producers such as Sven Vath and DJ Dag.

Though Dlugosh picked up limited attention as a remixer for artists including DJ Duke and New Jersey's Sabrina Johnston, he is best known for producing one of 1996's biggest club tracks, "Keep Pushin'". With its nagging vocal refrain, sub-heavy bass-line and Armand Van Helden-like cut 'n' paste dynamics, "Keep Pushin'" quickly rose to the top of the UK club charts and was championed by DJs stretching from New York's Danny Tenaglia to London's speed garage dons Tuff Jam and The Dreem Teem. 1997's follow-up, "Hold Your Head Up High", was even more popular and became an anthem at clubs such as Twice As Nice when injected with an even heavier dose of bass courtesy of 187 Lockdown producer Julian Jonah's "Bad Boy" remix.

Having released **The Deep Course** EP, featuring vocals from Mood II Swing's Lem Springsteen, Dlugosh has followed his singles' dance-floor success in 1998 with a remix of Jasper Street Company's "Love Changes" and his self-produced MFSB cut-up, "The Check Out", released under the guise of Peppermint Jam Allstars.

⊙ **"Keep Pushin'"**   Peppermint Jam,1996

One of the tunes of 1996: simple melodies, addictive vocal hooks and a gut-wrenching bass-line from hell.

Don Carlos

Unlike fellow Italo-House music acolytes Black Box, or superstar money DJs like Claudio Cocolutto, Don Carlos has remained a resolutely underground figure on the fringes of the scene. This is true despite the fact that he's been spinning since the late '70s, dabbling in

studio production since the late '80s and his debut single, "Alone" (1991), sold around 12,000 copies on the Calypso label and has been a coveted Deep House classic ever since.

Working as a professional DJ since his latter teenage years, playing at the Caminaccio club in Varese in the late '70s and later at various venues in Italy and abroad, most notably at the Morandi in Lugano, Switzerland, Don Carlos has achieved his standing through a series of jazz-washed instrumental 12". Rarely denting the club charts, they have nearly all referenced his passion for disco, Philly soul and subtle, Heard-esque Deep House, finding a small but influential fan base both in England and America.

One of Irma Records' most consistently impressive producers in the early '90s, Don Carlos followed "Alone" with the six-track **Mediterraneo** EP (1992). An under-rated triumph, the EP showcased his ability to blend mellow, yet uplifting, sax- and piano-led grooves with clean, crisp production, notably on the breathtaking synth stabs of "Free" and the subtle, Carl Craig-like electronic melodies of "Re Mida Overture".

The well-received Montego Bay project followed with long-time collaborator Stefano Tirone. 1993's "Everything" caused his reputation to blossom in England and he released the disco-inspired "Anitugua Managua" for Andrew "Doc" Livingstone's London-based Centrestage label.

oped, ironically, by American producer Kelly G (who remixed Tina Moore's "Never Gonna Let You Go", a key anthem on the London scene), was the style was taken to another level when the Dreem Teem added distinct London flavour. The combination of sweet R&B-style vocals (for the girls) and ruff beats and bass-lines (for the boys) proved to be the perfect combination of US and UK styles at a time when London's black clubbers were crying out for an alternative to drum 'n' bass. A string of key remixes (Amira's "My Desire", Kwesi's "Lovely", All Saints' "Booty Call" and Colourgirl's "Tears") followed, putting the "two-step" style in the dance music spotlight.

But it was their own production, "The Theme" (1997), which really introduced The Dreem Teem to the general public. A huge Ibiza anthem and already a solid underground hit, the track received heavy support from London's Kiss FM and went on to be a Top 30 hit in December 1997.

Meanwhile, Spoony was consolidating their position through his residency at Twice As Nice, London's leading underground garage club night. Together with the cream of London's underground DJs, he has continued to push "two-step". A much-anticipated second single mysteriously failed to materialise, though at the end of 1998 the trio landed a weekly Sunday night show on Kiss FM.

⊙ Dreem Teem In Session Vol 1   4 Liberty, 1997

Showcasing the Dreem Teem's unique two-step style, this was markedly different from the crop of "speed garage"-related mix albums on the market.

⊙ Dreem Teem In Session Vol 2   Deconstruction/4 Liberty, 1997

Lacks the novelty value and basic raw underground vibe of its predecessor, but worth checking for the inclusion of "The Theme" and Amira's "My Desire".

DJ Duke

One of the main reasons for House music's mid-'90s shift towards NYC was DJ Duke. While Junior Vasquez, DJ Pierre and Danny Tenaglia may have carved out the "progressive garage" sound, it was the entrepreneurial Greenwich Village-based break-dancer who helped slam the hard-edged groove onto the map with his collection of Power Music record labels.

A publicity-shy character who has only ever agreed to a couple of interviews, Duke combined his own disco heritage with a taste for Chicago's minimalist 4/4 rhythm in 1990 to create his first vocal track, Club People's "Club Dancing".

With the Power Music logo aping the famous Trax insignia, it was clear where his ultimate ambitions and musical reference points lay. The imprint's debut, Inner Soul's "Make Things Happen" (1992), followed a similar musical path to "Club Dancing", but gave little indication of the scope both he and the label would shortly embark on. While essential emotive vocal singles like The Music Choir's "Get Down to Love", Freedom's "Closer" and Inner Soul's "Celebrate" were all well received, Duke also began turning his hand to darker instrumental cuts on the offshoot Power Music Trax.

Favouring a heavily percussive, tribal-rhythmic style, but never entirely abandoning disco's sensibilities, Duke's third release on Power Music Trax, Black Rhythms Vol.2's "Blow Your Whistle" (1993), became a surprise crossover commercial hit in the UK after months of club exposure. With its thundering bass-line, rave-esque whistle stabs and snatched Hamilton Bohannon excerpt, "Blow Your Whistle" led to formulaic follow-ups "Can U Feel It?" and "Turn It Up".

1994 found Duke continuing with his various vocal projects

(including Freedom's excellent "Loving You") and dark dubs under the guise of Tribal Liberation, Music Madness and Black Rhythms Vol.4, yet 1995 ushered in a surprising list of new names to the Power Music roster. More sub-labels – Power Music Distribution, DJ Exclusive Records and Sex Trax Records – were started to host seminal works by the Windy City's leading lights: there were albums by Roy Davis Jr and Felix Da Housecat (as Aphrohead) and monstrous, wild-pitch-style singles from LA Williams, Mark the 909 King, Spanky and Nate Williams. New York heads like Jason Nevins, Fred Jorio and Kings Of Tomorrow also found a label where they could freely release material, and Power stood alongside Tribal Records and Chicago's Cajual/Relief labels as one of the key moulders in House music's second coming.

Despite claiming in a rare 1995 interview that his "heart is in songs with melody", Duke remained an innovative and exploratory figure in the dance community, switching from vocal, piano-enthused singles to percussive, dark dubs. 1996 witnessed his own fierce, trance-inflected productions on Sex Mania using The Pleasure Dome (check "12 Minutes Of Dreams"), Music Freaks and Factory Kids monikers and a series of five sample-heavy, rough-edged, instrumental **Techdisco** EPs. He also found time

to create a bout of caustic Techfunkers singles and a series of subtle, late-night sax-led soirees as the Funky Horns with "Blow" and "Night Sessions" (1995–6) which were collected on the excellent **Music 4 Ya Ears** (1996), as well as recruit Daniell Dixon and Mood II Swing to the Power roster.

Since late 1996 Power Music has been a non-existent force and Duke has produced little of note, but 1998 witnessed a mild return to form with the hard-edged "Heat" 12" for Miami's Bassline Records (as Inferno Reaction) and the more melodic, Manuel Göttsching-sampling "E2-E4" for New York's Henry Street imprint.

◉ Power Mastermix   X:treme, 1995

A seamless label mastermix which spans dark, hypnotic slates from Aphrohead and Roy Davis Jr, Acid-overkill courtesy of Spank Spank and four inimitable Duke instrumental workouts, including Techfunkers' "Looking For Da Perfect Beat" and Black Rhythms Vol.4's under-rated "Throw Ya Hands in the Air".

Easy Street Records

A forerunner to the New York strongholds of Strictly Rhythm, Nervous and King Street Records, Easy Street provided the main outlet for the Big Apple's producers to transmute disco into garage and soulful House. Following the demise of the disco-era labels Prelude, West End and Salsoul, it was both Easy Street and Big Beat Records who showcased the emerging sounds so prominent on the dance-floors of Larry Levan's Paradise Garage and Tony Humphries' Zanzibar clubs. Furthermore, Easy Street introduced to the world seminal producers such as Paul Simpson and Blaze and important garage vocalists like Adeva and Alexander Hope.

Reflecting the trends in NYC nightlife, early releases were typically freestyle club cuts and included the John "Jellybean" Benitez-produced "Body Work" (by Hot Streak), World Premiere's "Share The Night" and Monyaka's dubious "Reggaematic Funk". Though interspersed with the inevitable dross, vocal goodies like 1984's "Picking Up Promises" by Jocelyn Brown indicated the label was moving in an upward trajectory.

That move was solidified with 1985's "You Don't Know", produced by the hand of New Jersey's Paul Simpson (who later achieved huge club success with his much sampled "Musical Freedom"). Serious Intention's phenomenal "You Don't Know" wasn't just one of Larry Levan's classic cuts, but formed a clear blueprint for garage with its skipping hi-hats, heavy bass-line and male vocal dropouts. Shot's disco-driven "Main Thing" was also a big hit, while Cultural Vibe's "Ma Foom Bey" (1987), produced in part by Tony Humphries, sliced up soulful melodies with Acid overtones to become one of the year's most important dance singles.

As the New Jersey scene grew in stature around the popularity of Tony Humphries' club nights at Zanzibar, Easy Street released Blaze productions like In-Sync's "Sometimes Love" (1987) and Adeva's gloriously funky "In & Out of My Life", which would spark off her musical career. Other 12"s of note included Todd Terry's "Voices In My House" and "Check This Out" (as HardHouse), Joanna Law's "First Time Ever" (1990) and Extortion's massive "How Do You See Me Now?", which became a favourite with London's Boys Own crew, whose label it was subsequently licensed to, and sent to the top of the dance charts thanks to a Joey Negro remix.

Further soul-dripping deepness arrived from long-time Blaze collaborator Cassio Ware in 1993 with both the "Baby Love" and "Loose

Booty" 12"s, while Blaze released Alexander Hope's "Let The Music Take You". In 1995, Easy Street again hit the dancefloor in emphatic fashion – it was the original home to De'Lacy's pop chart-topping "Hideaway".

⊙ The Very Best Of Easy Street   Easy Street Records, 1992

Includes the essential Humphries-mixed club classic "Ma Foom Bey" by Cultural Vibe and Serious Intention's proto-garage masterpiece "You Don't Know".

808 State

The old age pensioners of British electronica, 808 State can truly lay claim to be part of that select number of dance acts who've successfully crossed the near fatal fence dividing underground credibility and commercial success. Unfortunately, in over ten years of production they've never quite managed to regain the sheer anthemic brilliance of their first European hit single, "Pacific State" (1989).

Originally formed as a trio – Graham Massey (keyboards and various instruments), Gerald Simpson (DJ) and Martin Price (frontman) – 808 State combined the trend-setting Ambient, 303-tinged groove of "Pacific State" with two raw Acid House albums, **Newbuild** (1988) and **Quadrastate** (1989). Released through Price's influential record shop Eastern Bloc, **Quadrastate** clearly signalled that 808 State intended to be more than just one-hit wonders and introduced a more lightweight, commercial sound which, coupled with their studio prowess, ensured a stream of club anthems like "State to State" and "State Ritual" (both 1989).

But at their creative peak, Simpson (who had already been producing as a solo artist for some time) bitterly split from the collective to record as A Guy Called Gerald. Local DJs Andrew Barker and Darren Partington were quickly recruited into the fold and the hit factory continued with "Cubik" in 1990 and "In Yer Face" (1991), both of which were featured on the post-Acid hangover album **90** (1990).

Fresh collaborations with hardcore Moss-Side rapper MC Tunes yielded the breakbeat singles, "The Only Rhyme That Bites" and "Tunes Splits The Atom" (1990), while "Ooops" (1991) featured Icelandic nymphet Björk in her first dance-rooted work. These singles were included on UK Top 10 album **EX:EL** (1991), alongside more softly spoken vocals from New Order's Bernard Sumner on the standout track, "Spanish Heart". Yet only a few months later, the band's shape changed again as Price declined to tour the States and chose instead to work on solo projects. Various remixing duties followed for the remaining trio, including work with David Bowie, Quincy Jones, Primal Scream, REM and even Rolf Harris.

1994's "Bombardin" signalled a return to more welcome, underground roots with its inspired, rough-and-ready drum breaks and mellow atmospherics, while **State to State** (1994) – a free CD compilation of new and classic cuts released exclusively to their fan club – cemented the new direction. 1996's eagerly awaited **Don Solaris** long-player was something of a disappointment, though. Despite featuring an extensive cast of new collaborators, including the Manic Street Preachers' James Dean Bradfield, only the superb ethereal breakbeat of "Azura" (with Lamb's Louise Rhodes) stood out from the confused Techno soundscape.

No real surprise then, that the tenth anniversary of 808 State's finest moment heralded the cash-in opportunity to re-release, and remix, "Pacific State" along with a follow-up Greatest Hits album. With its nautical electronics "inspired" by Manuel Göttshching's proto-Techno album E2-E4, "Pacific State" might well have provided the soundtrack for a generation, not to mention a handy sampling tool for a host of drum 'n' bass producers, but it has also saddled 808 State with their longest hangover.

◉ **808; 88: 98**   ZTT, 1998

A near perfect Greatest Hits package, which includes both versions of "Pacific State", alongside "Cubik", "In Yer Face" and "Ooops".

Electribe 101

tar-struck vocalist Billy Ray Martin spent her early career on the Berlin club circuit with the eleven-piece Motown-inspired soul band Billie and the Deep, but, disillusioned with her lack of immediate success, the Hamburg-born chanteuse moved to London in 1985. It wasn't until 1987, after Martin had placed an advert in the music press pleading, "Soul Rebel seeks genius", that the Birmingham-born quartet of Joe Stevens, Les Fleming, Rob Cimarosti and Brian Nordhoff came together to form Electribe 101.

After a delayed start, in which time the boys found time to construct their own studio in Birmingham, the band released their debut hit single, "Talking With Myself" (1988). Fusing Martin's dramatic vocal range with moody, four-to-the-floor electronics (influenced by Julian Jonah's "Jealousy & Lies"), lush pianos and a cheeky hook from cult '60s TV show *Mission Impossible*, the record's status was ensured with a Frankie Knuckles remix. "Tell Me When The Fever Ended" followed a similar path to commercial and critical success, with a short-sighted music press drooling over the band's "unique" ability to combine House music with thoughtful lyrics. The Acid generation loved them regardless, and the ensuing album, **Electribal Memories** (1990), still provides the perfect backdrop to any after-hours comedown session.

Yet despite the acclaim, Electribe 101 split shortly afterward. The ambitious Martin moved on to a still more successful career as a solo artist where she drew even stronger comparisons with Marlene Dietrich and Aretha Franklin. The styling worked: 1995's pop-dance debut, "Your Loving Arms", sold over 200,000 units and became a Top 10 hit in the UK and a #1 club hit in the States. "Imitation of Life" followed suit and her subsequent album harnessed the production skills of Junior Vasquez, Eric Kupper and Arthur Baker alongside Martin's own considerable programming talents. Recorded in just two and a half months, **Deadline For My Memories** (1996) was a reasonable pop-dance effort that often revelled in Martin's mid-tempo musings, but lacked much of the conviction and emotive content of **Electribal Memories**.

The other members of Electribe 101, meanwhile, had gone back to Birmingham to work with local rappers, singers and reggae movers, producing the under-rated **Co-Operation** (1994) as Groove Corporation.

◉ Electribal Memories   Mercury, 1990

Gorgeous mid-tempo rhythms, lush pianos and weightless strings provide the perfect backdrop for Billie Ray Martin's dramatic vocals and conscious lyrics. Frankie Knuckles and Larry Heard 12" remixes come as an added bonus.

Emotive Records

Although Emotive Records' first release was licensed from Italy (Maude's "Get On the Move"), it is for tracking the House sound of NYC that the label will be remembered. Despite never spawning a major hit, Emotive nonetheless released a host of dancefloor-wreckin' singles stretching from upbeat garage paeans like James Howard's "We Can Do It (Wake Up)" to Felix Da Housecat's ultimate moment of twisted wild-pitch paranoia, "In the Dark We Live (Thee Lite)".

Early Emotive club favourites included the swinging groove of Matt Di Mario's "Feel the Drums" (1990), Valerie Johnson's "Step Into My Life", Michael Lavel's "Do Me This Way" and Michelle Ayers' upbeat "Share My Love". In 1991, one of garage's most impressive vocalists, James Howard, helped propel Emotive onto dancefloors with one of the year's best songs, "We Can Do It (Wake Up)". 1992's "Feeling Good" wasn't far behind with its equally uplifting, trickling piano lines and propulsive groove. Productions by Baltimore's Charles Dockins, New Jersey's Smack team and Brooklyn's Victor Simonelli (as Instant Exposure and Groove Committee) helped solidify Emotive's reputation both at home and abroad.

Deep House arrived courtesy of the unique Jovonn – whose Gold-tone label is distributed through Emotive – with well-regarded 12"s like the **Out All Nite** EP and the hypnotic 3am classic "Deep". As the darker rhythms of tribal became the dominant sound on NYC dancefloors, Emotive wasn't to be found resting on its laurels and cuts by DJ Pierre, Aphrohead, EG Fullalove, Project 4007, Spank Spank and That Kid Chris became staples of the new sub-genre.

Since the 1995 singles by Butch Quick ("Always"), Lenny Fontana ("Music") and 95 North ("Still of the Night"), the quality levels have been inconsistent at best. Yet for fans of New York House, Emotive will always hold a special place in any record collection.

⊙ The Future Sound Of New York   Emotive/Ministry Of Sound, 1995

Mixed by Junior Vasquez, this tribal/progressive garage collection includes merciless cuts by DJ Pierre, Aphrohead and EG Fullalove.

Faithless

A multi-faceted, four-piece dance outfit, Faithless have managed to create a successful niche for themselves in late '90s club culture. Formed by Mensa-member/philosophy graduate/producer/remixer Rollo Armstrong in 1995, Faithless also comprises DJ Sister Bliss, rapper Maxi Jazz and folk singer Jamie Catto.

Rollo had already achieved success in 1992 as the producer of Felix's "Don't You Want Me". Costing £300 to make, the single pre-dated the explosion of trance and reached #3 in the UK national charts while Rollo was still working in his local job centre. Remixes of material by Simply Red, U2, Pet Shop Boys and M-People, his own

tunes (the "Rollo Goes" series) and projects such as Kristine W established the Rollo sound: melodic, poppy and upbeat. This work led to a close relationship with House DJ Sister Bliss and a number of releases as a duo followed, although Bliss is also an established producer/artist in her own right, thanks to dancefloor hits such as "Badman" and "Life's a Bitch". Maxi Jazz was formely a DJ with the London-based The Soul Food Café Show and had released a number of EPs and played with acts such as Soul II Soul and Jamiroquai, while Jamie Catto had previously been a member of the little-known The Big Truth Band.

Together they recorded a debut album, **Reverence** (1995), which showcased a wilfully eclectic mix of House, hip-hop, folk and Ambient musics, tempering Rollo's more upbeat tendencies with a downbeat melancholia. Hampered by a lack of money for promotion, their debut single, "Salva Mea (Save Me)", reached #30 in the UK charts in July, 1995, while its follow-up, "Insomnia", reached #27. In Europe, however, "Insomnia" sold massively (1 million copies in Germany alone), and a British re-release in October 1996 saw it climb to #3, while the re-released "Salva Mea" reached #9.

Having toured Europe extensively as an expanded ten-piece collective, the group consolidated their previous hits in 1998 with the trance-inflected dancefloor perfection, "God Is a DJ", and a second album, **Sunday 8PM**.

⊙ Reverence Cheeky, 1996

Originally overlooked, the band's eclectic debut set ended up going gold in 22 countries on the back of the success of re-released singles "Insomnia" and "Salva Mea". Even REM's Michael Stipe named it as his album of the year.

Farley "Jackmaster" Funk

Originally rising to prominence as the DJ at Chicago's infamous Playground club (where he held a residency from 1981 to 1987), Farley "Jackmaster" Funk exerted a crucial influence over the course of House music's early direction through his radio show on WBMX 102.7FM.

Known until 1986 as Farley "Funkin'" Keith, his virtuoso spinning of Italian disco imports and Philly classics – often underpinned with the heavy kick drum sound of his Roland TR-808 drum machine – held sway over the airwaves. Together with the Hot Mix Five DJ team of Ralphi Rosario, Mickey "Mixin'" Oliver, Scott "Smokin'" Seals and Kenny "Jammin'" Jason, Farley is largely credited with bringing House music to the citizens of Chicago. Farley's lunchtime and weekend shows were so revered that he became the acknowledged influence for younger producers such as Felix Da Housecat to enter the studio, and when he made the station switch to WGCI with his "Jackmaster 5" in 1986, 1.5 million listeners were regularly tuning in. As Trax Records producer and visionary Vince Lawrence remembers, "Jamie [Principle] lent the music style and personality, but it was Farley who commercialised it and gave it a firm identity."

Like those of Jamie Principle, Vince Lawrence and Jesse Saunders, Farley's productions drew heavily on the synthesised, European sounds of bands like Depeche Mode, Kraftwerk and Telex. Farley's 1985 debut epitomised the overtly simplistic style and structure of most of his releases: "Funkin' With the Drums" merely looped a repetition of his name ("Farley, Farley, Farley") over the sound of an 808 drum machine and a stolen bass-line from one of disco's most over-played anthems, MFSB's "Love Is the Message".

The formula did hit the mark once, on the 12" now synonymous with his name, 1986's "Love Can't Turn Around". A cover of Isaac Hayes' "I Can't Turn Around", which Steve "Silk" Hurley accused Farley of stealing from him, the single was licensed to London's ffrr records and became the first House record to gain commercial success, reaching the UK Top 10 that year.

Farley's subsequent attempts at R&B and rap fell flat, however. A mid-'90s deal with London's 4 Liberty Records saw the re-release of "Love Can't Turn Around". Since then, Farley has returned to his original career, DJing, joining the UK's guest circuit, regularly playing his mix of vocal House at clubs such as Birmingham's Miss Monneypenny's and Coalville's Passion.

◉ House Music Movement – Farley "Jackmaster" Funk

Mastertone, 1998

Hardly inspirational stuff, but this beatmix collection of popular House/garage cuts by DJ Pierre, Roger S, Ultra Naté and others is probably the easiest place to find Farley's anthemic "Love Can't Turn Around".

Terry Farley

I f British clubbers are unsure as to what is "proper", "real" and "soulful" in dance music, then they have only to ask West-London-born DJ, producer and scenester Terence Farley. A guardian of the nation's dancefloors for over a decade, Farley has never been slow in championing the best and forgetting the rest.

From a young age Farley was avidly listening to radio jocks Robbie Vincent and Greg Edwards and he soon began collecting soul, reggae and hip-hop. His passion drew him into London's club and wareHouse scene and to soul weekenders and all-nighters across the country. With his knowledge, enthusiasm and hedonistic head, it was no surprise that he was asked to play his records out more often and by 1985 the former gas-fitter had joined Pete Tong as a warm-up DJ at Tottenham Court Road's Raid club, playing Studio One reggae and New York hip-hop.

In 1987 Farley was dragged away from his West London raregroove hangouts and taken to witness the capers occurring at Danny Rampling's South London Shoom club. He was soon installed in the back room playing reggae, but as the club became more popular and the vibe more upbeat, Farley dug deep into the boogie crates and pulled out old soul tracks which flowed smoothly into the E vein. Having also taken up a back-room residency at Paul Oakenfold's Spectrum, he began to be gripped by the Ibizan haze and his musical tastes opened up.

Already an integral part of the era's most important magazine, *Boys Own*, Farley also played a part in the release of two essential compilations. In 1988 ffrr released **Balearic Beats**, which stands as a testament to the diversity and rather ludicrous nature of some of the tracks that had gained favour with Farley and his all-seeing, all-knowing gang (Farley's favourites from the time included "Why, Why, Why" by the Woodentops and Code 61's "Drop the Deal"). By 1989 Farley had helped switched the capital on to the sounds of Italo House, again pencilling the accompanying sleeve notes to another significant compilation, **The House Sound Of Europe**.

Farley was working the capital's coolest dancefloors, so it was logical that groove-smitten indie groups like Primal Scream, Happy Mondays and The Farm should call upon him to add the necessary ingredients to satisfy the dancers. Consequently Farley took to the studio controls and (whilst often in the shadows of Andrew Weatherall) served up majestic versions of Primal Scream's "Loaded" and "Come Together" (both 1990) and also assisted Oakenfold with the early works of the Happy Mondays. However, the closest meeting of minds occurred with The Farm, a partnership which was cemented by a north versus south football and fashion rivalry. The result was the "Ghost Dance" mix of "Stepping Stone" and the triumphant "Altogether Now" (1990).

Farley also took to remixing acts from different ends of the musical spectrum, stretching from Bananarama's "Only Your Love" to Better Day's "Love Is the Message". This trait has continued throughout his career as he has taken on work by The Soup Dragons, Lisa Stansfield,

which lack the distinction of individual vision that separates the new Titans: Green Velvet, Moodymann, and Daft Punk.

Farris' releases on Relief, Cajual, Communique, Soma and most notably on Germany's Force Inc. label work on the interface between the hard bass-drum licks of Chi-town's past and the recesses of a huge disco collection. That in itself is not uncommon, and his choice of samples can veer too close to the commercially recognisable (check "Good Feeling" on **Planet House**). The trick with sampling, as DJ Sneak proved with "You Can't Hide From Your Bud" and Daft Punk's Thomas Bangalter took to its peak with Stardust, is to inject so much new joy into a track dominated by a recognisable sample that the listener can soon forget the source's presence. With Farris' records, the sample is all too often the object of fascination, rather than the track itself.

There was nothing disagreeable on Farris' two albums for Force Inc. **Planet House** (1997) was an exacting continuation of the first weed-dedicated slab, **The Fruity Green** (1996). His methods of filtering connect with the 909 hammer-blows to fine dancefloor effect, yet over the course of ten album tracks those methods never differentiate themselves enough to command repeat listening. When Farris DJs, he cranks the social dynamics of the dance to the max, but only occasionally do his tracks match this brilliance of disco and steel.

⊙ **The Fruity Green**   Force Inc., 1996

Solid debut that never veers from its dancefloor aims and never panders to the broader desires of the home listener.

Faze Action

Since 1995, brothers Simon and Robin Lee have been producing their own take on electronic disco as Faze Action with great success, providing the necessary funk for dancefloors whilst using original sounds and unusual instruments. Of the growing breed of artists attempting to mix a combination of House and disco, Faze Action bear the closest resemblance to the late '70s /early '80s blueprint of dubbed-out dance grooves produced by the likes of Arthur Russell. The emphasis is placed on a combination of live instrumentation (including cello, clarinet and Chapman Stick) and studio trickery – experimenting with modern technology in ways comparable to the adventures of earlier producers like the Mizell Brothers or François Kervorkian.

Robin, a multi-talented musician living in Osaka, Japan, receives basic ideas and beats from Simon, upon which he writes melodies and bass-lines. Back in England, Simon uses his brother's live input to pro-

duce the finished track. Their first release on Nuphonic Records, the silky smooth "Original Disco Motion" (1995), immediately propelled them into the spotlight with its gliding Rhodes and bass funk.

For their debut single to be supported by the likes of François K and Glenn Underground was impressive, but greater accolades followed when they unleashed "In the Trees" in early 1996. One of the year's best singles, the adventurous mixture of cello, Moog and crisp beats assured the release plenty of exposure, and promptly directed all eyes upon both Faze Action and Nuphonic. Following their next funk-fuelled single, "Turn the Point", Simon and Robin were ready to release their debut album, **Plans and Designs** (1997). More a rewarding home listening experience than a collection of devastating club tracks, it provides clear evidence of the brothers' ambition in the inclusion of a small orchestra on the string-led title track. Within months **Plans and Designs** had broken outside the underground House scene and the brothers were hyped by the British media as the forerunners of "nu-House".

Following the release of Simon Lee's mixed compendium of disco-House cuts, **Through the Skies** (1998), the brothers returned in October 1998 with yet another original groove, "Kariba". Combining Brazilian bossa with Zeke Manyika's Afro-Latin vocals, the single set the precedent for Faze Action's follow-up album which was released by Nuphonic in June 1999.

◉ Plans and Designs   Nuphonic, 1997

Impressive debut set which includes the essential "In the Trees" and "Original Disco Motion".

Felix Stallings (Felix Da Housecat)

Raised in Chicago's affluent suburbs, 14-year-old Felix Stallings formed his short-lived high-school band, Shades of Black, in the image of Prince & the Revolution. Catalysed into solo action by WBMX's lunchtime Hot Mix show, this self-taught keyboard player changed musical directions the following year to create the raw, 303-embedded track behind 1986's jacked-up Acid House classic "Phantasy Girl".

With lyrics and additional production provided by DJ Pierre, the track was released on Chicago's little-known SRO imprint and subsequently became one of the most popular records the city had produced. But while Pierre went on to greater things with Phantasy Club, Stallings' parents blocked any of his early ambitions of becoming a full-fledged teenage prodigy. It wasn't until he flunked out of Alabama State and returned to the Windy City's Columbia performing arts college that he met his wife-to-be and was persuaded to get back to his natural habitat behind the recording desk.

From then on, Stallings became one of House music's most enigmatic and compelling characters. Felix's moments of genius have often been encumbered by his paranoia about the music industry, which at stages has manifested itself in terrifying apocalyptic visions – music that he calls "Vapournoise".

Ironically, it was Pierre's wild-pitch blueprint single, "Generate Power", that motivated Stallings to give his former friend a call and get things moving again in 1991. The duo's trip to England shortly after heralded Felix's similarly styled debut single, "Thee Dawn", on Guerilla Records, released under the pseudonym of his favourite cartoon character, Felix Da Housecat. In a successful attempt to carve out a clearly definable style of his own, Stallings made his grooves more minimal, distorted and often faster than Pierre's, without destroying their dancefloor appeal. The early '90s bore a host of well-received cuts for labels such as Strictly Rhythm, Freetown Inc., Djax Up-Beats, Nervous, Bush and Global Cuts under a spectrum of monikers including Aphrohead, Wonderboy, Sharimaxx and Aurra and Thee Dove.

As a sign of his growing popularity in the UK, 1994 saw him ink a deal with the Deep Distraction label and subsequently his most effective release to that point, the stunning **Madkatt Courtship** EP. The captivating ensuing album, **Dawn's Early Light** (1994), took Pierre's influence to new heights by mixing up minimal beats, distorted rhythms and tweaking frequencies with semi-mangled vocals and lush emotive strings.

Under his Aphrohead guise, 1994 saw perhaps his most effective single, the twisted club classic "In the Dark We Live (Thee Lite)". But the following album, **Thee Industry Made Me Do It** (1995), was an aggressive tirade that at times just stated the obvious with tracks like "Manik Needs" and "Demented Syndrome".

Back under Thee Madkatt Courtship pseudonym, Felix's critically acclaimed **Alone In the Dark** (1995) was a completely different proposition. Although the panic-attack visions continued on cuts like the title track and "Alone", incredible grooves, gorgeous filmic backdrops and Harrison

Crump's intense vocals gave way to a sense of melancholy romance on the breathtaking "Under Water", "Ballad of the Rain" and "Claire".

Yet the same year bore the disappointing **Metropolis Presents Day? Thee Album** (1995) on his own Radikal Fear imprint. Though the romance continued on such standouts as "Some Kinda Special" and the impressive tranced-out funk of "Submarine", the album only appealed to his hardened fans.

With the tragic death of his friend and Radikal Fear's head of A&R, Armando, in 1996, the label disappeared, while Felix too has been unusually quiet. One of his last memorable releases, a remix of Kylie Minogue's "Where's the Feeling?" (1996), proved that Felix could still turn on the magic in an instant. Having indicated he has an abundance of tracks ready to be released, in 1998 he inked a deal with London Records, and looks set to make a full comeback in the near future.

⊙ Felix Da Housecat presents Thee Madkatt Courtship:
Alone In The Dark   Deep Distraction, 1995

Felix's most complete album. The trademark rising dramatics veer from the emotive to the extreme, but remain utterly compelling throughout.

Terry Francis

nspired by the soulful legacies of Blaze and Larry Heard, Terry Francis held his first residency at a bar in Leatherhead. But it was when he moved to the notorious Sterns club in Brighton, spinning alongside Acid-era deities Colin Dale, Mr.C and "Evil" Eddie Richards, that he began to find a truly appreciative audience for his dynamic segues of dubby House, celestial breakbeat and ethereal vocals. It would be Richards, himself a pioneer at merging House and Techno since the late '80s, who proved to be Francis' mentor. Like him, Francis took the route of DJing at small underground parties rather than commercial Meccas, acquiring a deep-held passion for the music and commitment to setting up his own club nights.

By 1994 he had established what would become one of London's most popular nights, Wiggle. Run by Francis, DJ Nathan Coles and their girlfriends, Wiggle has continued to be a road-blocked affair of tech-House tunes, chemical abuse and serious dancing. The fact that it has sold out every month since it started pretty much speaks for itself.

Francis has also been able to transfer his DJing prowess onto vinyl. He runs and records for both the Wiggle and Eye For Sound labels, though it is with Richard Breeden's Pagan Records that he reached a wider audience. Although he has released 12"s both under his own name and under the guise of Housey Doingz, it has been the two acclaimed volumes of his mixed albums, **Architecture** (1997, 1998), that have really put his name on the map.

⊙ Terry Francis presents Architecture
Volume 2   Pagan Records, 1998

Better than its predecessor, this mixes up moments of subsonic deepness, atmospheric breakbeat and even a full vocal cut (Presence's sublime "Sense of Danger").

Gemini

A s Gemini, Spencer Kinsey has developed a strong reputation as a producer to watch. Never much in the public eye, and with no big tune or album with which people can immediately associate him, he has achieved a model of underground status: near anonymity, but total respect. His sound has grown into a distinctively low-key version of House music's exuberance, a facet which is interesting, but which is not without its problems for the listener.

Born in Chicago, Kinsey moved to LA, returning fifteen years later to discover the growing scene that would set his mind spinning through excited tangents. Gradually moving into mixing, five years of learning, experimenting, and listening led to a union with Chicago's key second-generation labels, Cajual and Relief. It was Cajual that released his debut, 1993's "Tangled Thoughts".

It's with these two labels that Gemini has spent most of his career, gradually defining his own version of the tough, militant grooves that Relief promotes, whilst using elements of Cajual Records' madcap neo-funk to whet the appetite. Cajual is the home for the peak of his work so far, 1995's brilliant "Le Fusion". A cousin to Innerzone Orchestra's "Bug in the Bassbin", it's a spiralling chaos of cabaret compere giggles, synth drones and dedications to "Chicago, c'est la fusion", which never rests in one groove for long before tripping off into another double bass-line, another percussion fill.

As Kinsey moved into album work with **In & Out of Fog-Lights** and **In Neutral** (both 1997), a conflict emerged between Kinsey's development in pure Chicago House and his music's move into introspective self-absorption. While reworking his basic rhythm – strengthening House's double third beat so that it's closer to breakbeat – Kinsey has moved towards the "intelligent Techno" scene that the Warp label fostered in England in the early '90s and has found the same limits – his minor-key jazz inflections the Chicago equivalents of string pans and fades. The range of sound is too limited, the production too muted to involve, leaving the listener looking in at someone toying with a personal vision, but with no dynamic to grasp onto and no element to excite. At the most immediate level it means that the tunes fade into a background space that's skeletal enough not to offend, but too distant to involve.

There's always hope for Gemini in that dazzling moment "Le Fusion", a moment that doesn't define his career but stands outside it as a path that might have been.

◉ The Future Sound Of Chicago   Ministry Of Sound, 1995

Completely essential selection from Cajual/Relief's glory days. The exquisite "Le Fusion", one of second-generation House's highlights, is at the zenith of the whole thing.

◉ In Neutral   Distance, 1997

Probably the best of the three albums, but never special. "DeBass" and "?" show his single-minded aesthetic catching fire for brief moments before the pale wash returns.

Walter Gibbons

While Tom Moulton may have invented the disco remix with his razor-blade reconstructions of The Trammps, Walter Gibbons was the person who explicitly connected the art of the dance remix with the mixing desk wizardry of Jamaican dub producers and engineers. By applying dub techniques like instrumental drop-out, phasing and echo to the floor-burning functionality of disco's 4/4 beat, Gibbons teased dancers with instrumental foreplay and created the blueprint for the piano breakdown so beloved of present-day DJs like Sasha and Digweed. His stretched-out mixes often teetered on the edge of a bare-bones minimalism which provided a working model for the early jack trax of Chicago House.

Even without his undeniable craftsmanship behind a studio board, Gibbons would go down in history as the remixer of the first commercially available 12" single, Double Exposure's "Ten Percent" (1976). Extending the pleasure of Ronnie Baker, Norman Harris and Earl Young's production to a full nine minutes, Gibbons' first "disco blend" (as it said on the label) was more purely functional than mind-bending. But by emphasising those skipping hi-hats in the breakdown, Gibbons almost single-handedly created what would become garage.

Other fine early Gibbons mixes included Salsoul Orchestra's "Nice 'n' Nasty" (1976) and "Magic Bird of Fire" (1977), but perhaps his best, and most audacious, mix for Salsoul was his eleven-minute overhaul of Loleatta Holloway's "Hit and Run" (1977). These and other early remixes were included on **Disco Madness** (1979), a double-12" EP of Gibbons masterpieces.

His remix of Bettye Lavette's "Doin' the Best That I Can" (1978) was (and probably remains) the furthest any dance track has gone into dub's shadowy realm of echo. With the conga pattern about the only relatively stable element of the track, Gibbons brought the horns forward only to drop them out before the bar finished, mixed the triangle chimes higher than anything else including the vocals, phased the drums, used ludicrous sound effects and based the breakdown on a two-note mellow church organ riff. It was one of the few dance records that sounded as though it could have come out of Lee Perry's Black Ark studio. As journalist David Toop has said, "Walter Gibbons could make a dancefloor move to a glockenspiel."

Gibbons went even further out with his collaborations with dancefloor experimentalist Arthur Russell. Based on the connection that Russell made between disco's rhythmic repetitiveness and the repeating figures of minimalists like Philip Glass and Steve Reich, "Let's Go Swimming" (1983) was an improbable combination of Chinese water torture percussion and huge, enveloping bass chords and synth washes. As Indian Ocean, Russell and Gibbons released "Treehouse/School Bell" (1983) whose sumptuous textures prefigured the Deep House of Larry Heard by several years.

Another model for the stripped-down feel of early Chicago House was Gibbons' stunning mix of Strafe's "Set it Off" (1984). The drums that sound like they were recorded down the block from the studio let you know immediately that this was the result of Gibbons' handiwork, and "Set it Off" continued down this unrelentingly stark and moody path for nine minutes – the only respite from the claustrophobic sub-bass and mad scientist synth figures were the outrageous percussion effects that would creep up every once in a while, until they became as maddening as the synths. Gibbons has since settled down to a career as a behind-the-scenes studio technician, but tracks like Black Science Orchestra's "Walter's Room" (1996) continue to pay tribute to the man who paved the way for mega-bucks mixing stars like Armand Van Helden.

⊙ Disco Madness Salsoul, 1979

If you can find it, this is a collection of some of the most famous mixes in dance music history. His mixes of "Ten Percent" and "Nice 'n' Nasty" are available on **Classic Salsoul Volume 1** (Mastercuts, 1993).

⊙ Strafe: "Set it Off" Jus' Born, 1984

Another one to track down in the used bins, but worth the time and effort for its implausible audaciousness.

Glasgow Underground

Alongside Atlantic Jaxx, Glasgow Underground has been the UK's strongest outlet for new, dynamic House since its formation in 1996. Kevin McKay's small imprint is doing more, and better, than most other British labels to see Deep House as an international underground network. Guitars ripple and soothe whilst the distinctively globular production, warm and wide, adds to the feeling that this is a unified vision of House.

The label's first release, "Just a Mood" (1996) by Studio Blue (McKay and Andy Carrick), defined the tone immediately, its widescreen guitar so thickly enshrined in distant gazes that it carried listeners into a personal state. The other most potent highlights so far come from British House's two most feted young producers, DJ Q and 16B. Q's "The Original Porn King" (1997) may lift its riff from an old funk tune, but Q tweaked and phased a piece that floated between faint oriental strings and an addictive bass-line that moved with a simple regularity. Working with Mackay as Sixteen Souls, Omid Nourizadeh (aka 16B) surpassed his more acclaimed solo work, and, with the brilliant "Late Night Jam" (1997), created a minor masterpiece. Stripped to the essential its melody was a tickle in the upper register. It was a prime example of the hugely addictive qualities of Glasgow Underground's oeuvre.

In 1998 the label released two critically acclaimed 4am specialities: full-length albums from Powder Productions (**Pipe Dreams**) and Daniel Ibbotson (**Stream Lines**), both mixing deep grooves and warm melodies. Other artists on the label include Mateo & Matos and Romanthony, who released **Instinctual** in 1999.

◉ Glasgow Underground
Volume One   Glasgow Underground, 1997

Stunningly addictive first label sampler that works its way into your
mind as a late-night fadeout.

Global
Communication

Since joining forces in Taunton, Somerset in 1992, Tom Middleton and Mark Pritchard have become recognised as one of the
UK's most innovative production teams. House, Techno, electro, disco,
rap, funk, jazz and even classical music have eminated from their mixing desks and manifested themselves across many guises – Reload
(hard, industrial Techno), Link, E621 (trance Techno), Jedi Knights
(electro funk), The Chameleon (drum 'n' bass), Secret Ingredients
(Deep House), The Modwheel (experimental), Pulusha and Amba
(Ambient).

Classically trained Tom was doing a graphic design course and
approached Mark, a guitarist, while he was DJing in a club, after being
surprised at the Techno and Strictly Rhythm House that he was dropping. Middleton moved on to DJ and collaborate with Richard James,
allegedly as the other Aphex Twin. When Pritchard heard the material,
he set up the Evolution label with Middleton, inspired by Carl Craig's
track of that name.

They served notice of their intentions with some radical remixes of

Chapterhouse's **Blood Music,** re-named **The Pentamerous Metamorphosis** (1993), before delivering their defining moment, Global Communication's **76:14** (1994), an album rich in texture and ambience which combined haunting melody, inventive rhythmic patterns and a powerful sense of spirituality and emotion.

Their limited edition Evolution 12" releases have now become collectors' items, some of them pulled together on the Warp compilation, **The Theory of Evolution** (1995). In 1995, they were described by *The Wire* as "new complexity Techno" before going on to make a one-off

drum 'n' bass single, "Close Your Eyes and Listen/Amenity" for LTJ Bukem's Looking Good label. Their diversity and refusal to be pigeonholed was already evident.

The Evolution imprint subsequently grew into Universal Language, putting out ground-breaking 12"s by The Horn, Wishmountain, Jak and Stepper, Paul Hester, LA

Synthesis, Gerd and Max 404 as well as their own **New School Science** (1996), recorded under the Jedi Knights alias. At the same time, they released two excellent EPs in House and disco-funk styles, **The Way/The Deep** (1996), which entered the lower reaches of the British singles charts, and **The Groove** (1997), recorded with live musicians including Jethro Tull's Martin Barre on flute.

The long-awaited follow-up to **76:14** hasn't appeared yet. Pritchard has been concentrating on producing partner Kirsty Hawkshaw as well as side projects including Pulusha. Middleton has been developing his own live set with keyboard player Johnny Astro (aka Chris Johnson), as well as taking time to record his own atmospheric material under the name of Amba.

⊙ Global Communication:
A Jedi's Night Out   Mixmag/DMC, 1999

Mixed by Tom Middleton, this funk-fuelled mix of Deep House, drum 'n' bass and Ambient includes Global Communication's "The Way" alongside must-haves from Black Science Orchestra, A Man Called Adam and Ian Pooley.

Crispin J Glover

Though South London-based producer Crispin J Glover has been so often cast as one of the capital's "nu-House scenesters" alongside Faze Action and the Idjut Boys, his background marks him out as an original and distinct dance music technician.

Expelled from school aged 15, Glover quickly brushed aside a short-lived career as a painter and decorator when he blagged a job as "tea boy" at a recording studio. After moving to London, Glover cut his teeth with a wide range of pop musicians, including Level 42, Terence Trent D'Arby and Joyce Sims. Combining this pop sensibility, engineering expertise and a passion for '80s funkateers like Rick James, Prince and Grace Jones, Glover has since produced an array of well-received singles for a spectrum of UK labels that left him tagged "King of the nu-soul sound".

His debut 12", "Happy", recorded with Tonka sound system DJ Rev, made little dancefloor impact, but his subsequent bootleg remixes of Michael Jackson's "Power of Love" (with DJ Harvey) and Mariah Carey's "Someday" (with Japanese DJ Marbo) ripped up leftfield London dancefloors in the early '90s.

Unfortunately, they also brought Glover's name into the limelight, resulting in a police raid of his home and a three-year suspended sentence from the BPI (the first prosecution of this nature in the UK).

In 1993 Glover produced one of the year's most memorable four-to-the-floor releases based around the Roland TB303. Recorded as Caucasian Boy, "Northern Lights" – all soft Acid squelches, crisp kick drums and incisive melodies – made him only the third British producer to have work licensed to Strictly Rhythm.

Having started his own label, Matrix Records, in 1992 with South Central's maximal "I'll Be Right There", the majority of Glover's ensuing recordings established his sound. Coupling his influences from disco, funk, boogie and soul to the use of live instrumentation in the studio, Glover's singles (under monikers such as House Of Labasia, Century Falls, Masterbuilders, Bubblehead, Boogie Buffet, Sleazy, New Chapters In Funk and Baby Rock) for labels including Matrix, Junior Boys Own, Sony, Strictly4Groovers and Other prefigured the rise to media popularity of "nu-House" and established him as one of the country's most well-respected producers, though none came close to commercial success.

Recording under the alias of Crime, he has produced three of his best singles. 1994's police-siren-charged "Rhythm Graffiti", 1996's orchestral "Don't Fake It" and 1998's fusionist "Electra-Boogie In Dub" proved that retro-styled "live" House could keep the dancefloors rocking as well as any harder-pitched grooves had done and became staple fodder for DJs Ashley Beedle, Terry Farley and Harvey.

Together with Glover's acclaimed remixes for Bam Bam, Idjut Boys and Crue-L Orchestra, Matrix has remained one of the UK's best-loved independent House labels, with 1998 releases including Motif's ultra-funky "New Booty" and Masterbuilders' "London Town", which featured the vocals of Basement Jaxx singer Corrina Joseph.

◉ Matrix Records: Expressions   Dust II Dust/Rumour/Matrix, 1998

Fairly complete selection of Glover's 12"s for his own label, Other Records and Strictly Rhythm. Includes the cut which made his name, 1993's 303 classic, "Northern Lights", and a batch of funky, disco-bending, "live" percussive grooves like "Tonite", "Brazil" and "Zombie Dawn".

Chris Gray

Mississippi State University graduate Chris Gray's stunning debut, the **Moonchildren** EP (1995), immediately drew comparisons with Chicago pioneer Larry Heard with its warm, blue-textured melodies and reflective string arrangements. Gray's subsequent album, **A Deeper Level Of Understanding** (1997), confirmed his early promise with a wonderful selection of emotional Deep House grooves.

Brought up on a diet of jazz and Southern blues, music was an ever-present companion for Chris Gray in the isolated Delta farmlands of Mississippi. However, it took a poorly dubbed mix-tape from the airwaves of Chicago's WKKC 89.3FM to inspire him to turn his own creative energies towards music, forming The Deephouse Projeckt in 1990.

As much a studious obsession as anything else, Gray's alter-ego is, he says "an ongoing search to understand the roots of House music, and its perpetual migrations". It was this impulse which culminated in his own migration to Chicago two years later to begin his musical career.

Following three relatively obscure remixes for the city's DC10 label, Gray followed up his Subwoofer Records debut with the exceptional and self-explanatory **Very Moody** EP (1996). Though its smooth and building, hypnotic chords clearly harnessed influences from Kerri Chandler's groundbreaking 1993 **Atmosphere** EP, by now Gray was already establishing himself as a major new talent of startling ability amongst the House fraternity.

In 1998 Gray moved to Kickin' Records subsidiary Fragmented, and a prolific stream of deep slates, including the essential "Blueprints For Your Mind", the melancholy "For Jazzmyn" and the sublime **Tranquil Solutions** EP, followed. His acclaimed second long-player, **Fish & Luvconfushun** (1998), sealed the momentum with his finest collection of deep electronic soul yet.

⊙**Fish & Luvconfushun**   Fragmented, 1998

Fills in the few inconsistencies apparent on Gray's debut while stretching out his warm, evocative soundscapes into the realms of both ambience and drum 'n' bass. The oceanic "Sun Needs Planet" and angular "Yoruba" are glimpses of pure tech-House genius.

Scott Grooves

The son of a jazz guitarist, Scott Grooves (real name Patrick) spent his youth teaching himself how to play the drums, guitar and piano and working as a valet driver with Mark Kinchen, before starting to DJ himself in and around the Detroit area in 1989.

Grooves began contemplating his jazz-inflected testament in the mid-'90s, but it wasn't until he heard a Funk D'Void Techno track while working at Detroit's Record Time shop in 1997 that he contacted the artist's label, Scotland's Soma Records, with DATs and plans for his project.

His excellent Soma debut single, "New Day" (1998), had its roots clearly set in the early-Atkins, piano-led Techno signature and made little impact. But its follow-up, a cover of Lonnie Liston Smith's 1975 jazz-funk classic "Expansions" with Roy Ayers on scat vocals, picked up a wealth of press acclaim.

Pieces of a Dream (1998) continued in a similar vein with a hyped-up 4/4 re-edit of Parliament's "Mothership Connection". Based on one of the most startling records ever committed to vinyl when released in 1977, Grooves' update seemed a likeable, but pointless pastiche in comparison. It was the under-appreciated remainder of the album, though, which really marked him out as a producer of note. Grooves effectively utilised local Motown jazz guitarist Perry Hues on a wonderful cover of Wes Montgomery's "Bumpin' on the Street" and blues vocalist Gwen Fox on the be-bop-inspired "The Scat Groove".

⊙ Pieces of a Dream Soma Recordings, 1998

A flowing, jazz-soaked debut that you can listen to from start to finish without hitting the fast-forward button once.

Glenn Underground

For many, Larry Heard is the original godfather of Deep House, having honed the basic formula regardless of trends or commercial pressures since the mid-'80s. While others have tried and failed, arguably few have managed both to successfully re-create Heard's template and to develop his principles to a new level as effectively as Glenn Underground. Since rising to notoriety in the early '90s, Underground has built a reputation as one of the most consistently compelling House producers of his generation.

Encouraged by his musical family to take up the piano at the age of eleven, Underground taught himself to play the Fender Rhodes keyboard by imitating the music of his childhood – Philly soul and disco. Influenced by acts such as The Detroit Spinners, The Trammps and P & P Productions (aka Patrick Adams and Greg Carmichael), his keyboard skills soon developed. Together with Heard's predominance and the central role religion plays in his life, these elements fused to form the basis for his music.

Having begun experimenting in the studio in 1987, his debut, "Entercourse of the New Age", appeared on the Chicago Underground label four years later. Yet this passed by largely unnoticed, and it wasn't until 1995's **Beyond** EP that GU first came to prominence in the UK, providing the basis for his impressive, but mostly unheard, back catalogue of productions to be released. **Beyond** was the perfect disco groove for 1995: ten minutes of simple Moroder-flecked synth stabs and hypnotic Herb Alpert-sampled trumpet lines sequenced to a compulsive groove. The early '80s fascination spilled over to his next release, an energised reconstruction of Donna Summer's "I Feel Love" (1995). Issued on white label to an incredible reaction in the UK's clubs and music magazines, by the time the mystery producer was revealed as Underground the track was in high demand and fetching upwards of £10–15.

But Underground wasn't alone in his rise to prominence: Chi-town was experiencing a musical renaissance which found a number of new labels – Relief, Cajual, Prescription, Balance – and artists (such as Gemini, Boo Williams, Stacey Kidd, Gene Farris, Tim Harper, Paul Johnson) develop with exceptional speed. In a relatively short space of time, the Chicago "nu-school" stamped their authority on the global House map by injecting tried and tested production techniques with fresh ideas. Arguably, an element of this prevailing trend for often hard-edged instrumental House was partly hype-induced, and consequently dwindled as quickly as it arrived, but artists such as Glenn Underground continued to release a phenomenal amount of consistent, quality material which defied such confined definitions.

Following the release of the **Beyond** EP and several other well-rated gems for both Cajual and Balance (check "Party Time" and "Just Can't Stop" under his C.V.O pseudonym), a 1996 UK licensing deal with St Albans-based Peacefrog Records resulted in the release of Underground's astonishing **Atmosfear** (1996), a collection of tracks covering his work since the early '90s. Solidifying his already burgeoning reputation, its melding of intricate reflective melodies, jacking rhythms and sophisticated musicianship has since established it as one of Deep House's most accomplished works.

Later in 1996, Glenn Underground's collaboration with Boo Williams (his flat-mate and long-time friend), Brian Harden and Timothy Jaz as The S.J.U. Project (Strictly Jaz Unit) and a licensing deal with the UK-based Defender label produced **The Parables of S.J.U.** (1996). The collaboration had already manifested on vinyl earlier in the year with the well-received Cajual release "Take Me Back" as GU featuring CeiBei. Though the album continued with the same seamless deep grooves evident on previous GU releases, it also showcased Underground's broadening palette, marking his ability to shift toward an increasingly jazz-influenced sound at times. But his production skills didn't stop there, and an ability to harness vocals to a smoother style became evident with 1996's **Don't Stop The Feelin'** EP which featured the vocals of Terence FM layered over a silky '70s groove.

Although his follow-up album for Defender under the S.J.U. banner, **Future Parables** (1997), kept up the creativity levels, perhaps more impressive was his acclaimed **Jerusalem EPs** compilation (1997). Sure, the subterranean tendencies were still fully in check and some tracks employed a greater use of live instrumentation, but it was GU's emotive and deep-rooted spiritualism

which shone through. Using the simplest of warm melodies, songs steeped in religious, political and proud sentiment such as "Black Slave = Israel", "Negro Cry" and "To the King O.I" put his work on a different pedestal from other Deep House disciples and confirmed his place as perhaps Heard's natural successor.

After an unusually quiet period, in 1998 Glenn Underground returned with two of his best releases to date for the Windy City's Guidance imprint. The **House of Blues** EP and "Burning (The Midnite Oil)/Pancake Jaz" again segued live instrumentation to vintage Deep

House grooves, suggesting that the talent he's shown thus far should continue well into the future.

⊙ Atmosfear   Peacefrog, 1996

Stunning collection of Deep House and emotive Techno: this was the album that confirmed GU's place on the podium.

⊙ The Jerusalem EPs   Peacefrog, 1997

A collection of timeless, spiritual mood music – Deep House rarely gets better than this.

Guerilla Records

With Acid a hazy memory and the early '90s highlighting the decline of Chicago stalwarts Trax and DJ International, a batch of disillusioned British producers fused Balearic's pop/rock/dance fusion with the Windy City's 4/4 ethic and spearheaded a new sound, characterised by its lengthy, heavily percussive building intros, breakdowns and vocal absenteeism. Pretentiously labelled "progressive House" by journalists desperate for a new British musical movement to harp on about, huge dirty riffs replaced disco's soulful infusion and Acid's 303-soaked mantle and the pace upped to around 130 bpm. Arguably led by Leftfield and African drummer Djum Djum's 1991 single "Difference", the labels at the forefront of the explosion were Rhythm King, Cowboy, Limbo, JBO and, most importantly of all, London's Guerilla Records.

Conceived by producer William Orbit and Y Records owner **Dick O'Dell** in 1990, Guerilla was originally formed solely to provide an outlet for Orbit's Bass-O-Matic collective, whose debut, "In the Realm of the

Senses", soon saw them off in the direction of Virgin, from where they bombarded the UK Top 10 with "Fascinating Rhythm".

Guerilla, though, stayed distinctly underground, establishing itself as a major player in moulding British House over the next four years, spawning new talent like Techno front-runners React 2 Rhythm, London DJs Kevin Hurry and Kevin Swain's Visage-sampling D.O.P (Dance Only Productions), Spooky, DJ Charlie Hall's dub-tech collective The Drum Club and Tony Thorpe's Moodyboyz, among others. With the label's clearly defined camouflage sleeves, releases like React 2 Rhythm's "Intoxication", D.O.P's "Groovy Beat", Spooky's "Don't Panic" and Supereal's "One Nation" were immediate club favourites at venues like Slough's Full Circle, Manchester's Most Excellent and London's Love Ranch and helped take British House on its own semi-radical direction. In turn many of the label's cuts were remixed by the UK's "progressive" forerunners such as Leftfield and Justin Robertson.

Alongside British innovations, Guerilla were also quick to pick up on harder-tinged US grooves, releasing the single which first brought attention to Felix Da Housecat ("Thee Dawn") alongside well-regarded releases by Murk and DJ Pierre ("Atom Bomb"). With Guerilla licensing its output to IRS in the States, these tracks were picked up by NYC DJs like Duke, Vasquez and Tenaglia, who forged the Big Apple's drive to kick-start its own harder-styled imprints, most notably Tribal Records.

As the label's reputation flourished, single releases were collected together on the compilations **Dub House Disco** (1992) and **Dub House Disco 2000** (1993). While React 2 Rhythm released the thumping Techno of **Whatever You Dream** (1992), other well-received albums included D.O.P's **Musicians of the Mind**, Spooky's **Gargantuan** (1993) and Moody Boyz's **Product of the Environment** (1994).

Whether O'Dell liked it or not, the "progressive" tag stuck until the label sank without trace in 1995 after the ever-fickle dance music world

had split, with many of the scene's front-runners – not least DJ
Andrew Weatherall – pursuing a head-on rollercoaster ride into the
reaches of Techno, while American producers took up the Hard-House
mantle and turned it out better than the British could ever dream of.

Since then, however, a new wave of similarly minded UK producers, including Way Out West, Slacker and Van Basten, have taken up
the cause. Even Guerilla's back catalogue looks set for a comeback at
some point; it was acquired in 1997 by London label Jackpot
Records.

⊙**Dub House Disco**   Guerilla Records, 1992

Good compilation of the label's early tracks, including D.O.P's "Groovy
Beat" and Spooky's piano-chugging "Don't Panic".

Guidance Records

O riginally formed in Chicago in 1996 by producer Spencer Kinsey (aka Gemini), Guidance Records is now run by Sid Stary,
Ivan Pavlovich and Rob Kouchoukos, who all share a common
vision of wanting to expand House music's commercial boundaries
beyond the DJ/dancefloor ethos.

The label's third release, Blueboy's **Scattered Emotions** EP (1997),
crossed over to the UK charts with the irresistible retro-funk-fuelled,
Down Tempo "Remember Me". But this commercial success didn't set
a precedent for the majority of Deep House 12"s which have emanated
from the stable since. A better reference point was Guidance's second
release, 1996's cosmic flute jam, "When the Voice Come" by Project:
PM.

Accolades were heaped on Kevin Yost's debut, the **Unprotected Sax** EP, and Italian House producer Don Carlos was brought back from the brink of obscurity with The Aquanauts' "The Voyage". Austin Bascom's Abacus continued the momentum with radical black sentiments riding over his twisted groove on "Opinion Rated R", while Callisto's calypso-inflected "The Groove" and Larry Heard's **Calm & Chaos** EP (1997) cemented Guidance's reputation as the new home of Deep House.

The imprint has gone from strength to strength, continuing to push new local talent like Mark Grant, Justin Tewn and Detroit's Alton Miller, as well as recruiting the disco-charged Glenn Underground, the Wamdue Kids' Chris Brann and Scotland's Paul Hunter (aka Deep Sensation) to the roster.

Despite its generic sleeves, Guidance has demonstrated a sense of marketing savvy which should see it last well into the future, releasing two CD-only compilation albums and a timely summer 1998 collection of Afro-Latin inspired slates, **Copamundial Muzique**, to coincide with the World Cup.

◉ Hi-Fidelity House: Imprint One　　　　　Guidance, 1997

Essential compilation of cosmic, deep, funky grooves from then newcomers Project PM, Kevin Yost and Charly Brown alongside mandatory magic from old-timers Larry Heard and Don Carlos.

DJ Harvey

Regarded as one of the UK's most open-minded DJs, Harvey began his career as a drummer for various obscure New Wave bands throughout the '70s. With hip-hop taking a firm grip on early '80s UK street culture, Harvey became interested in the idea of cutting up records and using breaks to create new rhythms from the old. It was an idea that appealed to him as an extension of his musical background: instead of sitting behind a drum-kit playing to an audience, why not do it with two decks and a bag of vinyl?

It wasn't long before he began DJing at local warehouse parties, progressing to his first London club night, Wet, where his forward-looking eclectic sets forged a mark he still maintains to this day: a belief that a truly modern sound is one which never rules anything out. By the second half of the '80s Harvey and a group of friends from Cambridge formed the Tonka Sound System, taking their prevalent mix of electro, dub and hip-hop to work at warehouses across the country and gaining notoriety for their monthly parties at Brighton's beach-front club, The Zap.

As his reputation began to bloom, in 1991 Harvey began his now legendary Moist Friday night club sessions at London's Gardening Club where he drew attention both for his own sets and for luring NYC luminaries François Kervorkian and Larry Levan to play at a time when most people's conception of a good DJ revolved around someone who took the crowd "harder as the night progressed".

When Moist closed its doors, Harvey made the move south of the river to the Ministry Of Sound. Playing between 6am and 9am in his residency at Jim Master's Open nights offered him the opportunity to take his selection of choice tunes to the extreme, dropping a diverse selection which would range from Jah Shaka's dub projections to Little Louie Vega's House slates. Before long, Harvey found himself Saturday night resident alongside Tony Humphries at Rulin', and it's due in no small measure to both DJs' deeply personal choice of music that the corporate machine has become so successful. Yet it was at his mid-'90s nights at East London's Blue Note club, New Hard Left, where he finally came into his element. While the term eclectic has now become something of a worn cliché, Harvey's sets were exactly that, dropping anything from orchestrated disco to The Rolling Stones to Trouble Funk into the mix alongside obscure favourites like Donald Fagen's "New Frontier", Cerrone's "Music of Life" and "Macho City" by the Steve Miller Band, often using his own re-edits to extend breaks in the mould of his NYC heroes Larry Levan and Walter Gibbons. Harvey's nights are an education in music history but, by keeping an open mind and always looking to the future, he manages to avoid the chin-stroking musical purism that so often causes scenes to implode under their own weight.

While his association with the Ministry Of Sound led to an acclaimed mix album, **Late Night Sessions** (1996), and a well-received percussive reworking of Trip-Hop meister DJ Food's "Peace", his own re-edits have also crossed over into the public eye, most notably with his releases on the Noid and Moton Inc. labels. He produced well-regarded reworkings of Billy Paul's Philly classic "East" and Macho's "I'm a Man", while his own tongue-in-cheek-titled Black Cock label has released a sporadic batch of under-achieving gems such as the wired-psychedelia of Dick Hyman's rendition of James Brown's "Give It Up, Turn It Loose".

In 1998 even the label that kick-started the career of The Chemical Brothers, Heavenly Records, pricked up their ears and sponsored his vaunted Leftorium nights at London's Smithfields club. Despite the fact that these are now at an end, it seems the career of Harvey – though already well into its adulthood – is sure to make its mark on a wider audience again sometime soon.

◉ Late Night Sessions   Ministry Of Sound, 1996

Harvey's impeccable selection of Deep House, funky nu-disco and twilight grooves includes a smattering of his own percussive workouts (Persuasion's "The Bone" and a remix of DJ Food's "Peace") alongside essentials by Black Science Orchestra and St Germain.

Larry Heard

While legendary is a much-overused term in dance music journalism, Larry Heard can justly lay claim to this description, having created some of House music's most inspirational and experimental moments over a fifteen-year career. Unlike his contemporaries, Heard's blend of intricate melodies and memorable synthesised refrains has never borrowed from the past. On some of House's most important singles and dance music's most complete albums, his unique musical vision has remained subtle, soulful and emotive. As testament to this, producers as disparate as British drum 'n' bass pioneer LTJ Bukem and Detroit Techno deity Derrick May have cited him as the crucial influence, if not the sole motivation behind their music. But despite this, Heard has never achieved the fame of most of his peers and his career has been dogged by the demands of commerce. He has constantly disputed the royalty payments he received from Trax Records, has struggled to carve out a major album deal and has so far failed to find a long-term home for his output.

Born on the South Side of Chicago on 31 May, 1960, Heard graduated from college with a law degree. But jazz and Motown were always strong influences at home and from an early age Heard could play a variety of instruments. At 17 he learned to play drums and subsequently joined a friend's jazz-fusion cover group, Infinity (with Adonis), before switching to another band, Manhattan Transfer. Frustrated by the lack of musical input into this band, and fascinated by early '80s electronica and the creative possibilities offered by the new wave of cheap recording equipment, Heard decided to pursue a solo career in 1983.

A daytime job as a benefit authoriser for the US government enabled Heard to finance his home studio. Working independently of the mainly disco-dominated club scene that had been fostered in Chicago by DJs Frankie Knuckles and Ron Hardy, Heard wrote two of dance music's most important tracks in 1985 on a drum machine (Roland TR707) and a simple keyboard (Roland Juno 106). Neither showed any evidence of disco's musical roots, but referenced instead

Heard's soul-searching Ambient sensibilities and subtle mastery of synthesised refrains. "Mystery of Love" (1985), later released on DJ International, drew the blueprint for Deep House with its blues-inflected melodies and soft synth washes, while "Washing Machine" (1985) – a brutally crazed clashing of angular bleeps – was the prototype Acid workout, predating Phuture's "Acid Trax" by two years.

While the 110 bpm groove of "Mystery of Love" later

found its way into the all-time Top 5 of DJ Larry Levan, it was "Washing Machine" that stood out on the dancefloor of Ron Hardy's then disco-charged Music Box. "Washing Machine" was released on Trax Records in 1986, as part of a triple-headed 12" that contained another incredible spaced-out classic, "Can U Feel It?" While Heard's first two releases were incomparable genre-definers, their influence abroad at the time wasn't overly extensive. By dramatic contrast, the resolutely uplifting "Can U Feel It?", whose release coincided with the arrival of Ecstasy in British clubs, affected nearly every DJ, clubber and music producer in some way during that period.

"Mystery of Love" had been credited to Heard as Mr. Fingers, a nickname he'd acquired when he started DJing, and it was as Fingers Inc that he subsequently recorded. A collaboration with fellow benefit employee Ron Wilson and vocalist Robert Owens yielded mid-'80s gems like "Bring Down the Walls", "I'm Strong" and "Bye Bye", culminating in what some critics have described as the greatest House album of all time, Fingers Inc's **Another Side** (1988). Whatever the cognoscenti made of it, **Another Side** found Heard breaking new ground again simply by releasing the first ever House music album onto the shelves.

In 1989, Heard wrote and produced material for Kym Mazelle ("Treat Me Right") and Lil' Louis ("Touch Me"), remixed Adamski, Massive Attack and Electribe 101. While commercial recognition beckoned, Trax released a double album of his early instrumental demos, **Amnesia** (1989), without his consent.

In 1990 his reputation as one of the genre's most gifted producers was strengthened with the release of The It's **On Top of the World** (1990) for Big Life Records. The It – Heard and Chicago street-poet Harry Dennis – had already caused underground rumblings with 1988's wonderful "Gallimaufry Gallery", named after a Windy City nightspot.

But their debut album took House music one step further toward an integrated musical sound. Combining blues, funk and jazz with lyrics that dealt with issues like homelessness and inner-city angst on tracks such as "State of the World" and "This Place Called Nowhere", **On Top Of The World** should have guaranteed Heard widespread acclaim and commercial success, but Harry Dennis became addicted to heroin and the duo split.

A major album deal was struck with MCA in 1992. The ironically titled **Introduction** spawned the poppy club hit "Closer", but also contained the melancholy brilliance of "On a Corner Called Jazz", recorded with Robert Owens. MCA failed to release his follow-up **Back To Love** album, however. With aspirations centred around the success of UK artists, he was dropped from their books soon after.

Since that date, Heard has only released instrumental solo albums. Having referenced Pat Metheny as one of his strongest musical influences, **Sceneries Not Songs** (1994) and **Sceneries Not Songs Volume 2** (1995) drew deeply personal, and often incredible, pictures of blissed-out ambience, pulling together jazz and soul soundscapes. 1996's critically acclaimed **Alien** also came close to genius, fusing elements of Techno into the mix to become a favourite of DJs like Dave Clarke and Andrew Weatherall.

Having set up his own Alleviated imprint in 1988, Heard also released a number of 12"s that appealed across dancefloors. "Black Oceans" (1991), a dramatic vision of post-millennium soul, became an all-time classic at Scotland's infamous Slam club, while the vocal cut, "Premonition of Love Lost" (1994), was lauded by London's best-loved garage DJ, Paul "Trouble" Anderson. Heard became Ron Trent's partner in Prescription Records for a short time in 1996, releasing a single under the Ram Project moniker and signing up, and remixing, A Man Called Adam's "Que Tal America?"

In 1997, following his **Calm & Chaos** EP for Guidance Records, he announced his shock retirement from the music industry with the release of what was proclaimed "his last album", **Dance 2000** (1997). A flock of journalists eagerly tracked him down to his new home in Memphis, where he'd relocated to escape family pressures in Chicago and take up a job as a computer programmer for a financial company. Although tracks entitled "Psychotic Fantasy" and "Calm to Panic" referenced his disillusionment with the ever-cynical music industry, interviews revealed that his music career was far from over, that he had kept most of his equipment intact and had over a hundred tracks already recorded and yet to be released.

In 1998, French label Distance issued **Dance 2000 Part 2**, another set of soothing Ambient-House tracks, even though it is believed Heard had intended the material to be released as one package. The same year, his hard-to-find **Sceneries Not Songs Volume 2** (originally released on the tiny Miami-based MIA label) was repackaged and re-marketed as **Ice Castles**. Although it was perhaps not as fulfilled as earlier projects, Heard's effect on modern producers like Glenn Underground, House Of 909, Charles Webster, Chris Gray and Muzique Tropique nonetheless remains apparent.

◉ Mr Fingers: "Can You Feel It?"   Trax, 1986

The greatest House music single ever? A beautiful record that had an influence on virtually every key modern music producer. If you don't already own this, then your record collection isn't complete. Available on **The House That Trax Built II**.

◉ Mr Fingers: "Washing Machine"   Trax, 1986

Released long before Acid House became a way of life, this was the prototype which inspired DJ Pierre and Spanky to make music when they first heard it at Ron Hardy's Music Box in '85. Available on **The House That Trax Built II** (Trax/PRD, 1996).

◉ **Larry Heard: Sceneries Not Songs**

Volume One   Black Market Int, 1994

Ambient jazz and deep, deep, deep soul: eight emotional and evocative moods. As close to the inner sanctum of the man's mind as you're likely to get – and all recorded in the space of only ten days.

Herbert

Matthew Herbert has operated under a bewildering array of pseudonyms over the course of his career. As Dr Rockit he was a bedroom boffin of electronica, a circuit-breaker of analogue timbres who fused ear-shattering loops with ethereal visions. With his Wishmountain guise, he sampled the sound of clattering kitchen utensils and thudding blocks of wood and stole the voices of old-time radio personalities for his Radio Boy project. As Herbert, he creates jazzy Deep House offset with a quirky English eccentricity.

His material as Herbert draws on classic Chicago and New York styles, but also owes much to a Brit House tradition that includes free party terrorists DiY and Nottingham's Time Recordings, as well as avant-garde heads like Brian Eno and David Byrne. Nowhere was this idiosyncrasy better displayed than on 1998's **Around The House**. The follow-up to 1996's more dancefloor-leaning **100 Lbs.**, it featured the vocal talents of Dani Siciliano, whose vocal technique was devastating.

Herbert recognises that he's a product of the '90s cut 'n' paste ethic but tries to justify his sampling. "The '90s has produced a real nostalgia culture," he has said. "Everyone begs, borrows and steals to achieve a little piece of authenticity [but] I try to take one element from history and recontextualise it. It's not about giving people what they want. It's experimenting in public, I guess."

⊙ Around The House Phonography, 1998

Liquid House for the 3am faithful.

Hi-Bias Records

I n the fall-out from the collapse of Big Shot Records, producer Ron Allen formed Strobe Records, co-founder Andrew Komis created First Choice, while producer/founder Nick Fiorucci started Hi-Bias. With its name culled from a Big Shot recording artist of little note, the label has since provided one of the few credible outlets for Canada's House producers, building an esteemed reputation in the early '90s.

Hi-Bias' most effective cuts have all been marked by a deep, often jazz-influenced sound. Most of these have been produced by Nick Fiorucci with like-minded technicians under the pseudonyms Oval Emotion, Red Light, Willow, DJs Rule and Groove Sector.

The label didn't pick up any attention until it released the piano-charged, vocal dancefloor smash "Get Into the Music" (1991). More like an Italo House happy anthem than the majority of the imprint's deep grooves, the song remains the label's biggest dancefloor filler to date. 1991 bore more trademark minimal Deep House tracks like Z Formation's dubby **Intense** EP and Oval Emotion's warmly received "Do It".

By this time, Hi-Bias had gained enough underground respect to merit its sub-title "The DJs Label" with a slew of acclaimed releases like Red Light's **Rhythm Formula** EP and Groove Sector's "The Love I Lost". 1994 saw the release of Victor Simonelli's remixes of Red Light's glorious garage cut, "Thankful", Oval Emotion's piano-driven "Reach Out" and Groove Council's propulsive slab of disco-House, "You Won't Be Happy".

Since the mid-'90s the label has failed to ignite the same spark, largely moving toward a more commercial outlook with releases like pop act Temperance's **Virtues of Life**. It's not all doom and gloom though. Despite their fading prowess amongst hardened House fans, Hi-Bias have still come up trumps from time to time, releasing gems like Love Drop's "Take Me Higher" (1995), Spin That Wheel's tribal "Wake Up" (1996) and Oval Emotion's **Reach** (1996).

⊙ The Hi-Bias Experience   Hi-Bias/X:treme Records, 1995

The best of the label's compilations to date, featuring a selection of both deep and uplifting grooves. Includes Red Light's "Thankful", Groove Council's "You Won't Be Happy", DJs Rule's "Get Into the Music" and Oval Emotion's "Reach Out".

Nick Holder/ DNH Records

Although producer Nick Holder had released singles on Toronto's Hi-Bias label, it wasn't until he started his DNH (David Nick Holder) imprint in 1992 that he began to establish himself as one of Canada's leading dance music exponents.

Clearly influenced by a combination of the bare-bones minimalism of early Chicago House trax and the angularity/ambience of Detroit technicians like Derrick May and Carl Craig, Holder's spaced-out deep and dubby 12"s have provided DNH with the vast majority of its acclaimed output. Early releases like the warm **Summer Grooves** EP, **Underground Alternatives** EP and the **Private Selections** EP (all 1993) merged samples with groovy melodies and paved the way for the label's biggest success, 1993's **Phat Trax** EP. Remaining only an underground phenomenon – selling around 5,000 copies – **Phat Trax** sampled the voice of Bill Cosby from the cartoon show *Fat Albert* to a driving, bass-heavy groove. At around the same time, Holder's "Erotic Illusions" became a favourite on Junior Vasquez's Sound Factory dancefloor.

1994 releases by Strobe Records producer Ron Allen (the excellent jazzy "Tonight" as Hooked On Tracks) and relatively unknown studio technician Marcus Turcotte ("Sax Appeal" and the **Deep Experiments** EP) – alongside wired Holder groovers like "Get It Up" and the bumpin' "Track In The Box" – further served to enhance DNH's reputation both at home and abroad. But while 1995 and 1996 releases – including the mellow **After Hours** EP and **Deep 'N Delicious** EP – continued in a similar musical vein, 1997's debut album, **One Night In the Disco**, surprisingly betrayed a less original approach. The retrofuelled long-player disappointed with pointless reworkings of standard '70s favourites "He's The Greatest Dancer" (Sister Sledge) and Sylvester's "You Make Me Feel (Mighty Real)" rubbing up against simple disco-looped instrumentals.

⊙**Phat Trax**   DNH, 1993

The label's biggest dancefloor hit, though it's worth trawling through the back catalogue to search out Deep House goodies like "Tonight" and "After Hours".

Loleatta Holloway

I f sampling were regarded as some form of tribute to the original artist, then "Disco Queen" Loleatta Holloway would surely be the most admired vocalist in the Western hemisphere. Indeed, no part of her 1980 Salsoul screamer "Love Sensation" remains untouched. She's been sampled wholesale on Black Box's worldwide hit "Ride On Time" and Marky Mark and the Funky Bunch's tacky US Top 10 single "Good Vibrations", while DJ/producer Johnny Vicious, in particular, took to remixing her anthems in emphatic fashion in the early '90s. In 1997 even the Masters At Work paid homage to her with their cover of "Runaway".

A child prodigy, Holloway began her career singing as early as five; by her teens she'd turned professional, travelling with the Holloway Community Singers, managed by her mother. At 17 she joined The Caravans, a renowned all-female gospel group led by Albertina Walker, before striking out on her own with Loleatta Holloway and Her Review.

In 1971, following her starring role in the Chicago cast of Miki Grant's hit musical *Don't Bother Me I Can't Cope*, she met her producer, personal manager and husband-to-be, Floyd Smith and turned toward gospel, soul and R&B, recording her debut "Rainbow" (written by Curtis Mayfield) on indie label Apache, before being licensed to Galaxy Records.

Her powerful, soaring vocals soon reached the ears of entrepreneur Mike Thevis, who signed her as the first act for his Aware label, for whom Holloway recorded five singles and two albums produced by Floyd Smith. Although she came to R&B prominence with "Cry to Me" (1975), most of her work until 1976 centred around forgettable MOR soul ballads.

The 1976 switch to Salsoul Records resulted in yet another under-produced ballad, "Worn Out Broken Heart". The single's b-side, the wonderful "Dreaming", and follow-up, "Hit and Run", were produced by MFSB's Norman Harris and showcased her progression towards a more upbeat R&B-meets-Philly sound which served as a far better platform for her emotive vocals and put her firmly on the road to becoming a disco sensation.

The move toward disco was solidified with her debut Salsoul long-player, **Loleatta** (1977). With nearly two-thirds of the tracks produced at Philly's Sigma Sounds, the album utilised MFSB luminaries Ron Kersey (keyboards), Larry Washington (percussion) and the genius of Vince Montana Jr (vibes), amongst others. It was Montana and his Salsoul Orchestra who provided the platform for some of Holloway's finest productions, first pencilling the hit "Runaway" and her two most accomplished albums to date, **Queen Of The Night** (1978) and **Loleatta** (1979), which between them spawned the disco classics "Mama Don't, Papa Won't" and "The Greatest Performance of My Life".

In 1979 Dan Hartman called her in to sing on "Relight My Fire". He returned the favour a year later by producing her masterpiece, "Love Sensation" (1980). Holloway's semi-screaming, towering delivery, Hartman's incessant piano hook and a hi-hat shuffle delivered straight from the gates of heaven, ensured Holloway's place in the history books as the ultimate disco diva. **Love Sensation** (1980) highlighted her growing popularity within the industry itself, featuring the Bobby Womack-produced "My Way" alongside a soul rendition of Otis Redding's "I've Been Loving You Too Long".

Another collaboration with the Salsoul Orchestra, the under-rated club hit "Seconds" (produced by Prelude's wonderboy Patrick Adams), was released in 1982. After Salsoul was sold to RCA in 1984, however, Holloway struggled to find a suitable home for the rest of the '80s and produced little of note.

On the back of the Black Box fiasco, 1991 found Holloway teaming up with François Kervorkian to release the excellent "Strong Enough" single. Johnny Vicious then slammed her back on the dancefloor with his punk-disco soundclash mixes of her back catalogue, while in 1998 Farley & Heller cast her into the dance charts yet again with their pointless cover of The Style Council's "Shout to the Top". Her voice has been sampled on countless other House tracks besides and no doubt will be for years to come. It would be a hard task to find anyone to replace Holloway's passion, depth and soul.

⊙ **Classic Salsoul Volume 1**   Mastercuts/Beechwood Music, 1993

Although it's well worth picking up Holloway's albums **Loleatta**, **Queen of the Night** and **Love Sensation**, this label compilation is probably the best and certainly the easiest to find introduction to some of her best singles. Includes "Love Sensation", "Dreaming" and "Runaway".

Hooj Choons

Formed in the Spring of 1991, Hooj Choons emerged from the dying embers of the failing Greedy Beat Records. Jerry Dickens, Greedy's A&R man, had helped set the company up after leaving college, later abandoning the project to set up his own publishing deal. Having spent much of his time clubbing at London's Acid House venues, Dickens and his friend Phil Hawes began to release records inspired by the Balearic scene. The duo's debut release, "Carnival De Casa" by Rio Rhythm Band, appeared from their base in a tiny South London office and immediately established the Hooj philosophy: upbeat, good-time tunes.

Originally founded as a means to keep a roof over Dickens' head – and to provide cashflow for his clubland exploits – Hooj continued to be highly successful on the dancefloor. The big hits began in 1992 with Andronicus' uplifting soundscape "Make You Whole" and the European smash single "Don't You Want Me" by Felix, which was conceived with the help of House producer and future Faithless founder Rollo. Dickens began trading under the moniker Red Jerry and Hooj Choons established itself as one of Britain's most consistently successful "handbag" and "hardbag" labels. A love of Euro dance music, hi-NRG and clubs such as London's gay institution Trade informed Red Jerry's sensibilities. Gloworm's "I Lift My Cup" (1992), Restless Rockers' reggae-tinged "Dem Dem", Hyper Go Go's "High" (1993), the gay nu-energy anthem Dis-cuss' "Pissed Apache" (1993) and JX's ultra-poppy "Son of a Gun" (1994) were typical Hooj tunes and huge club successes. Most of these were collected together on the compilation album **Some of These Were Hooj** (1994), with the follow-ups, **Some of These Were Hooj Two** and **Some of These Were Hooj Three**, released a few years later. While "handbag" has drifted from dancefloor popularity since its mid-'90s zenith, Hooj Choons have kept both their credibility and momentum intact, releasing harder-edged tracks through their Prolekut subsidiary label and deeper rhythms from the likes of Nalin & Kane ("Beachball"), LSO, Lost Tribe and Energy 52, most of which were collected together on the excellent **Deeper Shades** compilation (1998).

⊙ Some Of These Were Hooj   Hooj Choons, 1994

The best collection of the label's most famous nu-energy anthems: includes Felix's "Don't You Want Me", Andronicus' "You Make Me Whole" and Dis-cuss' fierce "Pissed Apache".

House Of 909

The House Of 909 record label was conceived in 1995 by DJ/promoter Nigel Casey and Techno producer Affie Yussuf (who'd already impressed with recordings for labels such as Force Inc. and Ferox) as an offshoot of Yussuf's 909 Perversions label. House Of 909's first two releases, **Voices From Beyond** EP and **Future Soul Orchestra** EP, set the deep and groovy precedent with their corpulent, warm chords and jazz-inflected rhythms.

But it wasn't until south-coast producers Trevor Loveys, Jamie Cox and Martin Howes were signed up that the House Of 909 as a collective really began to take shape and the music was opened up to a broader audience. Snapped up by Richard Breeden's Pagan label, ensuing EPs revealed a more sophisticated, crisp production sound, though still clearly drawing their influence from a

combination of jazz and swinging New York House. 1997's **Deep Distraction** EP drew particular attention with its Deep Dish-style, fleshed-out bass-driven rhythm and floating chords evident on "The Main Event". Its follow-up, the **Moodswings** EP, a languid collection of cool grooves that was equally at home on the dancefloor or on the headphones, served to further hone their UK House associations with a remix from Muzique Tropique's Kevin McKay. **Soul Rebels** (1997) showcased the extent of both the label's and collective's work. Since then House Of 909 have remained fairly quiet. In late 1997, they expressed ambitions to take their sound further toward the use of live instrumentation and vocals, which gives a likely indication the route their musical direction will take.

⊙ Soul Rebels   Pagan, 1997

A perfect overview of both the label's and the collective's Deep House releases. Mixed by Nigel Casey, the aquatic flavour stretches from the chilled grooves of "Distant Cry" to the twisted vocal yearnings of "Deep Inside".

Tony Humphries

P laying his first gig at Manhattan's little-known El Morocco club in 1978, by the early '80s Tony Humphries had earned an influential slot on New York's Kiss FM after impressing DJ Shep Pettibone with his smoothly crafted mix-tapes. His blending of disco, soul and song-based dance tracks led to Zanzibar club owner Larry Patterson offering him a residency at the venue a year later, from where Humphries was to exert a decisive influence on the course of House music.

While in Chicago the pre-House emphasis had been on fast, Italian disco records, much of New York's club heritage rests firmly on the shoulders of slower R&B and the lush, orchestral sound of Salsoul. Humphries' early '80s sessions found him mixing up these styles, but

also broadening out to include rock and pop dance tracks (Talking Heads' "Once In a Lifetime" and The B-52s' "Mesopotamia" were huge on Zanzibar's dancefloor).

Having always focused on the soulful part of a record in his mixes, when House music broke, Humphries melded the essentially drum-kick tracks with powerful vocal disco and soul cuts. It was his penchant for pushing vocal dance releases like Park Avenue's "Don't Turn Your Love", Freestyle Orchestra's "You're Gonna Miss Me", Adeva's "In and Out of My Life" and Jomanda's "Make My Body Rock" rather than dubs which influenced local New Jersey producers to create tracks for him to "break" at the club. At New York's New Music Seminar, his organ-fired, soulful vocal groove was labelled "the New Jersey Sound" after the location where it was created.

As well as continuing to break new music – most notably Crystal Waters' commercial blockbuster "Gypsy Woman" and Djamin's "Give You" – his early DJing trips to Europe were met with delirium and in 1992 he took up a Saturday night residency at the Ministry Of Sound, from where he played a crucial role in bringing the garage vibe over to English shores. It's in no small measure due to Humphries' creativity and passion in the early '90s that the Ministry has since become such a commercially successful concept.

Although he's mixed well over a hundred records since the mid-'80s – including club hits like Cultural Vibe's "Ma Foom Bey" (1988), Ultra Naté's "It's Over Now" (1989), Desiya's "Comin' on Strong" (1991) and Mass Order's "Lift Every Voice" (1992) – Humphries has never really been a producer of note. Despite the fact that he's always been welcomed with open arms as a remixer by major labels on a mission for commercial and critical recognition, most of his mixes have amplified the singles' original melodies rather than taking them in any radical or incisive new direction.

In 1994 Romanthony summed up House music's appreciation of his talents, dedicating the club monster "In the Mix" to Humphries. Humphries' influence is still apparent by the number of mix albums and label compilations he's asked to blend together (check 1997's excellent King St Records' **Mix the Vibe**). That influence looks set to continue into the future: in 1998 Humphries launched his first record label, Yellorange, to showcase vocal talent.

⊙ Sessions Volume 1　　　　　　　　　　　　Ministry Of Sound, 1993

Humphries mixed this commercial selection of party favourites soon after he'd taken up an inspirational residency at the venue. A smooth blend of American vocal cuts and UK pumping House.

⊙ Classic garage　　　　　　　　　　　　　　Beechwood Music, 1999

Superlative compendium of garage hits that Humphries made famous, including Mass Order's "Lift Every Voice".

Terry Hunter

Unlike many Chicago House producers, Terry Hunter has mostly layered his smooth, soulful grooves with the sweetest of vocals. Like the majority of his contemporaries, Hunter's career began as a teenage DJ after his cousin had passed him a tape of Frankie Knuckles spinning at the Powerplant club. It's perhaps of little surprise then that Hunter has followed Knuckles' smoother, more vocal-orientated blend of House music than the raw, frenzied vibe created by the sets of the legendary DJ Ron Hardy.

One of the notorious "Chicago Bad Boys" set alongside Steve Poindexter, Robert Armani and DJ Rush, Hunter was well placed to observe the developments in the Windy City's nightlife scene. His debut single, "Madness", blew up on Chicago dancefloors and led to an introduction to producer Aaron Smith and the formation of the UBQ collective with another House pioneer, Ron Trent. The collective's raw urban soul sound was sketched on their debut single, "Into the Night", released on the House 'N' Effect label, but fully realised on 1992's beautiful "When I Fell In Luv". Harnessing the vocals of Kathy Summers to an emotive 4/4 groove, the single immediately found its way into every American jocks' playlist, later becoming a cult classic on the dancefloors of Ibiza clubs like Pacha and Space.

Ron Trent soon departed for a solo career, but Hunter and Smith's ascendancy continued with the formation of Vibe Records with producers Maurice Joshua and Georgie Porgie. While the duo found themselves popular vocal remixers (Brownstone, Zhane, Crystal Waters), Vibe established itself as one of Chicago's premier House imprints alongside Relief and Cajual Records. 12" releases like 1993's jazzy **House Union** EP (by Watanabe) and 1995's "Now I Know He's the Man" (by Blak Beat Niks) typified the label's upbeat, soul-infused

159

output. Smith and Hunter produced one of Vibe's best cuts, 1994's sample-splashed **Headhunter** EP. Disco-fuelled fillers like the **Smith & Hunter** EP for NYC's Henry Street label helped make their records a popular draw on dancefloors stretching from London's Loft to Naples' Angels Of Love.

Hunter returned from a lengthy production hiatus in 1998 with another slice of unstoppable vocal House, a piano-happy cover of the Isley Brothers' "Harvest for the World", while one of his Vibe Records compadres, E Smoove, also hit form with the anthemic "Deja Vu" (1998) topping club charts.

⊙ Chicago House Jam   Slip N Slide/Kickin Records, 1997

Features some of Terry Hunter/UBQ's finest moments, from the classic "When I Fell In Luv" to the more upbeat "We Can Make It" and "Feel My Soul".

Steve "Silk" Hurley

W ith a host of commercially successful, smoothly crafted vocal releases stretching from the beginning of the House era to the present, Steve "Silk" Hurley remains one of the genre's greatest producers. While journos continue to debate whether it was Jesse Saunders, Jamie Principle or Colonel Abrams who created the first recognisable House cut, there's little doubt that Hurley was the man with the commercial Midas touch enabling him to bring the music out to a wider audience.

Given his school playground nickname "Silk" because of his shiny hair, Hurley had intended to pursue a career in engineering but flunked his exams at the University of Illinois as a result of too much after-hours DJing. Inspired by the mandatory Parliament and Chic, Hurley began his upward DJing trajectory playing Philly and Salsoul disco tracks at local House parties and weddings in South Chicago before winning a DJ contest at a downtown bar/restaurant called Sauer's in 1981. A year later he moved on to promote his own club night with friend and flat-mate DJ Farley Keith. Inspired by the crowd's reaction to the simply produced "Your Love" by Jamie Principle, he made the transition from cutting re-edits for his club and radio spots to production.

What happened next provided yet another twist and turn in House music's murky past. Hurley claims to have created the vocal track "Love Can't Turn Around" in 1984 – hooking up lyrics and melody from Isaac Hayes' "I Can't Turn Around" to a simple drum kick and bass-line – and then been ripped off by his friend DJ Farley Keith, who added Darryl Pandy's vocals to the mix and released his version first to massive world-wide commercial success.

Whatever the case, Hurley's credentials proved themselves almost immediately with his first pressing, "Music Is the Key" (1985). Made as J.M Silk – with vocalist Keith Nunally – as a response to New Yorker Colonel Abrams' club hit "Music Is the Answer", it set the precedent for his future work. Marrying fat bass-lines and simple piano hooks to Nunally's vocals, the single was used to launch Rocky Jones' DJ International label, subsequently climbing to #9 on the Billboard dance chart.

J.M Silk kept up the momentum with "Shadows of Your Love" and "I Can't Turn Around", but in 1987 Hurley became the first producer to take House to the top of the pop charts, making UK #1 thanks to the incredibly simplistic "Jack Your Body". Typical of his commercial nous, "Jack Your Body"'s bass-line was lifted wholesale from First Choice's

disco classic "Let No Man Put Asunder", while the entire song only
contained the three words in its title. JM Silk's more commercial traits
were evident on "Let the Music Take Control", produced for RCA, and
"Hearts of Passion" (1987), but the duo soon split and Nunally left to
pursue a solo career.

Having formed his own ID record label in 1988, Hurley's rise continued with the production of a major-label debut album, **Work It Out**
(1989), for Atlantic Records. Indeed, from 1990 to 1993 it was virtually
impossible to escape from a Hurley remix. His joyous piano hooks and
obvious, but expertly crafted, bass-lines attached themselves to artists
stretching from Michael Jackson ("Remember the Time") to Roberta
Flack ("Uh Uh Ooh Ooh Look Out") and proved capable of making
practically any pop starlet into a dancefloor sensation. For proof look
no further than his shockingly credible reworkings of Danii Minogue's
"Baby Love" and MOR nightmare Simply Red's "Something's Got Me
Started". In 1991 he was voted "remixer of the year" at the British
Dance Awards, and a year later the Miami Winter Music Conference
bestowed on him the same blank cheque.

Alongside the big-name reworks were under-rated gems like D'Bo-
ra's "Dream About You" and "ESP", while his own ID imprint bore Shay
Jones' wonderful "Are You Gonna Be There" and Kym Sims' "Too Blind
To See It". Hurley also produced Jamie Principle's **Midnight Hour** and
M.Doc's well-rated **Universal Poet** albums during the early '90s.

But with the exception of less effective remixes, a few R&B forays
and work for Ce Ce Penniston, Hurley was relatively quiet on the production front from around 1993 to 1996. He was actually spending the
time fighting a court case with his label partner which almost resulted in
the demise of his mini-empire. "The Silkster" hit back on two fronts in
1997. Having created a new imprint, Silk Entertainment, both the revisionist R&B of Chantay Savage's "I Will Survive" and Voices Of Life's

gospel-styled "The Word Is Love" (both 1997) sealed his position as one of dance music's most complete vocal producers. 1998's highly regarded smooth re-union with Ce Ce Penniston, "Nobody Else", cemented it.

⊙ JM Silk: Music Is The Key   DJ International, 1985

The track that first brought attention the way of both Hurley and DJ International. One of House music's first soulful anthems and perhaps his most emotive. Available on **Classic House Volume 2** (Beechwood Music, 1994).

⊙ Shay Jones: "Are You Gonna Be There"   ID Records, 1991

Alongside DSK's "What Would We Do", this set the pattern for Hurley's ascent into piano-happy remix overdrive.

I:Cube

U sing the neo-chic of Dimitri From Paris as a basis for more texturally diverse work, Nicholas Chaix has quickly emerged as French House's shining talent. The blends of smooth hip-hop, electro and jazz alongside House showcased on DJ Gilb'R's shows on the French pirate radio stations Radio Nova and France Culture caught Chaix's attention and have been the almost unseen template for "la style Française".

Chaix's deal with Gilb'R's label in 1995 led to a remix of Cheek's "Venus" and then his debut single as I:Cube, "Disco Cubizm" (1996). Centred around a distant keyboard riff with snatches of easy listening, "Disco Cubizm" kept attention spans locked by never letting one riff linger too long. Daft Punk's stripped revision of the track moved it into DJ boxes, but as a debut single it hinted at a promising future.

That promise was realised with his well-regarded debut album, **Picnic Attack** (1997), which featured a multitude of sounds shifting through varying rhythmic matrices, electro-breakbeat, solid Motor City grooves and beatless passages of static and off-cut voices. The precocious "Mingus In My Pocket" was jazz-House intensified to pointillism.

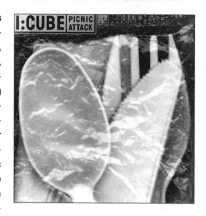

1997 also bore I:Cube's collaboration with his mentor, DJ Gilb'R, on the exotic "Chateau Flight". I:Cube rests alongside Daft Punk as one of the few French acts who will still be left standing long after the fashion parade has moved on.

◉ Picnic Attack   Versatile, 1997

One of the better debut albums of recent times, assured and fascinating.

Idjut Boys

Since U-Star Records formed in 1994, its releases have been characterised by the use of studio techniques that draw their inspiration from the type of heavily effected sounds that original

DJs/mixers such as François Kevorkian and Larry Levan used during their more creative dub-based disco phase. After owners Dan Tyler and Conrad McDonnell (aka Idjut Boys) forged a useful partnership with like-minded studio producer Laj (Raj Gupta), early releases such as "Oh La La Teaparty" and "Funkyland" by Bam Bam proved that an impressive and humorous talent was already developing. Unfortunately, these extremely limited releases ensured that The Idjut Boys were kept a well-hidden secret.

The first U-Star record to receive any recognition was the **Not Reggae** EP (1995), which stood out from the vast majority of new releases because of its originality and the quality of production. Mixing live instrumentation with deep, dubby, heavy four-to-the-floor grooves, it was the sketch for the London "nu-House" sound prevalent in recent years. Included on the b-side were extended beat-based instrumentals which used heavily effected studio tricks to create a sound that shocked, then rocked dancefloors. Tracks such as these are a staple element of their DJing, tying vocal-led cuts between percussive grooves or original disco tracks between modern House, using techniques similar to DJ Harvey.

Ben Davies' **The Quakerman** EP followed suit with the piano-led "Cream Cheese" and the electro/House fusion of "Schlam Me". The **Beatin' On Dave** EP and the **Beard Law** EP (both 1996) continued in a similar vein, but also marked a progression in the intricacies of their pot-fuelled music which would later become evident on their debut album.

Although still an enigma to most, The Idjut Boys received sufficient attention in London and from abroad to work on dub-remixes, as opposed to complete reconstructions, for a variety of like-minded artists. One of their earliest efforts, a remix of Century Falls' "It's Music" (1996), produced live instrumentation above and beyond the normal artificial House sounds, managing to mix live Salsoul-styled disco with dubbed-out House. Their remix work has involved A Man Called Adam, 16B, Dimitri From Paris and DJ Gilb'R, as well as re-editing classic jazz-funk records such as Kabbala's "Ashewo Ara" (1997) and Atmosphear's "Deep Space Nine".

Alongside London's Faze Action, DJ Harvey, Crispin J Glover and Ashley Beedle, Idjut Boys were placed at the centre of the media vaunted "nu-House" scene. While live instrumentation had become the fresh sound of House, the Idjuts marked themselves out by veering clear of aimless "jazz noodling" and by making records people could dance to.

Alongside their U-Star and Noid imprints, the Idjuts have launched the Fiasco label (featuring a Tabasco bottle on the front cover), with Laj and Quakerman providing the music, and the Disfunctional label, offering a diverse range of tracks from artists around the world. In 1997 they picked up more club play with the Fela Kuti-influenced drum sounds of **The Whoktish** EP and perhaps their most complete production to date, the **Roll Over and Snore** EP (1997), with a title track which uncharacteristically kicked into life with killer piano hook similar to those used on early Chicago House cuts by the likes of Marshall Jefferson and Sterling Void.

1998 witnessed their debut album, **Noid Long Player**. Although it featured none of their singles to date, it had the Idjuts' mark clearly stamped over every track. Using a wealth of jazz-funk/disco samples as a common thread, cuts like "Highway 167" and "Steinworld" were nothing but ludicrous drum breaks, extreme sound effects and crazy Marx Brothers samples all the way.

⊙ **Roll Over and Snore EP** Nuphonic, 1997

A much-hidden secret, this EP should've have been massive. Infectious disco b-lines and gloriously irreverent piano breakdown = dancefloor perfection.

◉ Noid Long Player Noid, 1998

Maybe not as impressive as fans would've expected, but, just like their DJ sets, it's all good times, stupid-dumb sound effects and disco licks.

Inner City

In 1987, Brooklyn-born producer Kevin Saunderson, then a 22-year-old Detroit telecommunications student struggling to pass his exams and make a success of his Techno label KMS, recorded a backing track in a makeshift studio stuck in the basement of his apartment. In need of a female vocalist who could also supply lyrics, he flew in Paris Grey from Chicago, having had her recommended by friend and WBMX Hot Mix 5 radio DJ Terry "Housemaster" Baldwin.

The duo's first effort "Big Fun" was born, but incredibly the tape was subsequently filed away and almost forgotten. It was only some months later, when UK dance aficionado Neil Rushton (who owned Northern Soul label Inferno) was visiting the Motor City to put together the compilation album **Techno – The New Dance Sound Of Detroit**, that he stumbled upon Saunderson's track, subsequently licensed it and set it loose for world-wide commercial success as a single.

But, despite the success, Grey hung on to her job as a sales assistant in a Chicago store until the duo's next release, "Good Life" (1988), outsold their debut. Backed by Saunderson's driving strings and mesmerising rhythms, it acted as a clear indication of the direction of Inner City's critically acclaimed debut album, **Paradise** (1988). Combining pop sensibilities and resolutely positive, anthemic songs

which expanded upon Detroit's abrasive Techno blueprint, the album sold over six million copies world-wide.

Unlike most of his Motor City counterparts, Saunderson had been influenced by Larry Levan's disco sets at the Paradise garage. Although gospel and R&B were always evident in Inner City's vocal projections, Saunderson's European white-synth group influences were more apparent on the under-rated **Paradise Remixed**, which featured wonderful, stretched-out, emotive remixes from his Belleville High school friends Derrick May and Juan Atkins.

Another hit single followed with a cover of Stephanie Mills' "Whatcha Gonna Do With My Lovin'" while Saunderson launched a career as a remixer, working on major-label pop acts including New Order, The Pet Shop Boys, Paula Abdul and The Charlatans. Despite narrow-minded accusations of "selling out" from Detroit, Saunderson was still capable of breaking new ground. His extreme remix of Wee Pappa Girl Rappers set a new precedent in that it was the first to totally strip out the original track and start from scratch, virtually standard fare amongst many of today's producers.

And although Inner City's follow-up, Fire (1990), was a disappointingly bland pop album which failed to make any lasting impression, **Praise** (1992) spawned "Pennies From Heaven" and the gospel-driven title track, which was accompanied by a mesmeric Derrick May remix.

In 1992 the duo were dropped from Virgin amidst claims of decreasing album sales and moved over to Neil Rushton's (Saunderson's manager) Network label. The **Testament 93** compilation album was released which featured remixes of their best-known songs by CJ Mackintosh, Leftfield and The Future Sound Of London.

Following Inner City's stop-gap single cover of Roberta Flack's "Back Together Again", Saunderson shifted the focus firmly underground with the release of two commercially unavailable DJ-only tunes. "Ahnongay" was an untamed slab of raw Detroit Techno that's widely regarded as one of the genre's most important productions, while the dubbed-out experimental remixes of "Share My Life" hinted at a more left-field approach for the expected fourth album.

Nothing emerged, and whilst 1994's trademark string-constructed "Do Ya" got back to basics, 1996's "Your Love/Hiatus" mixed an uplifting pop-dance track with a darker, experimental, Techno-rooted groove. **Hiatus** (1996) featuring vocals from both Paris Grey and Saunderson's wife, Ann, never saw the light of day as Network folded (though most of the early promo reviews suggested it was regressive and disappointing).

In 1998 Saunderson finally released his more experimental tracks on the **Faces and Phases** compilation. The following year Inner City returned to the UK charts with a disappointing remix of "Good Life", entitled "Buena Vida".

◉ Paradise   Ten/Virgin Records, 1988

Accessible Techno/House which features all their early anthemic hits, including "Big Fun" and "Good Life".

◉ Praise   Virgin Records, 1992

Essential if only for one track – the sublime "Pennies From Heaven". Though the rest of the album isn't bad either.

Irma Records

I taly may well be better known as the birthplace of thundering hands-in-the-air piano anthems, but Irma Records has always taken its cue from jazz and disco. Conceived by music enthusiasts/producers Umbi Damiani, Cesare Collina and Massimo Benini, the imprint has established itself world-wide as the leading Italian proponent of quality dance music, setting the standards for European melodic House music in the early to mid-'90s.

While the Italo House explosion of 1989/1990 prompted European clubbers to throw in the Ibizan towel for a summer spent on the dirty Adriatic Riveria seaside towns of Rimini and Riccione, most of the Italians were already dancing to a far cooler, Mediterranean jazz-washed groove at clubs like Paradiso, Ethos Mama and Baia Imperiale. Bored with the pop-ethos of Black Box-esque party hits, influential DJs Flavio Vecchi and Ricky Montanari were leading the drive toward soul-infused

US-style House and garage which Irma had quietly begun in 1988.

1988's debut, Kekkotronics and LTJ's (aka DJ Luca Trevisi) "First Job", combined House's four-to-the-floor rhythm with soul, funk and jazz influences to forge one of the label's most effective electronic grooves and heaviest bass-lines. It was quickly followed by the similarly styled "Gimme the Funk", Be Noir's soul-injected "Big Hit" and later Collina's sax-swamped "Babe What's Goin' On" (1989).

It wasn't until 1990, though, that Irma gained widespread attention with the release of three sure-fire sparkling club classics: K-Tronics Ensemble's jazzy "House of Calypso", Soft House Company's timeless, ivory-tinkling "What You Need/A Little Piano", and the biggest international hit of the lot, Angelino Albanesa and Claudio Rispoli's infectious piano-stomper "Found Love" (as Double Dee) which was licensed to CBS, given the Danny Tenaglia remix seal of approval and crashed into the UK charts.

Though Hip-Housers Master Freez and TJ Saunders, amongst other unmemorable acts, are best left consigned to the history books, much of the label's output retained the consistency levels over the early '90s. The K-Tronics team produced some of Irma's finest outings – "You X Me" (1990) and "Music You Got Me" (1993) – alongside Be Noir's gorgeous "Give Me Your Love", "Serious" and "Love Themes", and Nikita Warren's vibrant disco-ditty "I Need You" (1991).

Whilst Don Carlos got deep and ultra-jazzy on the stunning "Alone" (1991) and **Meditteraneo** EP for Irma's Calypso subsidiary, DJ Ricky Montanari used warm emotive grooves on "Never Can Get Enough" and "Antares" (both 1991) for the imprint's Onizom offshoot.

Reflecting Irma's growing appeal Stateside, the label opened an office in New York, and 1992 heralded the bass-heavy, Kerri Chandler-like "Marble Arch" by Subway Ground Master, while Tito Valdez's Latin monster "Tumbe" received the remix treatment from Murk's Oscar G and Philadelphia's King Britt recorded the jazzy "Into The Kick With Tito" as D.A.P.

Since then though, Irma's musical direction has moved away from its jazz-House blueprint to focus on jazz itself. Having released one of Italo House's best cuts in 1991 with Jestofunk's Peech Boys-sampling "I'm Gonna Love You", 1995 saw the creation of the Molto Jazz subsidiary, which has since released Jestofunk's acclaimed **Love In a Black Dimension** (1997). The 1998 inception of Instinctual, under the production team of DJs Uovo, Rame and Dino Angioletti, has signalled that a return to more exceptional House grooves could be back on the agenda.

⊙ **Riviera House Traxx**　　　　　　　　　Irma Records, 1997

Impeccable collection of Irma's finest jazz-inflected slates, including Don Carlos' "Alone", Kekkotronics' "House of Calypso", Jestofunk's "I'm Gonna Love You" and Soft House Company's "A Little Piano".

Jaydee

S ometimes one unforgettable record is all it takes to become a permanent fixture in the chronicles of clubbing folklore. Robin "Jaydee" Albers sealed his place when he emerged from nowhere in 1993 with one of House's most enduring anthems, "Plastic Dreams". Albers was something of a media celeb back home in Holland, having been three times winner of the Dutch arm-wrestling championship and a member of the national baseball team. Since the early '80s, he'd been both a TV presenter and radio DJ, reputedly only turning his hand to production after he'd lost his slot on the airwaves.

Originally recorded for Belgium's R&S records, "Plastic Dreams" – a ten-minute-long dark tribal groove, underpinned by a devastatingly simple breakbeat and incessantly addictive Hammond B3 organ signature – was immediately picked up on by nearly every DJ from London to New York (where it perfectly fitted Junior Vasquez's then dominant tribal sound).

Albers meanwhile seemed to disappear from sight almost as quickly as he'd emerged. Though he subsequently released a couple of largely ignored trance cuts under the guise of Graylock, he did return as Jaydee for the reasonable tribal-instrumental track "The Hunter" for Dutch label Clubstitute in 1994, and has since produced two brooding four-to-the-floor slates on George Morel's Groove On Records with the singles "S.U.A.D" and "Hidden Strength" (both 1995).

⊙ "Plastic Dreams"   R&S Records, 1993

Albers' only track of any real note, but an absolutely essential one nevertheless – ten minutes of innovative, breakbeat-driven, totally addictive House music. Available on **A Retrospective of House 1991–1995 Volume One** (BMG, 1996).

Jazzy M

Although he has never achieved either the media profile or widespread adulation heaped upon pioneering UK House DJs like Mike Pickering or Graeme Park, Jazzy M was an equally important figure in first bringing the sound of Chicago's jackin' rhythms to British shores. While Pickering introduced Manchester to House via his residency at the Haçienda, and Park did likewise through his influential stint at Nottingham's garage, it was Jazzy M who first brought the music to the nation's capital via his regular House show on pirate radio. In doing so, he provided much of the inspiration for DJs like Nicky Holloway, Johnny Walker and Darren Emerson to spearhead London's own club and musical soundtrack.

Born Michael Schiniou, Jazzy M began DJing aged 17, progressing to work behind the counter at Spin-Offs record shop on Fulham Palace Road in the mid-'80s. From there, he blagged his way onto the airwaves of London's predominantly reggae-orientated pirate radio station LWR. Perfectly placed to seize upon the raw, elemental tracks trickling into the shop (the only one to stock House in the south of England at that time) from Windy City DJs/producers like Jesse Saunders, Vince Lawrence and Mike Dunn, Jazzy began to incorporate House music into his radio show alongside releases from Prince, Walter Gibbons and New York's Easy Street Records. As the trickle turned into a flood with the launch of Chicago labels like Trax, WareHouse and Dance Mania, Jazzy's three-hour Jackin' Zone show, which began in 1986, became essential listening for virtually all the new wave of London-based DJs, promoters and producers who would forge 1987's Acid explosion.

Through his increasingly influential position, he worked with Pete Tong to compile ffrr's seminal **The House Sound Of Chicago** compilation, a key album in spreading the House gospel to a wider mainstream audience. A further edition in the series would House Jazzy's debut release, "Living In a World Of Fantasy". The relationship between Tong and Jazzy also bore fruit when his label, Oh-Zone, unwittingly launched one of the era's biggest rave anthems, Orbital's seminal "Chime" (1990). Originally passed to Jazzy on TDK cassette, the single went on to crash the national charts and establish Orbital as one of England's first bona fide rave pop stars, selling over 66,000 copies.

But although Jazzy began a second label, Delphinus Delphis, to release garage and House 12"s (notably Cuddles' "Hold On") and a third label, Spankin' (check Dub Nation's "I Can't Help Myself"), neither his recording nor his DJing career took off in the spectacular fashion one might have expected. Never one to succumb to the fashion-centric club set, Jazzy nonetheless took up an influential '90s residency at London's Release The Pressure (at Café De Paris) and has since become a regular on both the Ministry Of Sound's world-wide club tours and a resident at Saturday's long-established Rulin' club night.

His Saturday night residency at the Ministry Of Sound led to his first vinyl excursion for aeons, sampling George Duke's Latin-jazz classic "Brazilian Love Affair" for 1998's dancefloor smash, "Be Yourself Be Free".

⊙**Sao Paulo: "Be Yourself Be Free"**   Ministry Of Sound, 1998

Carnival vibes filtered direct from the summit of Sugar Loaf Mountain.

Marshall Jefferson

T he son of a school teacher and a policeman, Marshall Jefferson attended Chicago's Lindblom Technical High School and completed three years of accountancy at Western Illinois University before taking a post office job which paid twice as much as his first accounting jobs. He intended to return to his studies eventually, but never did.

At the age of 23, Jefferson visited the now legendary Chicago nightspots the Music Box and Frankie Knuckles' Powerplant. Among the early records that influenced him were Jamie Principle's "Your Love", Z Factor's "Fantasy" (a co-production from Jesse Saunders and Vince Lawrence) and Jesse Saunders' "On & On 117". Like other budding producers of the era, Jefferson felt that Saunders had developed an accessible sound that could be improved upon. At a time when the disco revolution was in full swing, he also cited rock legends Led Zeppelin and Black Sabbath as major influences, even playing guitar in a few bands.

Jefferson had quite a bit of spare cash as a result of his post office gig, and he channelled much of it into his music. He avidly bought records, sometimes up to thirty per week from local vinyl merchants like Imports Etc. He was intrigued by the equalising power of electronic gear being made available and promptly purchased a Roland TR808 drum machine, a Roland JX8P synthesizer and a Yamaha QX1 sequencer. Two days later he wrote "Free Yourself", which would later be released on his own Virgo Trax imprint on the **Go Wild Rhythm Tracks** EP, most of which was eventually recorded with Vince Lawrence in Jefferson's first ever studio sessions (he would later collaborate with Lawrence and Harry Dennis as Jungle Wonz).

He soon discovered another essential piece of Roland equipment, the TB303, and used it to write "I've Lost Control" in the summer of 1985 for Music Box compadre Sleazy D. It would be his first, and also one of the industry's first Acid House tracks. Though now recognised globally, at the time the track achieved only local success, selling about 70,000 units in the city and receiving as many spins at the Music Box.

Jefferson has alleged that he wrote records for the Trax label during this period that were never credited to him, but amongst those that the label has acknowledged as Jefferson's are Screamin Rachel's "My Main Man", a collaboration with Lil' Louis on "7 Ways To Jack" under the Hercules guise, and the track that would truly earn him a name, the

Ron Hardy-mixed "Move Your Body (House Music Anthem)" (1986), featuring vocals from Curtis Maclain. The track's energetic piano chords and vibrant emotion formed the blueprint for thousands of subsequent House releases.

Never publicised too loudly, in 1986 Jefferson produced "Acid Tracks" for the DJ Pierre-led outfit Phuture, a track that launched the Acid House movement abroad, as well as spawning a litany of knock-off tracks in Chicago alone. He quickly grew weary of the monster hit he had created, however, and began to map out the more melancholy, darker side of the genre, helping to define, alongside the productions of Larry Heard, what would become known as the sub-genre Deep House. Influenced by the seemingly unlikely source of Pink Floyd's **Dark Side of**

the Moon, the single which earmarked the new style was called "Open Our Eyes" (1987), recorded under the humble name Marshall Jefferson presents The Truth.

At around the same time, Jefferson also turned his energies to a more R&B-influenced, soulful blend of House, eventually turning his production skills to new Chicago band Ten City. House music's first marketable "act", Ten City signed direct to Atlantic Records, releasing their first single, the Jefferson-produced "Devotion", to a rave response at the clubs. Jefferson then produced the outfit's debut album, **Foundation**, whose single "That's the Way Love Is", hit the UK Top 10 in 1989. A follow-up album, **State of Mind**, incorporating the Chicago Symphony Orchestra, was released in 1990, but by the time Ten City had reached their third album they had parted company with their producer.

Jefferson went on to produce Kym Mazelle's debut album and also wrote tracks for Ce Ce Rodgers while at the same time cementing his reputation as a remixer with mainstream labels. His credits include artists such as Dusty Springfield, Pet Shop Boys, Tom Jones and Donna Summer. But it was his work with Ten City, Ce Ce Rodgers and Curtis McLean (check "Let's Get Busy") that established him as one of the finest songwriters of his generation.

The collection **This Is Other Side Records** (released by German label Tresor in 1993) traces the extended life of Jefferson's own label, gathering together several of his remixes and productions between 1989 and 1992 for artists like The Party Girls and Vicky Ryan. In 1993 he teamed up with Adonis, Farley "Jackmaster" Funk and Chip E to form Godfathers Inc., but their full-length album was never released. By 1996, he emerged with an album for Tresor called **The Day of the Onion**, a record which again revealed that his talent for sequencing emotive melodies with killer grooves had lost none of its potency.

Jefferson currently resides in London, having made his first visit in 1986 as part of a UK club tour called the 6 Chicago House Party that also featured Adonis, Fingers Inc and Kevin Irving. The tour promoted the release of a compilation of tracks from the DJ International label on London Records.

A heavily sampled source in the dance music world in his own right, Marshall Jefferson tends to eschew sampling and has always emphasised pure, original musicality over everything else. It's perhaps for this reason, coupled with the emotionally intense quality of his productions, that Marshall Jefferson is up there alongside some of the greatest legends of House music.

⦿ Past Classics Fierce/Trax, 1998

A superb collection bringing together most of Jefferson's early classics. The full-length version of his landmark 1986 anthem "Move Your Body" is here alongside the Acid-intensity of Sleazy D's "I've Lost Control". But, more pleasingly, so are his experimental and inventive Deep House grooves as Jungle Wonz (with Harry Dennis) and Virgo.

Paul Johnson

A longside Cajmere, DJ Sneak, Glenn Underground and Gemini, Paul Johnson stands as a central part of the vital force the Relief and Cajual labels let loose in both Chicago and the wider international underground in the mid-'90s. More associated with the sophisticated brutality of Relief, Johnson's career has gone on to be paradigmatic of the label's vital energy and of the difficulties that sound has in translating into broader contexts.

The Relief sound, for all its immediate stomp and circumstance, is rarely about the basic, clean 909 kick drum that drives European Techno, instead focusing on the tints and sheens of a simple drum pattern. Johnson's records rarely look to that kind of scrutiny, contenting themselves with the energy and erotic force of cranked-up rhythms. One particular beauty was on Dance Mania, a double a-side called "11p.m music/2a.m music" which exemplifies the style and his own special effect: the wiggle.

It's that wiggle that lures the listener back to Johnson, and sonically there's never been much going on of great interest. The wiggle continues into his first album, **Bump Talkin'** (1994), an assault of moments when the hips take over, but little more. With **Feel The Music** (1996), Johnson moved distinctly into Cajual's psycho-disco terrain. Although the influences have changed, taking in modern approximations of Latino-funk hero Joe Bataan, the method is still there, the wiggle happens, albeit more often from melody than rhythm. It is difficult to dislike, particularly at huge volume where it starts roomfuls of people smiling, shaking, but it's difficult not to want more.

⊙**Bump Talkin'**   Peacefrog, 1994

A sexed-up stormtrooper assault on the hips, depthless but massive fun.

François Kervorkian

François Kervorkian remains one of dance music's most innovative producers. Alongside Larry Levan, his unique early '80s dubbed-out disco mixes provided a raw blueprint for many of Chicago's basic House productions, while in the '90s his remixes and DJing residency at the Big Apple's Body & Soul Sunday afternoon sessions have helped inspire a legion of NYC producers to use more live instrumentation in their mixes.

Having given up his attempt to study pharmacy at Strasbourg University in the early '70s in favour of playing the drums and spinning in the city's bars, Kervorkian abandoned France altogether and headed for New York in September 1975, where, after an unsuccessful stint playing R&B covers with various bands, he was hired to drum live alongside DJ Walter Gibbons at Galaxy 21. Adapting to the heavily percussive, extended-mix sets, Kervorkian was given an initial insight into the possibilities of both disco and DJing/mixing/extending the original music. His perception was honed further when he moved on to work as an assistant at Experiment Four, where DJ John "Jellybean" Benitez's quick, cut-up, cross-fading technique held sway.

By the late '70s the NYC gay club scene had reached climax point and Kervorkian was not only DJing himself, but was beginning to cut his own exclusive dubby disco-medley edits. Soon after he held a residency at the celebrity hangout New York New York, he landed a position as A&R for Prelude Records from where he exerted his first tangible influence on dance music.

His career as in-House mixer for the disco label began in 1979 with a mix of Musique's "(Push, Push) In The Bush", whose b-side "Keep On Jumpin'" has since been covered by Todd Terry and the Lisa Marie Experience among others. While his mix of Martin Circus' bizarre "Disco Circus" (1979) perfectly encapsulated NYC's drug-crazed nightlife with its shamanic chants and wired, psychedelic effects, it was his dub-inflected early '80s instrumental remixes which provided House music with part of its basic soundtrack. Taking cues from both disco and reggae dub mixers like Augustus Pablo, Kervorkian's productions of D-Train's "You're the One For Me" and "D-Train Dub", The

Striker's "Contagious" and Dinosaur L's "Go Bang" (1982) were unique, often abandoning the need for vocals and stripping a track to just its basic groove and melody.

Having spread the sound as a part-time DJ at the most influential clubs in the city – Paradise garage, Studio 54, AM:PM, Zanzibar and Better Days – in 1983 Kervorkian abandoned the club scene to work for the next seven or so years solely as a pop producer, working with artists including Jah Wobble, Kraftwerk (check 1983's "Tour De France"), Ashford & Simpson and Thomas Dolby.

In 1987 he opened his own Axis recording studios in NYC, and indicated a move back to his disco roots with production work for Loleatta Holloway on the back of her Black Box court case, with the single "Strong Enough" (1991). He also took up the mantle of DJing once again, touring with Larry Levan on his last stint to Japan in 1992 and bringing his ten-hour sets to London's Ministry Of Sound.

But it wasn't until 1995, when he started his Wave Music imprint, that Kervorkian began to have his second real impact upon House. Though the label's output has been relatively small to date, its first few releases – Rob Rives' post-Ambient **Downtime** and Kervorkian's self-produced **FK** EP (both 1995) – made an immediate and important impact.

The **FK** EP is still widely regarded as Kervorkian's finest House release. With Freddie Turner's wailing voocals, a bad-ass Deep House groove and emotive, strung-out chords, "Hypnodelic" became one of the tracks of 1995, but the rest of the EP remains equally impressive.

At around the same time Kervorkian initiated his Sunday afternoon club, Body & Soul, with DJ/producer Joe Claussell, which showcased the duo's passion for live instrumentation, influencing producers world-wide. 1997 and 1998 have seen Kervorkian carry this same vibe over to remixes such as Ame Strong's dubby "Tout Est Bleu", Cesaria Evora's semi-Balearic "Sangue de Beirona" and Big Muff's "My Funny Valentine", while his Wave label has continued sporadically to meet the dancefloors' needs, releasing tracks like "Din Da Da" by Kevin Aviance (1998).

◉ Prelude – Deep Grooves   Sequel Records, 1993

A near perfect overview of the quintessential '80s disco label, which showcases some of Kervorkian's most popular mixes, including Musique's "In the Bush", D-Train's "Music" and "You're the One For Me".

◉ Body & Soul Vol. 1   Wave Music, 1998

The sound of Kervorkian & Claussell's Sunday afternoon sessions. Includes FK's beautiful "Time & Space", Jepthe Guillaume's acoustic gem "The Prayer" and the Claussell/Chandler Latin classic "Escravos de Jo" alongside productions by Mood II Swing, Murk and Mousse T.

King Street

F ew clubs have launched the careers of budding House DJs and artists as successfully as New York's Paradise Garage. Hisa Ishioka, an immigrant to America from Japan in the '80s, took his passion for nights spent at the Paradise Garage and channelled them into both an enduring tribute and a new venture when he started the BPM King Street Sounds label in 1993.

While Paradise Garage guru Larry Levan made garage from a wild combination of tracks ranging from Philadelphia soul to Van Halen, from The Trammps to The Clash on any given night, King Street, on the other hand, seemed intent on preserving the spiritual (and often deliciously hedonistic) vibe of the garage movement that had been launched inside that club. Rather than developing as radical a form of musical eclecticism as would doubtless have reigned if Levan were still alive, King Street, and sister label Nite Grooves, became a staple fixture with House purists for a certain type of late-night flavour. Their back catalogue is overflowing with House legends, having released platters from producers and artists such as David Morales, Masters At Work, Roger Sanchez, Lil' Louis, Satoshi Tomiee, Danny Tenaglia, Mateo & Matos, Ultra Naté and even Evelyn "Champagne" King.

Naturally, this ideology has meant that King Street's greatest support in its home country would lie in, but not be limited to, the gay clubs of New York City. The label has garnered at least three #1s on the Billboard dance chart: Kimara Lovelace's "Circles" (perhaps the label's signature track), Urban Soul's "Show Me" and Pump Friction's "That Sound", remixed by Ralphi Rosario.

King Street's main focus since its inception has been on the DJ consumer and 12" market, assuring waxmasters a steady flow of new banging trax to build up sets.

That being said, 1997 showed a marked interest in exploring a larger audience with some key mix CD releases: a collection of past King Street singles from New Jersey producer Kerri Chandler, the inception of the **Mix The Vibe** series, mixed by Tony Humphries, and jazz-House compilation **Abstract Jazz Lounge**, featuring David Morales, Little Louie Vega and Lenny Fontana. By 1998, however, they were poised to conquer this wider market with highly anticipated full-length releases from Kimara Lovelace, Urban Soul and Johnny Dangerous, as well as a five-year retrospective collection and **Abstract Afro Lounge**, a compilation featuring Spiritual Life's Joe Claussell, Ron Trent and Wamdue Kids.

◉ Mix The Vibe: Tony Humphries　　　King Street/SonyS3 UK, 1997

An essential look at both the tremendous DJ skills of Tony Humphries and some of King Street's most elegant tracks: "Only You" from Kimara Lovelace and Urban Soul's "Back Together" (featuring seasoned diva Sandy B). Also check the follow-up in the Mix The Vibe series, executed handily by Peter Rauhoffer (aka Club 69 / Size Queen).

Kings Of Tomorrow

The New York-based production team of Sandy Rivera and J. "Sinister" Sealee have an undeniable trademark in their music: their drums, always innovative, nothing less than energetic and relentless. Their appreciation for '70s-era disco, funk and gospel sensibilities, along with their own keen sense of the future of the garage dancefloor, have propelled them high above the glut of House tracks and distinguished themselves as real musicians. They've covered daunting funk classics like Lonnie Liston Smith's "Expansions" and The Blackbyrds' "Rock Creek Park" with maturity and effectiveness. Kings Of Tomorrow productions truly are "songs" in terms of structure, thoughtfulness and completeness, and each contains a perfect melding of those essential elements that never fail to move a crowd.

In an era where there are far too many awful wailing divas on House tracks, a vocal excursion from the Kings has an assured stamp of qual-

Kings Of Tomorrow

The beginning - Mixed by Sandy Rivera

ity. They favour voices with strong, gospel-ready backbones – check Sean Grant's astounding delivery on "I Hear My Calling" or Dawn Tallman's belting on "Let It Go" (1997) for prime examples.

In their career they have recorded for such labels as Blackwiz, Deep Vision, Zestland, Distance (and imprint Remedie), Slip 'N' Slide and Yoshitoshi. Since first emerging in the mid-'90s, they have rarely failed to garner critical acclaim from DJs and press, more recently hitting hard and funky with dancefloor fillers like "Fade to Black" (1997) and "Fly Away" (1998). Presently, K.O.T. have had a fairly low level of exposure in their own country, limited to vinyl-only single releases on obscure 12" labels.

Above all, what is most striking is that Kings Of Tomorrow are what one calls "musicians' musicians" – not only are many (larger) artists aware and respecting of their sound, many have attempted unsuccessfully to imitate it. But there's no mimicking the originality that lies behind those killer drums.

⊙ The Beginning: Mixed by Sandy Rivera   Distance UK, 1998

Released in the summer of 1998, **The Beginning** is a prospective listener's first chance to catch this duo on CD, and their bold, gospel-influenced brand of garage House is sure to please. This collection culls their most essential productions and remixes up to that point, including Sandy Rivera's solo outings as D'Menace and Aurei, whose stunning "Time" is an excellent closer.

K Klass

In late 1988 Andy Williams and Carl Thomas were still part of minor Welsh dance act Interstate. But a succession of evenings spent on the dancefloor of DJ Mike Pickering's Nude nights at the rainy city's Hacienda club led to a meeting with local lads Paul Roberts and Russ Morgan, and the birth of K Klass. 1990's **Wildlife** EP not only became a significant underground hit, but foregrounded K Klass' combination of a canny pop sensibility, sense of humour and anthemic breakdowns.

Martin Price of Manchester collective 808 State – whom K Klass successfully supported on tour in 1990 – recognised kindred spirits and released K Klass' second outing, "Rhythm Is a Mystery", on his Creed imprint in mid-1991. Featuring the vocals of soon-to-become mainstay Bobbi Depasois, "Rhythm Is a Mystery" blew dancefloors away with its immediate, chopping piano chords and outrageously hypnotic, but lush, melody, capturing both the hedonism of the moment and the tension necessary for a good dance track. K Klass' reputation in the North of England soon spread. Not only could they create anthemic tunes, but they proved themselves a formidable live experience, and it was on the gig circuit that they really bolstered their reputation.

Re-released six months later on Deconstruction Records, "Rhythm Is a Mystery" reached #3 in the UK charts. The commercial success continued with 1992's piano-washed anthems "Don't Stop" and "So Right", while 1993's "Let Me Show You" cranked up the excitement levels for the release of their debut album. The well-received **Universal** (1993) ventured into the unexpected, though, with "What You're Missing" betraying a darker edge, and "La Cassa" featuring ex-Smiths guitarist Johnny Marr.

Since then it's been a case of back to basics – churning out unashamedly mercantile, piano-heavy remixes for artists as diverse as New Order, Carleen Anderson and Bobby Brown. No commercial dance music compilation seems complete without a K Klass remix; surely a testament to their ability to harness the needs of the dance-floor through an essentially marketable aesthetic.

Even their own sporadic productions have followed an identical path. 1998 spawned the long-awaited follow-up to "What You're Missing". "Burnin'", released though the collective's second album, K2, showed a serious lack of progression and slipped by largely unnoticed. The same year's mixed compilation of funky US House, **Prohibition**, fared far better with the critics.

◉ Universal   Deconstruction, 1993

A reasonable pop-House debut that includes their most effective anthem, "Rhythm Is a Mystery".

Frankie Knuckles

Alongside DJ Ron Hardy, "House godfather" Frankie Knuckles remains the figure who altered the course of Chicago dance music more than any other. His influential residency at the Warehouse Club from 1978 to 1983 would not only give this new genre its name, "House", but more immediately changed the perception and popularity of dance music within Chicago, forming the basis for the Windy City explosion some years later.

When Knuckles arrived in 1977, *Saturday Night Fever* hadn't yet taken disco into the mainstream and most of Chicago's clubs were still soundtracked by pre-programmed sound systems. Knuckles single-handedly changed all that by bringing with him the smooth mixing techniques he'd learnt from NYC DJs Nicky Siano and Larry Levan.

A teenage friend of DJ Larry Levan, Knuckles began his club apprenticeship by allegedly spiking the punch at Nicky Siano's Gallery in Manhattan, before moving on to DJ first at Better Days disco and then at the gay leisure complex, the Continental Baths, alongside Levan. He stayed there until the venue closed in 1976, from where he took up the invitation to become resident at a new Chicago club, the Warehouse, after Levan had turned down the owner's initial offer. He brought with him the distinctly NYC vibe of playing Philly soul along-side Salsoul disco, funk and a wide selection of vocal dance 12"s.

As other DJs tuned into the faster sounds of Italian disco and Euro-pean electronica, Knuckles upped the pace, re-editing and remixing versions of songs from reel-to-reel tracks to please the crowds. His blending of disco's lush orchestration with faster, electronic melodies by the likes of Giorgio Moroder, often underpinned by his use of drum machines to add a fiercer kick, helped to create a constant rhythm that would, in due course, become known as "House music".

When Knuckles left the Warehouse in 1983 (after the owners doubled the admission price to $8) no one had yet made a recognisably four-to-the-floor House record, though the minimalist disco productions of NYC technicans like Arthur Russell and Kenton Nix, and the dub-inflected 12" edits of François Kervorkian and Larry Levan had set the precedents. Knuckles' influence within the city limits was becoming evident, though: in singer Jamie Principle's emotive, new-wave recordings, and in radio DJs Farley Keith (aka Farley "Jackmaster" Funk) and Steve Hurley own club, House Music Only, at the Playground.

In 1983, Knuckles began another influential DJing residency at the Powerplant club. Soon after, a Los Angeles emigré, DJ Ron Hardy, began to draw attention for his wilder and more experimental selection

of distinctly black soul and disco by the likes of Harold Melvin & The Bluenotes and Eddie Kendricks at the Music Box club on Chicago's South Side. Soon the competition between the two would result in both pushing the limits of their technical skills with Knuckles creating exclusive edits backed up by the drums of his Roland 909 machine. But, in the end it was Hardy's club which proved both the radical inspiration and testing ground for the city's pioneers Jesse Saunders, Larry Heard, Marshall Jefferson, Adonis and DJ Pierre.

Knuckles produced his first commercial remix for Salsoul in 1982, an extended re-versioning of First Choice's "Let No Man Put Asunder". But it was once the House explosion was under way that his vinyl excursions began to receive widespread attention. One of the studio mixers for both Trax and DJ International, his early work with Jamie Principle yielded two of House music's most important, and most imitated, 12"s: "Your Love" and "Baby Wants To Ride". In 1987 he also produced the Nightwriters' anthem "Let the Music Use You".

In the late '80s Knuckles moved back to New York and began phase two of his career, one that would eventually take House music to a wider mainstream audience. Having formed the Def Mix production team with David Morales, Knuckles set about remixing and recording for and with a wealth of vocalists and pop acts. In 1990 he produced Robert Owens' monumental "Tears" with keyboardist Satoshi Tomiee. The same year he co-worked Alison Limerick's "Where Love Lives" into a string-laden, piano-driven masterpiece, and he has since applied the same commercially succesful formula to artists including Electribe 101, Sounds Of Blackness, Chaka Khan, Michael Jackson, Luther Vandross, Toni Braxton and Janet Jackson.

In the interim, Knuckles also became an artist of note himself. Though his debut album, **Beyond the Mix** (1991), was a slick and sometimes predictable work, it yielded the singles "Rainfalls", "Workout" and "Whistle Song", the latter a chart hit in the UK. 1995's follow-up, the formulaic **Welcome To The Real World**, featuring Adeva, was also far from his best, though the smooth soul production did gel on the singles "Too Many Fish" and "I'm Walking".

As resident at NYC's Sound Factory Bar and numerous guest spots throughout the world, he continues to be a major influence in the late '90s and has proved that he has always remained true to the music.

◉ Nightwriters: "Let the Music (Use You)"   Dancia, 1987

One of those "Summer of Love" classics that just won't die. Available on **Classic House Volume 1** (Mastercuts/Beechwood Music, 1994).

◉ Sounds Of Blackness: "The Pressure"   A&M, 1992/1997

The power of religious celebration has never gelled as well on the dancefloor as when Knuckles took Atlanta's sixty-strong choir to new levels of intensity.

Bobby Konders

These days you're more likely to find the name Bobby Konders cropping up on the production credits for a killer dancehall reggae cut than a House 12". But back in the late '80s and early '90s his dub-inflected signature paved the way for Deep House with a unique selection of slow-burning singles released on imprints like Nu Groove and his own label, Massive B.

Konders first rose to fame around 1988 through his seminal *Saturday Lunch Mix* radio show on New York's WBLS station. Relocating to the Bronx, he found it was NYC's multi-racial, thriving after-hours club scene where dub, New Jersey-style vocal tracks and hip-hop were mixed up at clubs like The Choice and Ego Trip, that fuelled his urge to make the move into production in the late '80s.

First stop was Nu-Groove Records, where after a few initial attempts at fusing reggae with House, Konders produced the cut still synonymous with his name, "The Poem" (1990). With its softly spoken Last Poets-style intro and hypnotic, dubby skank, it has sold in excess of 50,000 copies.

He followed it with **Massive Sounds** EP and an excellent mini-album, **House Rhythms** (1991), which showcased his soothing dub-House production on cuts like "Nervous Acid", "Let There Be House" and "Masai Women". By this stage, he'd initiated Massive B with **Cool, Calm and Collective**, following it with perhaps his best vocal House track, the sublime "As One" (1991) with Robert Owens.

Having picked up attention from major labels, Dub Poet's "Black or White" (1992) and his remixes for Maxi Priest, Shabba Ranks and Shinehead acted to broaden his palette on the subsequent **Massive Sounds** (1992) album for Mercury Records. Though it includes a re-versioning of "The Poem", the album signalled Konders' move further away from House's beat to a more traditional dub, reggae and dance-hall vision, utilising vocalists like Mikey Jarrett, and spawning the massive reggae/hip-hop cut "Mack Daddy".

Konders has claimed he lost interest in House when the majority of the music became faster and harder. Since 1992, as a DJ Konders has gone from strength to strength on the reggae scene, forming the Massive B sound system with MC Jabba, touring the West Indies and Europe.

His weekly Sunday radio show has continued to strengthen his position in the scene and his production work has included the ragga anthem, "Ready to Fe" for General Levy's **Six Million Ways to Die** (1994) and a 1997 remix of Monkey Mafia's "Work Mi Body".

◉ "The Poem" Nu Groove, 1990

Konders' ultimate dub-House melange. Available on **Chill Out Too** (Avex, 1996).

⊙ House Rhythms Nu Groove, 1991

Soundclash alert. Konders' eclectic mini-album fuses reggae, dub and drawling four-to-the-floor rhythms into one fat joint and comes up with the necessary green.

Eric Kupper

I t should come as no suprise that Eric Kupper's self-produced album, **From The Deep** (1995), failed to propel him into the limelight, despite garnering slavish reviews from most of the dance music press. Kupper had already honed his keyboard and production skills to shape a wealth of classic club cuts since the early '90s without a sniff of public recognition.

Turning to studio work after jacking in his guitar and keyboard-playing days with various post-punk combos at the tail end of the '80s, Kupper's education in electronic experimentalism with electro-deity/"Planet Rock" producer Arthur Baker brought him well up to date with the endless possibilities of dance music.

A session of tinkling the ivories for the in-demand Def Mix team of Frankie Knuckles and David Morales provided Kupper with the base from which to launch his first solo outing, "The Whistle Song" (1990), although at the time nearly all the credit went to Frankie Knuckles (the track later appearing on his 1991 album, **Beyond the Mix**. Shying away from the obvious disco loops and vocal samples used by so many of his East Coast counterparts, its ethereal ambience and simple, mesmerising flute hook fitted the emerging aesthetic in House music previously evident on labels like Nu Groove, making it a favourite amongst clubbers and the cognoscenti alike. Testament to his modesty, it's still often mistakenly listed as one of Knuckles' finest works.

In the ensuing period, Kupper set up his aptly titled Hysteria production company, taking on remix and production work for Chanelle ("Work That Body"), Ru Paul ("Snapshot") and Sabrina Johnston ("I Wanna Sing") amongst others. Yet it was as a keyboard sessionist that his Midas touch extended over some of House music's most effective and commercially successful anthems, including Alison Limerick's "Where Love Lives" (1990), Ce Ce Penniston's "Finally" (1991), Degrees Of Motion's "Do You Want It Right Now" and Clubland's ballad "(I'm Under) Love Strain" (both 1992).

A mid-'90s affiliation with the Big Apple's Tribal Records enabled Kupper to continue with his own evocative, subterranean excursions evident on "Organism"'s warm synthetic textures. Kupper's **K-Scope Project** four-track EP of 1994, alongside works by Ludovic Navarre and Washington's Deep Dish, helped set much of the agenda for a more subtle twist on the formula which proved yet again that dance music could be as stimulating off the dancefloor as on it.

Though Tribal has since folded, Kupper has remained a constant NYC fixture, behind the scenes as a remixer for various vocalists and independent labels. Having signed as a solo artist to Twisted Records in 1998, Kupper released the four-track K-Scope 3 EP, followed some months later with an album for the label, **Instant Music**.

◉ From The Deep   Tribal United Kingdom/IRS Records, 1995

As you'd expect from the title, this is no hands-in-the-air collection of piano-pounding ditties. Kupper's tracks may be too subtle for their own good, but overall this is an album built for longevity.

Dave Lee

From the late '80s to the present, Dave Lee's sample-heavy, disco-marked tracks have rarely failed to hit the dancefloor head on, while his host of tongue-in-cheek pseudonyms have carved out intriguing public personas, most notably that of Joey Negro.

Lee first attracted attention in 1988, setting up the NYC-styled Republic Records in the UK with Mark Ryder. Over the next few years Republic proved instrumental in licensing and breaking the soulful wave of New Jersey garage from artists such as Blaze, Hippie Torales and Paul Simpson, opening up the music to a larger audience with a series of acclaimed compilation albums such as **The Garage Sound of Deepest New York** (1988).

Around the same time, Lee began to release a number of disco-flecked 12"s on both Republic and a host of New York labels under pseudonyms including M.D. Emm, Kid Valdez of Mystique, Masters of the Universe, Quest For Excellence, Life On Earth and Energize. It was 1989's "Forever Together", under the guise of Raven Maize, which provided the UK's clubs with Lee's first bona fide House hit. Welding Exodus' disco gem "Together Forever" to the back of a whistle-blowing carnival stampede and a ten-ton bass-line, the track became one of the year's clubland anthems. Having spread the scam that Raven was an ex-convict currently working in a Disneyland steel band, it also propelled Lee into the music press.

The tricks continued with his next and most successful alias, Joey Negro. Hijacking the pseudonym from a obscure disco track, "Shoot the Pump" by Walter J. Negro, Lee released the wonderful slab of slow-burning, groovy beats, "Do It Believe It" (1990) for New York's seminal Nu Groove Records. An immediate underground hit, a year later it was given vocals and a re-edit, Lee swiping from Michael Wilson's Prelude disco classic "Groove It With Your Body" to provide the cut with its spaced-out intro, and "Do What You Feel" was unleashed into the UK Top 40.

A major label deal with Virgin produced 1993's unashamedly disco-fied **Universe Of Love**, which fully realised Lee's ambitions of working with disco-era deities Gwen Guthrie and The Trammps, spawning updated singles of the latter's "What Happened to the Music" and The Gibson Brothers' "Oooh What A Life".

Although the duo of Lee and Andrew "Doc" Livingstone assembled club-happy sample cuts under the guise of Hedboys, Lee has continued to save his best singles for the label he had conceived in 1989, Z Records. 1991 heralded joyous vocal productions such as Pacha's "One Kiss" and Extortion's consummate "How Do You See Me Now?"

Since 1996 Lee has pushed out a wealth of club-storming instrumentals including the "Streetlife"-sampling "New York City Woman", Foreal People's "Does It Feel Good To You?", Z Factor's "Gotta Keep Pushin'" and Sunburst Band's electro-funk "Atlantic Forrest".

He's also kept up the humour: recording under the alias of an Australian soap-opera character, Doug Willis, with more disco-snatching tracks like the essential "Tonight's the Night" and "Two Tons of Doug", and releasing tracks such as the undeniable dancefloor stormer "I'm Back" as Sessomato – the name (Italian for "sex mad") culled from West End Records' first release.

With the late '90s disco revival fully under way, Lee has compiled the definitive **Jumpin'** compilations for Harmless Records and continues to release disco-inspired productions, most successfully with 1998's Here Comes The Sunburst Band.

⊙ Here Comes The Sunburst Band   Z Records, 1998

After five years, Lee returned with an expertly crafted selection of addictive '70s funk and disco soundtrack-style melodies courtesy of his first live group, The Sunburst Band. As you'd expect, the sound of soaring strings, wah-wah guitar hooks and breezing basslines are never far away.

Leftfield

Leftfield, formed by Paul Daley and Neil Barnes in 1990, have hardly been what one would call prolific, having released only a handful of singles and, at the time of writing, one album. Their output to date, albeit limited, indicates a finely crafted music

by perfectionists who are, quite rightly, regarded as pioneers of British House.

The pair first met at a club in Soho, run by the sadly defunct acid jazz group The Sandals. On discovering they shared a musical common ground (they are both drummers), it wasn't long before the two were working together. Leftfield's first release was Neil's version of "Not Forgotten" for Outer Rhythm Records in 1990, produced with Mat Clark, who is known for work with Big Life label mates A Man Called Adam, an outfit Paul Daley once played percussion with. The driving, groove-led beats and simple but affecting melody made for an impressive debut, but it was not until Paul's "Hard Hands" overhaul of the track, on the flip side of their "More Than I Know" single, that they really grabbed the attention of DJs and record buyers alike.

It was a landmark release, and presented an undoubtedly new, resolutely British sound that heralded the advent of "progressive House" in the early '90s.

The association with The Sandals led to Leftfield taking up production duties for the band. The bass-lines, steeped in dub roots, and the strong, percussive feel of both "A Profound Gas" and "Nothing" (1992) clearly demonstrated the pair's love of slow, funky dance music. 1992 also saw the release of two singles on their own Hard Hands imprint, "Release the Pressure", showcasing the vocal talents of Earl Sixteen, and "Song of Life". "Song of Life" was irresistible in its uncomplicated beauty and "Release The Pressure" managed perfectly to marry hard beats with a groovy, dubby feel, proving that hard-edged dance music did not necessarily have to be fast.

Leftfield returned in 1994, releasing "Open Up", featuring guest vocalist John Lydon of Sex Pistols and PiL fame. For many this was a pivotal point in their career and the track certainly proved to be their most commercially successful release, reaching the Top 20 in the UK singles chart. An aggressive, uncompromising record – in keeping with Lydon's vitriolic lyrical refrain, "Burn Hollywood burn" – it nonetheless disappointed some hardened fans who felt that, in achieving this aggression, much of the character and feel that marked the duo's earlier releases had been sacrificed.

In 1995, following a licensing deal with Sony, Leftfield's much-anticipated debut album, **Leftism**, was released to critical acclaim from all areas of the music press. Although perhaps not quite as consistent as some had hoped (the stand-out tracks were reworked versions of their previous singles), it featured contributions by African rapper Djum Djum, Manchester poet Lemn Sissay and Curve's Toni Halliday, whose breakbeat track, "Original", proved a fantastic single.

The album's eclectic range of material found **Leftism** nominated for the Mercury Music Prize, and led to soundtrack recordings for the films *Shallow Grave*, *Shopping* and *Trainspotting*.

Leftfield have been no less successful in their work as remixers. Inevitably, after a high-profile remix of David Bowie's "Jump They Say", they were offered work by other major artists wishing to exploit the new market. Displaying an admirably principled stance, however, Paul and Neil turned these various offers down, choosing to work exclusively on tracks that they themselves like. Such an approach has served them well and tracks to look out for include Ultra Naté's "Deeper Love" (1992) and their version of Renegade Soundwave's eponymously titled single (1994). A slow, dense and engrossing track when played at 33rpm, it could also be played at 45rpm pitched down to -8, as heard at clubs such as Andrew Weatherall's Sabresonic in London. "Intoxication" (1992) by React 2 Rhythm, a major signpost for British House, also received the Leftfield treatment and remains one their finest moments to date, still sounding fresh several years on.

Leftfield's importance to the British House scene cannot be overstated. Ignoring the transient trends that so often proliferate in dance music, they have doggedly followed their own path and created their own unique sound where many have been content to ape and emulate.

⊙ **"Not Forgotten – Hard Hands Mix"**   Outer Rhythm, 1990

One of British House's finest moments. A trend-setting, gloriously incessant moulding of beat and bass.

◎ **Leftism**   Sony/Hard Hands, 1995

Unique combination of spacey Techno, bassbin-shattering dub and distinctly British House that hints at subversive punk tendencies while rarely escaping the whims of the dancefloor.

Larry Levan

L arry Levan is a figure of clubland folklore, engendered by his God-like DJ/producer/remixer status and cemented by his cocaine-fuelled lifestyle of excess which eventually resulted in his death in November 1992. Perhaps Levan's greatest legacy is the number of House artists who were and still are directly inspired by both his own music and the way he crafted and adapted that of others. Disco classics like "Let No Man Put Asunder", MFSB's "Love Is the Message" and Gwen Guthrie's "Seventh Heaven" were played alongside singles such as The Clash's "Magnificent Seven", Talking Heads' "Once In a Lifetime", Eddie Grant's "Time Warp", ESG's "Moody" and Manuel Göttsching's proto-Techno masterpiece "E2-E4" to create a truly unique and largely unrivalled atmosphere.

Levan was initially spurred into action through teenage nights spent on the dancefloor at early '70s gay clubs. He was originally moved by the legacy of DJ Francis Grosso's shamanic and eclectic soul/rock sets at the drug-frenzied Sanctuary club in Manhattan's Hell's Kitchen neighbourhood.

By 1973, Levan had progressed to first working the lights, then DJing, at the Continental Baths, where he did so for a year, building up a loyal fan base. After a stint at the Soho Place he'd established his credentials and owner Michael Brody asked him not to play anywhere else until he opened his new venue at 84 King Street.

Built and opened in 1977 by Levan, Michael Brody and Mel Cheren (the co-owner of West End Records), the Paradise Garage was a million miles apart from the glitz, glam and cold-cash requirements of Studio 54. Essentially a tightly policed House party for 2,000 hedonistic, predominantly black and gay disco kids, the venue played host to amazing vocalists including Chaka Khan, Gloria Gaynor, Jocelyn Brown, Patti Labelle, The Jones Girls and Billy Ocean way before they were selling singles by the bucketload. There was no alcohol served, but, as in Chicago, there was plenty of drug consumption and in the early years the free "electric punch" was spiked with LSD.

A perfectionist (stories of him leaving the decks to clean the mirror balls for up to thirty minutes are commonplace), Levan resided in a balcony above the dancefloor with his three turntables, Bozak mixer and custom-built sound system, alternating vocal cuts like "Weekend" by Phreek and Lamont Dozier's "Going Back To My Roots" with disco dubs (many of which he'd produced in the studio), to create a unique fusion of sound. He would often leave spaces of silence, play videos between songs or specially edited, almost epic, Ambient introductions to convey a particular emotion or message.

But his influence even stretched to the roots and structure of dance music production itself. Levan's penchant for blending the instrumental sections of songs and cutting his own dubbed-out versions of tracks to play acapella vocals over helped persuade labels like West End and Prelude to issue b-side "dub" versions of the original vocal mix, now a

prerequisite for virtually any dance record.

His first move into the studio was a remix his fans would probably rather consign to the history books. The disco-novelty affair "C Is For Cookie" (1978) by *Sesame Street*'s Cookie Monster certainly didn't set a precedent for the stream of defining disco, proto-House and electro releases that followed in its wake. Between 1978 and 1983, when he was most prolific, Levan turned his mixing hand to Salsoul classics including First Choice's "Double Cross", Loleatta Holloway's "The Greatest Performance of My Life" (both 1979) and Inner Life's "Ain't No Mountain High Enough" (1981). But it was his propulsive re-versioning of Instant Funk's "I Got My Mind Made Up" (1978) that ranks as one of the greatest mixes of all time.

His minimally structured proto-House mix of Loose Joints' "Is It All Over My Face?" (1980) was followed by his (since countlessly sampled) mixes of The Striker's "Body Music" (1981), Central Line's "Walking Into Sunshine", Chaka Khan's "Tearin' It Up", Gwen Guthrie's "It Should Have Been You" and Tracy Weber's "Sure Shot" (all 1982). It was Levan's ability to transfer his energised trickery behind the decks – using sound effects, reverb, filters and beat clashing – over to vinyl which made these so exceptional and radical. This came to a zenith with his hypnotic reworking of Taana Gardner's "Heartbeat" (1980): a sleazy, sexy and utterly mesmeric 12" that truly epitomised everything the garage was about.

Levan's early '80s move from studio mixing into music production came with the release of The Peech Boys' "Don't Make Me Wait" (1982), recorded with singer Bernard Fowler, guitarist Robert Casper and Paradise garage keyboardist Michael deBenidictus. A proto-garage masterpiece, its groundbreaking electro-funk signature, psychedelic synth washes and sinuous bottom-heavy bass-line also set much of the standard for the electro revolution Arthur Baker began with "Planet Rock" (1982).

The mid-'80s saw his sets fuse Chicago and New Jersey House tracks, inspiring a legion of East Coast DJs (not least Junior Vasquez), while his mixes included the downright funky-as-hell "Seventh Heaven" by Gwen Guthrie (1985), Man Friday's "Jump" and Patti Austin's "Honey For The Bees" (both 1986).

But with the garage's co-owner Michael Brody ill with AIDS, the club closed on September 26, 1987 with Levan playing out with The Trammps' emotive seven-minute story of the 1976 NYC blackout, "Where Do We Go From Here?" Levan never again came close to capturing former glories as either a DJ or producer. His drug addiction spiralled and he found it hard to change his approach to work with subsequent record companies and clubs, though he did help set up the Ministry Of Sound's sound system and still found time to remix Italian-pop band DJH featuring Stefy's "C'mon Boy" into twelve minutes of sonic pleasure in 1992. His addiction and hereditary heart condition finally caught up with him toward the end of that year, though, and he died soon after his Harmony DJing tour of Japan on November 8.

◉ Larry Levan's Paradise Garage   Salsoul Records, 1996

Most of Levan's classic Salsoul disco mixes on one compilation, including Instant Funk's phenomenal "I Got My Mind Made Up", Skyy's "First Time Around" and First Choice's "Double Cross".

◉ NYC Peech Boys: "Don't Make Me Wait"   West End, 1982

Levan's move into production provided the missing link between gay-roots disco and cutting, street-edged electro. The edit can be found on **Classic Electro Volume One** (Mastercuts/Beechwood Music, 1994).

Lil' Louis

L il' Louis is not the conventional household name he might have become following the surprising #2 UK chart success of his 1989 X-rated groove, "French Kiss". A complex and passionate producer, he has never paid much heed to convention during a twenty-year career. Stages of his recording career have drawn their inspiration from an array of musical genres stretching from Acid rock to R&B, while his lyrics have often explored unusual, evocative territory. Even the simplistic "French Kiss" was a major landmark in that it was the first House 12" to vary the speed of its bpm, immediately extending the parameters of creativity within the confines of a 4/4 rhythm.

One of the Windy City's original and yet much overlooked pioneers, Louis began DJing in his early teens and by the late '70s was running his own club, the Future, at the same time Frankie Knuckles was in control at the Warehouse. After he had tentatively experimented with remixes in his home, Louis enrolled himself at Columbia Recording School at the beginning of the '80s and continued to DJ around town, earning a name for himself locally through his parties at the Hotel Continental. By the mid-'80s he was holding some of the largest parties in town at the Hotel Bismarck, and although his first self-financed record was the unremarkable "How I Feel" his name alone carried so much weight within the city limits that tracks would appear fraudulently labelled "remixed by Lil' Louis".

In 1985 he produced his own bona fide, raw House classic for Chicago's Trax Records – Hercules' "7 Ways to Jack" with Marshall Jefferson. Proving more diverse than most, however, he also stunned Detroit's close-knit Techno fraternity with his claustrophobic, futuristic visions, releasing the Euro-influenced singles "Frequency", "Video Clash", "Blackout" and "War Games" to underground acclaim.

Commercial success with "French Kiss" came as a complete surprise. Created in 1987, its release was held back by Louis for over a year, he used the mesmeric, pitch-shifting, female orgasmic moaning-groove as his signature DJing cut and building up a burning live following. Within weeks of its release on the tiny Diamond Records, however, Louis had signed a world-wide deal with CBS in the States and ffrr/London in England – where the single was initially banned by the BBC, and where it ultimately became one of the biggest-selling House records ever (estimated at over a million copies).

Although the sexually swamped, heavy-breathing shtick was carried over to his next UK Top 40 single, "I Called You" also placed Louie among the extraordinary batch of dance music lyricists who could create both evocative and club-friendly soundscapes: the subject matter was a panic-ridden tale of a disastrous relationship with an ex-girlfriend that gets so out of hand Louis is forced to take out a restraining order.

From The Mind Of Lil' Louis (1989) exceeded expectations and further boosted Louis' reputation as one of the genre's most compelling producers. The album drew its rock effects from Led Zeppelin (cited by Louis as a major influence), its jazz inflections from Louis' father – BB King's guitarist Bobby Simms – and employed the co-writing and production skills of industrial band Die Warzau, and Larry Heard on "Touch Me" and the sublime "6AM".

Louis' reflective, melancholy persona, which occasionally betrayed itself on his debut's jazz-infused Down Tempo tracks, was much more to the fore on his stunning follow-up, 1992's under-valued **Journey With the Lonely**. An increased sense of alienation filtered through the single "Club Lonely", which, along with the uplifting "Music Saved My Life", introduced one of the genre's most capable vocalists, Jo Caldwell.

Louis apparently disappeared from music until 1995, although it later emerged he'd simply stayed out of sight while shifting styles to take in R&B, producing for Babyface, Michelle N'DegeOcello and his own moderately successful girl group, Tomboy. He hit back on the less formulaic House tip first with the reflective, sexually charged poetry of "Freaky" as Lou 2 (with DJ Little Louie Vega) for his new home at NYC's Strictly Rhythm imprint, and then with one of 1995's most affective vocal grooves, "Freedom", under his new mysterious Black Magic guise.

Further fine singles, "Let It Go" and "Dance (Do That Thing)", were well received, though hardly spectacular by his standards, but he got back to his deep, tripped-out best on "Stormy Black" for NiteGrooves. Late 1997 found him pushing the R&B formula again alongside four-to-the-floor rhythms on the good-time cut "Clap Your Hands", finding a surprising new home at UK independent label Go Beat!

⊙ From The Mind Of Lil' Louis   London Records, 1989

A great dance album which weds soul, jazz, House and Techno. Contains Louis' ultimate House-as-sex allegories, "French Kiss" and "I Called You", alongside the essential tripped-out Heard co-production "6AM".

⊙ Journey With The Lonely   London Records, 1992

One of the most inspirational House-based long-players ever committed to vinyl. A consistently beautiful record of deep warmth, passion and pain that continues to explore Louis' evocative and unusual lyrical soundscapes through both upbeat dancefloor hits like "Club Lonely" and introspective, Down Tempo cuts such as "Share".

Limbo Records

Building on the success of similar House labels Guerilla and Cowboy, Limbo became one of the UK's prime exponents of "progressive House" in the early '90s, yielding a succession of dancefloor-friendly club cuts and helping British Techno acts like Havana gain recognition. 1992's debut release from Q-Tex, the **Equator** EP, created the label's blueprint. A funky, breakbeat-driven, accessible, yet almost instantly forgettable 12", the single's club success in Scotland paved the way for future releases.

Initially called 23rd Precinct records, the label was literally born "behind the counter" at Glasgow's influential record shop of the same name, and was run by local DJ Billy Kiltie and club organiser Davey Mackenzie. In 1992 the pair posted a dance newsletter around the city from the shop, and were almost immediately flooded with demo tapes, reflecting the growing frustration of Scottish producers who – with the notable exception of Soma – had no local outlet to press up their recordings.

By the time of Q-Tex's second release, the well-received **Natural High** EP, the imprint had national distribution through Revolver, and was quickly renamed Limbo. Havana's "Schtoom" (1992) alongside subsequent releases by Gypsy ("I Trance You"), Mukka, Deep Piece and Sublime epitomised the "progressive" genre with their driving bass-lines, heavy percussion and chunky, dirty riffs, garnering column inches in the UK dance music press and becoming staple fare for DJs like Sasha and Leftfield. As credibility ratings increased, the label licensed output from abroad, notably Josh Wink's "Thoughts of a Tranced Love".

But commercial success came at the expense of credibility, and despite the fact that Kiltie's Umboza project tracks – including the

Lionel Richie-sampling "Cry India" (1995) and "Sunshine" Fade's "So Good" and Ritmo de Vida's "The Spirit Is Justified" – were like-able club monsters up and down the UK, they've had no lasting impact.

Since 1997 Limbo has largely abandoned the hi-NRG pop-fluff and returned to its musical roots, forging two new labels, Peakin' and Progressin', releasing trance-styled cuts like "Crystallise", "Discoveries" and 1998's **Summation** EP from a new batch of rising "progressive House" stars like Channel Islands DJ Chris Sokrati (aka Seafield) and Scottish producers Steven McCreery and Ross McPharlin (Tipple). Whether they will capture the same response as Limbo's early releases, however, remains to be seen.

⊙ **House Of Limbo Trilogy**   Limbo, 1996

Mixed by S'Express' DJ Mark Moore, this includes most of the club hits from the Scottish "progressive" stable, notably Umboza's shamelessly cheesy "Sunshine" and "Cry India", Gypsy's excellent "I Trance You" and Wink's superior "Thoughts of a Tranced Love".

Alison Limerick

In 1991 Alison Limerick's debut "Where Love Lives" was voted "dance single of the year" in Billboard magazine, despite never gaining a Stateside release. With its stunning Morales- and Knuckles-conspired string and piano arrangement, it rightly remains a perennial club favourite the world over.

Although most of the '80s were spent doing session work in London studios, Limerick aimed to follow in the footsteps of her childhood heroes Stevie Wonder and Chaka Khan. But her career – which has witnessed the search for popular acclaim through an ever-shifting persona ranging from aggressive diva to a more earthy, marketable image – has ultimately always returned to the clubs and the four-to-the-floor backbone to find its commercial appeal.

Like her debut, Limerick's second single, "Come Back (For Real Love)" (1991), was also destined for dancefloor success. Mixed by Arthur Baker, with backing vocals courtesy of Papa Dee and Jocelyn Brown, "Come Back" was a garage cut. Her debut album, **And I Still Rise** (1992), showcased the full range of her impressive vocal talents, boasting collaborations with Tony Humphries for her third single, "Make It On My Own", and Malcolm McLaren on the Stock, Aitken and Waterman-produced rave tune, "Magic's Back" (both 1992).

The session work continued into 1993 and 1994, as Limerick utilised the mixing talents of the Def Mix duo again for her disappointing follow-up, **With a Twist** (1994). Failing to gain widespread commercial acceptance, single releases in the subsequent few years relied on names such as Jon and Helena Marsh from The Beloved, Romanthony and Paul Oakenfold to pull her back out onto the dancefloor – which she did most notably with the warmly welcomed disco cover, "Love Come Down" (1994).

Still, 1998's suprisingly consistent **Spirit Rising** found her alongside a tight quintet of musicians, and tracks like "How Happy" signalled that a return to past dancefloor glories remained possible.

O Club Classics   BMG, 1996

The title perhaps over-emphasises the status of most of Limerick's releases, but the album nonetheless includes the spine-tingling 1991 Morales & Knuckles mix of "Where Love Lives" alongside the excellent early singles, "Make It On My Own" and "Come Back (For Real Love)".

M/A/R/R/S

The ultimate one-hit wonder band, M/A/R/R/S, along with Bomb The Bass and S'Express, were one of the first dance outfits to turn the British charts on to the sound of House music with their infectious single, "Pump Up the Volume", which reached #1 in August 1987. M/A/R/R/S was a collaborative project involving DJs Dave Dorrell and CJ Mackintosh and two bands signed to the independent label 4AD, Colourbox and A R Kane. The acronym M/A/R/R/S came from M: Martyn Young (Colourbox), A: A R Kane, R: Rudi from A R Kane, R: Russell (who was connected with A R Kane at the time) and S: Stephen Young (Colourbox).

The single, which combined a sample from James Brown with the indie-guitar sound of A R Kane, was championed by daytime radio, which was beginning to familiarise itself with the new sound of dance music. An advance white label of "Pump Up the Volume" had been mailed to club DJs a month before its general release, a shrewd move that ensured demand was sufficiently high once the single arrived in high street shops. A suitably eye-catching video and a sleeve by design supremo Vaughan Oliver added to the hype.

A spat with chart-pop writing/production team Stock, Aitken and Waterman occurred when the trio accused M/A/R/R/S of sampling from their earlier hit that year, "Roadblock". Although M/A/R/R/S never released another record, CJ Mackintosh continued to be successful as a producer/remixer/DJ both in the UK and America, while Dave Dorrell ditched his DJing skills to manage grunge-lite rockers Bush, and sell twelve million albums world-wide.

⊙ **"Pump Up the Volume"** 4AD, 1987

The collective's only release helped turn on the UK charts to the sound of House and kick-start the sampling debate in the process.

David Mancuso

DJ David Mancuso and his NYC apartment, the Loft, have played a paternal and mythical role in the annals of House music's birth. Aficionados like DJ/producers Larry Levan, Frankie Knuckles, François Kervorkian, Joe Clausell and David Morales were all "Loft babies".

Every Saturday night from 1970 onwards, initially in an old factory space at the bottom of Broadway but after 1975, in its peak period, at 99 Prince Street in Soho, the home of designer David Mancuso provided the after-hours hangout for a New York sub-culture that would dance its way through to Sunday afternoon. But for the crowd of predominantly gay, black and Puerto Rican attendees, this party was more of a playground than a sophisticated bar. The buffet consisted of fruit and the juices were strictly non-alcoholic, consumed in an apartment decorated like a kid's jelly and ice cream fantasy with hundreds of brightly coloured balloons.

Mancuso's idea wasn't simply to create an irreverent party atmosphere, although the sexually liberated environment often took on a wild energy with the open use of drugs like mescalin and LSD. His method of segueing records with associated messages or emotions may have taken its cue from DJ Francis Grosso's wild sets at the hedonistic Sanctuary club, but it was radical in those early days in that it was designed to take people on a trip which would clearly later influence the style of both Larry Levan at the Paradise Garage and Frankie Knuckles at the Warehouse. Regarded by many of that crowd as a wizard of sorts, the long-haired, bearded figure of Mancuso in his prime stands as an icon in the well-worn story of disco's transition to House.

Despite his modesty, Mancuso played a crucial role in establishing a base from which DJs could access records in advance, writing the charter for the first DJ record pool in 1975 alongside Steve D'Aquisto and Vince Aletti. This, in turn, provided the structure from which Salsoul could release the first commercially available 12", Double Exposure's "Ten Percent". Obviously Mancuso's music varied drastically over the time period, but in the early days R&B (epitomised by Philadelphia International) was interspersed with rock, pop and reggae (Rolling Stones, Led Zeppelin and Brian Auger amongst others) before disco proper arrived and made Loft classics of songs like Fred Wesley's "House Party" and Third World's "Now That We Found Love".

After Mancuso's 1975 move to Prince Street (where he remained until the early '80s), his sound system was reputed to have been one of the world's finest. Prelude mixer François Kervorkian would even come down from his studio with the acetate of a track he'd been working on and test it out on the Loft system, then go back and make the necessary adjustments to get it perfect. At its peak in the mid-late '70s to early '80s, the venue quite simply provided a benchmark and testing ground for the music.

Mancuso abandoned the use of headphones and mixer in the early '80s and moved venues around 1983. When it re-opened in the early '90s the Loft attempted to regain some of its early energy, but today it is widely judged to be a pale shadow of its former self.

⊙ **Loft Classics**   1995–96

Search out this excellent series of specially edited re-released disco-funk-soul 12"s at your local specialist record store. They're a good representation of the tunes that were massive at the venue in its peak period and include such inspirational gems as "It Ain't No Use", "Whistle Bump", "Funkanova", "Rude Movements", "Outer Space" and "Powerline".

Masters At Work

Masters At Work have "flipped the script" time and time again –
surmounting the transient nature of the dancefloor by drawing
their inspiration from a wide musical spectrum. While the ever-fickle
world of House music has offered up a host of producers for a short-
lived spell in the limelight before banishing them back to their beloved
"underground" status, Kenny "Dope" Gonzalez and Little Louie Vega
have consistently found fresh ways to add Latin, jazz, hip-hop, disco
and soul to the four-to-the-floor conundrum and come out on top.

From a musical family (his uncle is legendary Latin musician Hector Lavoe), Bronx-born Vega began spinning aged 13, and was already an established name on the Big Apple's club circuit by the late '80s. Following in the footsteps of DJ John "Jellybean" Benitez's cut 'n' paste, percussive-hinged sessions at the Funhouse club, Vega rose through the ranks at venues like Devil's Nest, before graduating to Manhattan's Hearthrob, Studio 54, Roseland and Palladium clubs. Initially he became known for breaking and producing freestyle records (as Freestyle Orchestra).

Over the bridge, Brooklyn native Kenny "Dope" Gonzalez and his Masters At Work DJing crew (formed 1986) took their lead from pioneering radio hip-hop DJs like Marley Marl, Awesome Two and Teddy Ted. It was when Gonzalez's Hard-House 12", "A Touch of Salsa", caught the attention of Vega's ear that the two hooked up through mutual friend Todd Terry (who had already "borrowed" the MAW tag from Gonzalez to record two singles for Fourth Floor Records) in 1991.

MAW's debut single, "Blood Vibes" (1991), blueprinted the duo's refusal to be genre-conscious, drawing its inspiration from Vega's original turntable segueing of reggae artist Junior Reid's "One Blood" and A Tribe Called Quest's hip-hop excursion "Bonita Applebum". Nowhere is that refusal more apparent than on 1997's lauded **Nu Yorican Soul** album, which fully realised the duo's ambitions to showcase both their and New York's rich and diverse musical heritage moulding Latin jazz, abstract hip-hop, funk and Salsoul together. It also contained the single which epitomised their unique relationship, 1993's monumental "The Nervous Track", a ground-breaking fusion of jazz, Latin, breakbeat and House.

While the collaborators on the Nu Yorican Soul project (George Benson, Vince Montana, Jocelyn Brown, Roy Ayers, Tito Puente) reads like a list of musical greats, MAW have been able to apply the same innovative agenda to turn pale pop artists into credible dancefloor propositions. Their minimal early '90s b-side reconstructions of Debbie Gibson ("Out of the Blue"), Chris Cuevas ("Hip Hop"), St Etienne ("Only Love Can Break Your Heart") and others not only defined what would become known as "dub House", but also helped to set the modern precedent for big-name remixers like Armand Van Helden and Mousse T.

1991's "A Mute Horn" introduced the sound of real jazz with Ray Vega's live trumpet, while the duo's production of the *Mambo Kings* soundtrack and Tito Puente's "Ran Kan Kan" (1992) slammed Latin firmly onto the House agenda. All prefigured 1993's half-House, half-hip-hop album for Cutting Records which atypically spawned vocal anthems like the India-sung "I Can't Get No Sleep".

While Gonzalez pursued a sideline in hip-hop projects, Vega's three-and-a-half-year Wednesday night residency at the Sound Factory Bar kept NYC's vocal tradition alive and well at a time when Hard-House fetishism was all the rage. Barbara Tucker's "Beautiful People", Michael Watford's "My Love", MAW's "Voices", River Ocean's "Love & Happiness" (all 1994) all benefited from Vega's expert touch at the controls. In 1995 Kenny "Dope" achieved surprising commercial success with the Chicago-sampling single "The Bomb" (as The Bucketheads) reaching the UK Top 10.

MAW records, formed in 1995, has also refused to conform to any musical regulations. Since its jazz-fusion debut, "Moonshine" (1995), the imprint has released elemental hypnotic dubs (1995's "The Bounce") alongside emotive vocal cuts (1997's "To Be In Love", sung by India), acoustic Latin grooves (1998's "Pienso En Ti") and disco-charged floor-fillers (1998's "Odyssey").

⊙ **Masterworks - The Essential Kenlou Mixes**   Harmless, 1995

Exceptional collection which features some of MAW's best productions

("The Nervous Track" and the rare promo-only released 12" of "Voices In My Mind") together with many of their ground-breaking remixes.

○ Nu Yorican Soul: Nu Yorican Soul   Talkin Loud, 1997

Two years in the making, Vega and Gonzalez finally produced a long-player we all knew they were capable of. From the spellbinding soul of George Benson's "You Can Do It" to the remake of Rotary Connection's "Black Gold of the Sun", this is a truly remarkable record that deserves a place in everyone's collection.

Mateo & Matos

John "Roc" Mateo and Eddie "Ez" Matos could hardly be described as the coolest heads in House music. The disco obsessives met in 1985 after hooking up on those good old CB radio airwaves and began playing at street jams together, making friends with Little Louie Vega and moving into the studio in the early '90s. Since then, they've produced around forty tracks for a host of NYC labels including 4th Floor Records, Henry Street, Nervous, Freeze, King Street and Spiritual Life, building up a reputation for consistently danceable, if not always inspirational, instrumental House cuts.

As with so many of NYC's producers, the sound of disco has never been far removed from the vast majority of the duo's output, and their soulful, cut-up signature is only definable at times by their abundant abuse of discophonic loops and boogie bass-lines. But unlike Johnny Vicious or Armand Van Helden's aggressive mix-and-match ethos, Mateo & Matos have remained faithful to R&B/disco's inherent sense of rhythm and soul, and have proved capable at times of pushing the formula into deeper, more compelling dimensions.

Initial work appeared on their own label, the now defunct Final Cut, including a selection of rough disco cut-ups such as their debut "House Faze/Deep Dimensions" and the well-received, '70s-snatching **Raw Elements** series of EPs. Picked up by the NYC cognoscenti, these were followed by the **Early Reflections** EP and **Higher Octave** EP for the Big Apple's esteemed 4th Floor Records. Although these

were likeable club cuts which served their purpose well enough on the dancefloor, the duo's outstanding release was their 1995 **No Props** EP with its wonderful reworking of the Salsoul Orchestra's disco classic "Rainbow".

1996 and 1997, though, had them move toward deeper, jazz/ Latin/funk-inflected grooves such as "Deeper Dimensions" for NiteGrooves and the breathtaking, chilled vibes of "New York Style", "Madd Deep" and the **Love of Life** EP for Spiritual Life, while continuing with the plangent disco-synth stabs on cuts including the excellent "Disco Dance", "Something I Feel" and **Creative Logic** EP.

Mateo & Matos produced their well-received 1997 debut album, **New York Rhythms**, for Scotland's Glasgow Underground Records. 1998's **New York Rhythms Volume Two** continued in a similar disco-charged vein to its predecessor, its most effective moment being the Odyssey-sampling "Don't Give Up", but it still remains far from their best.

○ "Mixed Moods"   Spiritual Life, 1996

A wonderful slab of organ-led Deep House, available on **Spiritual Life Music** (Nuphonic Records, 1997).

MK

You can count the number of House music producers to emerge from the Motor City on one hand. Kevin Saunderson, Terrence Parker and Mark Kinchen (MK) have managed to break clear from Detroit's inherent obsession with all things Techno. It's not really surprising then, that the three producers have something of a shared history.

In 1988 Kinchen worked alongside Terence Parker as Separate Minds, producing the raw emotive Techno of "We Need Somebody". He was also adopted by Kevin Saunderson as something of a "studio mascot", engineering many of the early Inner City records (check "Do You Love What You Feel?") and most of the output of Saunderson's Techno imprint, KMS.

The experience paid off, and MK's first solo release, "Separate Minds" by First Bass, appeared on the acclaimed KMS **Techno 1** album, while "Somebody New" and "Get It Right" (both 1990) created the blueprint for smooth tech-House, followed by the more impressive "Mirror Mirror" and "Feel the Fire". All of these were licensed to Birmingham-based Network Records in the UK.

A move to New York in 1991 was followed by the single which really marked him out as a producer of note to a wider audience. "Play the

World", released on his own Area 10 label before being licensed to a Creation Records compilation in the UK, featured the basis of MK's unique production style with its short, sharp repetitive vocal snippets, shuffling hi-hats and pounding orchestral strings. Above all, though, the lethal combination was recognisably based on a House rhythm, but with the funk, energy and soul of Techno.

As with so many other Detroit dance music producers, MK's vital influences include Euro synth bands like Depeche Mode and the spaced-out future funk of Parliament-Funkadelic. Welding elements from these seemingly disparate styles to House music's incessant rhythm, Kinchen effectively re-invented boogie for the '90s. Its swinging bump 'n' hustle also forged a sketch for producers like Todd Edwards and Armand Van Helden, who replaced MK's silky smooth production with a rougher edge, but kept the mix 'n' match ethos intact.

MK firmly established himself on the global map with his next two releases, a stunning remix of Chez Damier's "Never Knew Love" for Saunderson's KMS label, and his first self-produced out and out vocal track, "Burning" (1991). Using singer Alana's raw, haunting vocal, "Burning" introduced Kinchen's penchant for juxtaposing xylophone melodies and short, sharp string arrangements, while its similarly styled follow-up, "Always" (1992), showcased his innovative use of Juan Atkins-like pianos and muted sax across its six mixes.

All of these traits were evident on the vast amount of remix work Kinchen undertook between 1992 and 1995 for artists stretching from the B-52s to D-Influence. Although many of these became too predictable, MK's piano-led mixes of MAW's "I Can't Get No Sleep" (1992) and his ultra-deep mixes of Captain Hollywood's "All I Want" (1993) and Saundra Williams' "I Want It, I Need It (Real Love)" rank amongst his best work. While some of Kinchen's most compelling productions were recorded under the guise of the often minimalist 4th

Measure Men ("Given", "The Need", "4U", "Just a Dream"), it was his anthemic UK Top 40 remix of little-known white-soul band The Night-crawlers' "Push the Feeling On (MK's Dub Of Doom)" that has since become a durable House classic in an age of mass dancefloor consumption.

Surrender (1995), an album shifting uneasily between Teddy Riley swingbeat and MK's more familiar slick grooves, ultimately disappointed most of his fans. In an interview the same year he revealed that he felt confined within the narrowing possibilities House could offer, solidifying the move toward formulaic R&B with his Down Tempo US smash single, "Love Changes". Since then, he has disappeared from sight.

⊙ **Nightcrawlers: "Push the Feeling On (MK's Dub Of Doom)"**   Island Records, 1992

Apparently it only took an hour for Kinchen to turn out one of House music's all-time anthemic dubs. Quintessential MK – deconstructed snippets, orchestral strings and smooth production.

⊙ **Remixed, Remade, Remodelled**   Activ Records, 1997

Essential album which includes MK's gorgeously deep workouts as 4th Measure Men ("The Need", "4U") and a selection of dope remixes from Basement Jaxx and Armand Van Helden.

Mood II Swing

Producers Lem Springsteen and John Ciafone (aka Mood II Swing) began working together in 1992, following the collapse of a proposed deal with Little Louie Vega to launch an R&B project. But the meeting with Vega proved profitable regardless, and the duo began hanging out with the Master At Work, picking up production tips as he turned releases from flailing pop artists into credible dancefloor dubs. With ex-hip-hop DJ Ciafone's self-taught drum programming skills and Springsteen's passion for R&B, this flawless appreciation of both the pop aesthetic and the needs of the dancefloor has established Mood II Swing as one of New York's most accomplished House production teams. Their trademark of simple, soulful melodies and hypnotic synth lines coupled with the freshest drum kick sounds around have produced some of NYC's most exceptional 12"s to date and some of the underground's biggest hits.

After Ciafone had provided the drum programming for various Masters At Work tracks – a relationship that would continue into the late '90s – Mood II Swing hit the dancefloor in emphatic fashion in their own right in 1992. Hardrive's instrumental "Sindae" (recorded with MAW) was pure dubbed-out, rhythm-crazed bliss, while Urbanized's "Helpless" moulded a Chris Isaak-like heartache vocal to smooth percussion and emotive synth washes to become one of the year's underground anthems.

Mood II Swing have achieved more success with a series of slamming singles for Nervous Records with diva Loni Clark. 1993's "U" (later followed by "Rushin'" and "Love's Got Me") became a huge club hit, vaunted by both the New York set and UK DJs like CJ Mackintosh and Graeme Park. One of garage's finest hours, Wall Of Sound's "Critical" (1993), followed, and introduced Mood II Swing's use of a live funk guitar sound, a signature which would re-emerge on their most successful single to date, Ultra Naté's "Free" (1997).

From 1993 to 1995, Ciafone and Springsteen recorded after-hours deep dubs, often inflected with jazzy melodies, for labels including Power Music, NightGrooves, Waako and Empire State. Perhaps the most impressive of the lot appeared in 1994, on King Street Records. "Closer", featuring the vocals of Carol Sylvan, foregrounded their bouncing bass-lines, simple "mood-altering" melodies and ability to harness strong vocals to a propulsive groove.

1996, though, was the year that the duo finally started to pick up press coverage in the UK. Their two breathtaking singles for Groove On Records, "All Night Long" and "I See You Dancing", became staples in the record boxes of everyone from Danny Tenaglia to Tony Humphries, while their productions of Fonda Rae's "Living In Ecstasy" and, in 1997, Loni Clark's "Searchin'", topped House DJ charts the world over and became classics on the dancefloor of NYC's influential Body & Soul club. Remixes inevitably followed as the major labels finally caught up with the duo (Everything But The Girl, George Michael), but Mood II Swing saved their best for Deep Dish's independent imprint, Yoshitoshi Recordings – a stunning re-interpretation of Mysterious People's "Love Revolution" (1997).

In 1997 the formula finally broke the pop charts too. Having already turned out an under-rated remix of Ultra Naté's "How Long" in 1994, Mood II Swing's 1997 production of the Baltimore singer's "Free" reached the UK Top 10 and #1 in Italy and Spain. The accolades haven't stopped there: their expansive remix of Kim English's "Learn to Love" and melodic re-versioning of Brian Transeau's "Remember" turned up in numerous DJs' top ten records of that year, confirming their position as one of NYC's most respected and successful production outfits.

⊙ **Wall Of Sound: "Critical"**   Eightball/Positiva, 1993

Classic garage mixed to perfection by Ciafone and Springsteen.

⊙ **Mood II Swing: "All Night Long"**   Groove On, 1996

Beautiful reflective strings, glowing melodies and the phattest of drums combine on Mood II Swing's most emotive instrumental.

Moodymann

Detroit's Kenny Dixon Jr stands virtually alone in a musical genre which strives to provide an outlet for escapism from the pressures and monotony of modern living. Like Techno's highly politicised Underground Resistance, Dixon's darker alter-ego, Moodymann, projects an enigmatic, secretive image while emerging as one of House music's most impressive producers.

Kenny Dixon Jr's career began with the well-regarded "Emotional Content" single for Terence Parker's Intangible imprint in 1996. Although this and his subsequent releases for the Grassroots label betrayed elements of the twisted, lo-fi sound which would characterise future work, it wasn't until he launched his own label, KDJ, that he began to achieve notable recognition.

KDJ's first commercially available 12", Moodymann's "Tribute (To The Soul We Lost)" (1996), patented his fusion of distorted disco grooves and black consciousness, opening with radio coverage of the shooting of Marvin Gaye, before twisting the soul legend's vocals into abstraction. Its follow-up, **The Dancer EP** (1996) introduced the sleazy vocals of Norma Jean Bell, who would later cause dancefloor devastation alongside Dixon on cuts like the insane after-hours groove "I'm the Baddest Bitch" (1996), and the gorgeously reflective "I Love the Things You Do to Me" (1997).

Subsequent Moodymann productions, including the Chic-sampling "I Can't Kick This Feeling When It Hits" and the hypnotic "Misled" (both 1997), forged forward with minimal sci-fi concepts and contorted atmospherics, teasing seconds of disco samples across each groove before filtering the loops into minutes of tense beauty. Single releases pictured parodies of Dixon with afro and shades, concealing a serious message about both the music industry and social exploitation.

Dixon's refusal to be interviewed by the UK dance music press has only added to his mystique and contributed to his cult status amongst his fans.

1997's **Silent Introduction** compiled most of his best work from his KDJ imprint, evoking his use of sampling and wired sequencing across its nine tracks, while again expressing political sentiments in its inside

cover. Having released the album on Carl Craig's Planet E label, Moodymann's appeal crossed over into the Techno camp when he released the harder, paranoid frequencies of "Dem Young Sconies" on the Detroit label. As his reputation flourished in the UK, the same year found him releasing singles and remixes for

labels including Ferox (remixing Synchrojack's "End of the Road" into a cool groove), Music Is, Three Chairs, Soul City and After Midnight, but still saving his best for his own label. Using distorted film and background bar-chatter samples alongside an ingenious oscillating breakbeat and bottom-heavy disco loop, "Black Mahogany" (1998) marked him clearly out as one of the genre's most experimental and forward-thinking artists.

1998's **Mahogany Brown** disappointed due to its avant-garde and ambitiously abstract approach. Despite haranguing pronouncements like "You can't learn how to make black music by listening to your record collection or reading books", much of the album still featured a selection of intricate rhythms and disco-tinged melodies, with cuts like the jazzy "Sunshine" and spaced-out synth washes of "Me and My People" proving instantly appealing. What is almost certain, though, is that if his innovation continues in the same vein, he'll remain one of the few producers capable of taking the genre into fresh directions.

◉ Silent Introduction Planet E, 1997

Inspired and essential collection of lo-fi, twisted robo-disco that's ultimately as addictive as it is initially hard to access. The nine tracks provide the best sample of Moodymann's work to date.

Angel Moraes

The influence of Junior Vasquez's sets at Manhattan's Sound Factory club reached such a peak in the mid-'90s that local and European producers began making homage tracks both to him and to the intense sweatbox he created. But no track paid more tribute than Brooklyn-born Angel Moraes' fifteen-minute groove, "Welcome to the Factory" (1995), which re-created the hyper-percussive, bass-driven dancefloor phenomena of the old meat warehouse.

Although Moraes' biggest track to date, "Welcome to the Factory" was by no means his first. Serving his mobile DJing apprenticeship in and around Brooklyn since his mid-teens, Moraes took his lead from heroes like David Morales' hard-edged sets at the Ozone club and John "Jellybean" Benitez's Latin hip-hop mixes at the Funhouse.

However, it wasn't until fate dealt a winning hand in 1992 that his career began to take shape. A chance meeting with Victor Simonelli led to the duo's collaborative remix of Ebony Soul's well-received 12" "Can't Hardly Wait", and the subsequent introduction to Roxy club DJ Johnny Vicious. The two struck up a friendship, and through Vicious, Moraes met Roxy club owner Jeffrey Rodman, who provided the financial support for Moraes to set up his own label.

Moraes' Hot 'N' Spycy Records debut, 1993's "Release Yourself", immediately marked him out as one of New York's hottest new talents. The single, alongside his follow-ups "Deep Inside Your Love" and "The Cure", showcased his stripped-down sound which builds slowly throughout each track, adding layers of percussion, bass and vocal snippets to the propulsive rhythm before reaching climax point.

Subsequent singles such as "I Like It" (with ex S.O.U.L System chanteuse Octavia Lambertis) and the initially overlooked "Heaven Knows" (with Basil Roderick) demonstrated that Moraes could produce more soulful songs. In fact, it was the re-release of "Heaven Knows" (1995) on the more media-friendly Tribal Records which solidified his reputation alongside established NYC producers like Danny Tenaglia and DJ Duke.

Following the success of "Welcome to the Factory", Moraes hit the remix paydirt roster in the UK, with mixes for the Pet Shop Boys' "Paninaro '95", Bensaid's "I'm So Grateful" and Fire Island's "White Powder Dreams", while on Hot 'N' Spycy he released the excellent "For Love and Peace". Moraes also continued his vocal projects with Blind Truth's "It's So Hard" for Minimal Records.

While he continued to DJ across the States, 1996 and 1997 were barren years on the production front, and his "To the Rhythm" and "Body Work" releases didn't really cut the mustard. 1998 signalled a return to form with an extreme Moraes signature build over an epic twenty minutes called "23 Minutes of Your Love", and a laid-back vocal mix of 4 Tune's "After Hours".

⊙ **Hot 'N' Spycy – The Album**   Hot 'N' Spycy Recordings
                                             Inc/Sound Storm Entertainment, 1996

The definitive Moraes collection. From his multi-layered, bass-driven signature, "Welcome to the Factory", to ambitious vocal cuts like "Heaven Knows" and "I Like It", Moraes remains one of NYC's most engaging producers. Not exactly coffee-table stuff, but play it loud and wait for those bassbins to blow!

David Morales

The story of David Morales' rise to prominence is almost a modern-day urban fairy tale. Brooklyn born and bred to a Puerto Rican family, he quit school after the ninth grade (around age 14) and would never complete his education. Despite daunting odds and teenage years marred by violence (he still bears scars from being shot), Morales would emerge as a world-renowned DJ as well as a ground-breaking producer and remixer. He has also become one of the most visible and influential dance music entities in America, both on his own and with Frankie Knuckles, his partner in the Def Mix production company and label.

He began DJing at age 14, and advanced his education in dance culture as a faithful "Loft baby", a devotee of the invite-only New York psychotropic disco after-hours club piloted by David Mancuso.

Morales' first public DJ gig would be for Ozone Layer, graduating to clubs like Inferno and Better Days. At age 21 he was invited to play for the first time at the Paradise Garage, ironically through Judy Weinstein, who ran a company called For The Record. Years later, Weinstein would become Morales' partner in their label Definity Records and act as manager for both Morales and Knuckles. By 1985 he had jacked in to the new sound of Chicago and became one of the first DJs in New York to spin House music. In 1989, the year he was first booked to DJ in London, he would be well on his way to cementing

his place in influencing the sound of popular dance music throughout the world.

It seems as though Morales returned from London with a keen understanding of how dance music could truly work on a populist level. Morales attacked a slew of remixes that year, naming them the "Red Zone" mixes after his club night at the time. These would twist the conventions of Techno and House into one united force years before journalists would invent the tech-House sub-genre.

Most importantly, his mixes added a certain cool cachet to artists who had begun to run dry, revitalizing acts like Darryl Hall, Thompson Twins and Pet Shop Boys in the elite confines of the dancefloor. In later years he would become a reliable source for major labels wanting to try to add some hipness to decidedly unhip artists, hence subsequent remixes for artists like Jon Secada, Ace Of Base and even comedian Eddie Murphy. His extended list of remix credits looks like a who's-who of pop music, including the likes of Diana Ross, Aretha Franklin, Tina Turner, Spice Girls, Annie Lennox, Michael and Janet Jackson, Whitney Houston and Gloria Estefan. At present he is quite probably the highest-paid remixer in the business.

He has produced full-length albums for Ce Ce Penniston and Robert Owens, mixing the latter's classic "I'll Be Your Friend", and singles for such House luminaries as Byron Stingley and Jocelyn Brown. He has written and produced several tracks for other artists as well, including Jody Watley's "I'm the One You Need", Ten City's "My Piece of Heaven" and Mariah Carey's "Fantasy", for which he was nominated for a Grammy in 1996. He received yet another Grammy nomination in 1997 for new category Remixer Of The Year, losing only to compatriot Frankie Knuckles.

Such a hectic schedule of demand has left Morales time to complete only one solo album so far. Made in 1991, David Morales and the

Bad Yard Club's **The Program** was released in 1993, to a somewhat lukewarm reaction. The BYC's ragga anthem, "In De Ghetto", however, was a smash club hit the next year.

Having gone back underground to record the respected "Philadelphia" (as Brooklyn Friends) for King Street Records in 1995, he launched Definity Records with Judy Weinstein in 1997. Their first release, Bobby D featuring Michelle Weeks' "Moment of My Life", reached the Top 40 in several countries. In 1998, David Morales Presents The Face emerged with "Needin' U" on Definity. The perfect Ibiza holiday anthem garnered a *Billboard* dance #1 and #8 on the UK pop charts.

◉ Mariah Carey: "Fantasy"　　　　　　　Columbia, 1996

Hundreds of Morales remixes could be examined to capture his magnetic style, but it is this simple pop song he produced for Mariah Carey – for which he was nominated for a Grammy – that demonstrates his flair for song structure and showcasing the female vocal.

George Morel

One of the Big Apple's most versatile producers, George Morel first rose to prominence with 2 In A Room's infectious Hip-House chart hit, "Wiggle It". Originally a DJ at clubs like Palladium, Tracks and Red Zone, Morel made his initial move into production with Dee Holloway's "Our Love Is Over", produced with C&C Music Factory's David Cole.

The same formula gave Strictly Rhythm, the Manhattan-based label whose direction Morel would help shape throughout the '90s, its first notable club smash, the ridiculously sleazy "Voices In the Club"

(1990). Together with DJ Pierre, the figure who would distinguish the majority of Strictly's harder, instrumental style (tagged "wild pitch"), Morel wrote one of 1991's most endearing vocal 12"s, Simone's "My Family Depends On Me". The two combined most effectively again on Joint Venture's double-headed gem, "The Move/Somewhere In Space" (1991).

While Morel continued to release fine garage 12"s including Ira Levi's "Free Your Mind", Shadi's "My People" and Mark Davis' stunning "So Special", 1992 heralded the beginnings of a series of stripped-down, abstract grooves. Staple fodder for US jocks David Morales, Erick Morillo and Roger Sanchez, the series of ten **Morel's Grooves** EPs have ranged from the self-explanatory "Touch of Jazz" (1994) through the piano-happy "I Feel It" to the carnival rhythms of "Todos Los Latinos En La Casa" (1995). Along with well-worn DJ tools, they've also provided Morel with one of his biggest underground hits in **Volume 4**'s killer instrumental, "Let's Groove" (1993), which suprisingly became something of an anthem across both "handbag" and Deep House dancefloors upon its 1996 UK re-release.

Having played a pivotal role in the success of Strictly, as both co-head of A&R and producer, in 1993 Morel set up his own Groove On Records imprint, home to a seething Hammond-driven remix of Ce Ce Rodgers' "No Love Lost" (1994). Morel, meanwhile, has also continued to produce for Strictly, proving his versatility again with garage rubs like Tafuri's "Running On Empty" and more militant, aggressive instrumentals like "Feel It, Work It, Touch It" which were collected on his solo album, **NYC Jam Session** (1995).

⊙ **The Best Of Morel's Grooves**   Strictly Rhythm, 1995

Raw, minimal instrumentals from start to finish: including the essential "Bouncing Sax" and anthemic "Let's Groove".

Erick "More" Morillo

Getting his nickname from his astounding ability to churn out mixes, Erick "More" Morillo's commercially viable production style has extended across ragga, salsa, drum 'n' bass and, of course, House. Having spent his childhood in Colombia, Morillo began DJing in his teens, chopping together disco, ragga, rap and Latin-tinged grooves. He continued to sample Jamaican toasting in his sets for a number of years, until he caught the attention of one of the artists he'd sampled, General. This resulted in a collaboration called "Funky Buddha" (1992) which previewed his trademark of wrapping ragga vocals around a bass-heavy drum kick and Todd Terry-style beats. The buzz created by this track and another Caribbean-flavoured cut called "Mueva La Cadera" (1992) resulted in the introduction to maverick reggae-rapper Mark Quashie (aka The Mad Stuntman) and the subsequent formation of the act for which Morillo is best known, Reel 2 Real.

The collective became one of the most commercially successful dance acts in America. Their first album, **Move It** (1994), bore the multi-million selling single, "I Like to Move It". Fusing The Mad Stuntman's gruff, street-wise toasting to a rocking House groove, the track became a party perennial on both sides of the Atlantic.

As owner of the Big Apple's Double Platinum studio, Morillo is a prolific producer of underground House projects including the sample-soaked Smooth Touch efforts of 1993 and 1994 with singer Althea McQueen. Morillo has also produced fierce rhythms including RAW's "Unbe", Smooth Touch's "Come and Take a Trip", Club Ultimate's Latin monster groove, "Carnival 93" (all 1993), "Reach" (1995) as Lil' Mo' Yin Yang with Master At Work Little Louie Vega and B-Crew's "Partay Feeling" (1997).

With the launch of his Subliminal Records in 1997 and 1998's residency at the Ministry Of Sound, Morillo has affirmed his place as one of House music's most popular characters. Subliminal, one of NY's most succesful House labels, has hitched on to the speed garage vibe in the UK with releases from the Pianoheads and R.I.P. Groove. Once again the ragga influences are strongly in evidence, showing that Morillo's Dominican-Colombian roots are never far away from the mix.

⊙ Reel 2 Real: Move It   Strictly Rhythm, 1994

One of the most successful US House albums of all time. An example of how Latin grooves, House and reggae vocalising equal one big party.

Motorbass

A longside Daft Punk, Dimitri From Paris and I:Cube, producers Philippe Zdar and Etienne De Crecy, who record together as Motorbass, have repositioned Paris as the most creative House music capital of mainland Europe. Since emerging from sound engineering backgrounds in the mid-'90s, both Frenchmen have helped destroy the poor-taste legacy of Vanessa Paradis and Johnny Hallyday through a series of inventive singles, a critically acclaimed album and numerous collaborative projects with fellow Parisian musicians including Air, Alex Gopher and Boombass.

It's been the celebratory mix of hip-hop, House and disco that has enabled the duo to rise above the ranks of underground notoriety and step unashamedly into the limelight. Having released a series of frequency-distorting 12"s, the duo first picked up sizeable attention with

their debut album, **Pansoul**. Recorded in 1995, it wasn't until the long-player gained a more widespread release in September the following year through Different Recordings that Motorbass picked up press coverage in virtually every UK dance magazine, receiving *Muzik*'s Album of the Month award.

A crazed mix of lo-fidelity atmospherics, raw disco samples and chugging, bottom-heavy bass-lines, **Pansoul** was never going to be as commercially popular as anything penned by Daft Punk, but it is widely accepted as one of the city's most accomplished House albums. Indeed, the duo's use of FX – often taking looped samples and funk b-lines to the point of abstraction – drew warm comparisons with Chicago's DJ Sneak and London's Basement Jaxx, and has undoubtedly influenced the new batch of rising Parisian producers.

As one-third owner of Solid Records, Etienne De Crecy's gloriously mellow series of 10" "Super Discount" singles (check the string-laden meanderings of "Prix Choc") led to 1997's compilation, **Super Discount**. An experimental grouping of jazzy sketches, disco loops, etheral atmospherics and soul samplings by De Crecy and Parisian producers Air, Alex Gopher and Mooloodjee (all remixed by De Crecy), **Super Discount** crossed from dance press recognition to make a virtually unprecedented dent in mainstream rock mags like *Q* and *Select*.

Meanwhile, De Crecy's Poumchak label established itself as one of the city's best with fresh releases from himself, Dimitri From Paris, Harrison Crump, Alex Gopher, Philippe Zdar and others, typically giving one side a four-to-the-floor dancefloor flavour and the other over to a laid-back groove.

Philippe Zdar meanwhile has re-invigorated his partnership with ex-La Funk Mob producer Boombass (aka Hubert Blanc-Francart). Recording under the moniker of Cassius, the duo have followed up 1995's party-rocking single, "Foxxy", with the Top 20 single "1999" (1999). Their mix of urban hip-hop and freaky House rhythms gained a wider audience with the release of their debut album, **Cassius 1999** (1999).

⊙ Pansoul   Different Recordings/Motorbass, 1996

A hugely innovative, distorted and often manic genre-spanning soundscape that sometimes veers into abstraction, but never loses its direction completely. As the sleeve illustrations sardonically state, "This Is Bass Music for Bass People".

⊙ Cassius: Cassius 1999   Virgin, 1999

Convoluted breaks and disco snatches are inter-woven to great effect on this eclectic album of real innovation.

Mousse T

A DJ for over ten years, Mousse T was still largely unheard of until he co-created the Peppermint Jam record label in 1994 and began to make his mark with a serious of well-timed, widely appealing pop remixes for artists such as Shabba Ranks and Inner Circle. His own early productions for the imprint – "Shake Your Ass!", "Mine" and "Dirty Beat – though unremarkable, prefigured his combination of garage-style vocals and smooth, heavy bass-lines which would become a commercially successful formula later in his career.

Well-crafted remixes for Ziggy Marley ("Power to Move Ya"), Randy Crawford ("Give Me the Night") and Quincy Jones ("Stomp") preceded 1996's dancefloor smash, a compulsive mix of ex-Sounds Of Blackness singer Ann Nesby's "Can I Get a Witness". Following an upbeat collaboration with London's Grant Nelson and a solo single ("Everybody") for the producer's Swing City label, Mousse T's excellent jazzy collaboration with vibes master Roy Ayers, Ferry Ultra's "Dangerous Vibes" (1996), became a firm favourite with many of NY's top DJs and set him on the path to remix overdrive. In amongst the inevitable dross, his subsequent re-versionings of Deepzone's vocal monster, "It's Gonna Be Alright" (1996), Jay Williams' "Testify" (1997) and Kim English's wonderful "Supernatural" (1997), proved he was a worthy Grammy nominee.

But even this success couldn't have prepared him for the reaction to his 1998 single, "Horny". The instrumental dub may crop up in sets by spinners as diverse as Angel Moraes and the mighty Kevin Saunderson, but the vocal track, with its irritating, repetitive vocal refrain and naff lyrics coupled by Mousse T's snappy hi-hats, shuffling funky sax lines and booming bass-lines rang out on dancefloors stretching from Streatham's Ritzy to Ibiza's Pacha.

⊙ **Mousse T's Mastercuts**   Peppermint Jam, 1998

The best compilation of Mousse T's own releases and remixes available.
Includes the Roy Ayers collaboration, "Dangerous Vibes".

Murk

O scar G and Ralph Falcon's (aka Murk) bottom-heavy bass-lines
have become instantly recognisable on dancefloors stretching
from New York to London to Tokyo since 1991's monumental deep
slate, "Outta Limits", was recorded under the guise of Mission Control.

Both Cuban-born exiles, Ralph's DJing career took off at Miami's
leading 8 Avenue underground House parties. There he built invaluable
friendships with DJ/producer Danny Tenaglia and engineer Aldo Her-
nandez, with whom the duo began recording at the Deep South studios in 1991.

Debuting as the trio Deep Six, "We're Going Under" previewed
Oscar and Ralph's patented mix of heart-pounding bass-lines and
sparse driving rhythms. It was followed by 1991's "Outta Limits". After
the trio's third and largely forgettable single recorded as Hex, Hernan-
dez departed company and the Murk record label launched in March
1992 with the exceptionally deep and minimal male vocal gem,
"Together", under yet another pseudonym, Interceptor. Intruder's
"You Got Me" proved that the duo's ability to segue bass-heavy oscillations with well-carved songs was no fluke, and, masked as Liberty
City, the Murk boys provided the increasingly influential NYC Music
Seminar with its tune for 1992, "Some Lovin'".

For their next project, they brought in Shana, backing singer of Miami pop group Exposé, to sing on Funky Green Dogs From Outer Space's "Reach For Me" (1992). 1993 saw a link-up with NYC's Tribal Records for the release of Liberty City's bass-led vocal anthem, "If You Really Love Someone", and a label compilation, **Murk - The Singles Collection** (1995).

Ralph's Miami Soul label showcased his own Deep House classic, "Every Now and Then" (1992), and The Fog's "Been a Long Time" (1993), while 1995 gave birth to Oscar's tribal Kumba label and "Reaching Up" with soul vocalist Mark Michel, as well as work by Danny Tenaglia and Don Carlos.

1996's return as Funky Green Dogs bore the fierce single, "Fired Up", and the well-received album, **Get Fired Up** (1997), which heralded a more aggressive, instrumental style evident on singles like the Acid-tinged "The Way" (1998). In 1999 they produced another album,

Star, with new vocalist Tamara, for New York's Twisted Records.

Although many feel that Murk haven't veered that far from the original musical grid they drew in 1991, their combination of gut-wrenching bass-lines, narcotic grooves and killer melodies rarely fails to deliver on the dancefloor.

⬤ Miami Deep   Harmless Records, 1998

The best introduction to the Murk sound. Combining bottom-heavy grooves and strong soul vocals, the compilation includes Funky Green Dogs' "Reach For Me", Liberty City's "Some Lovin'" and Ralph Falcon's melancholy masterpiece, "Every Now and Then".

Tommy Musto

With his father owning a television and radio repair shop, access to recording equipment never posed a serious problem for teenager Tommy Musto. Having started DJing in the late '70s, in 1981 he won the Tommy Boy Records Mix Contest and soon gained a slot on the airwaves of the Big Apple's WKTU station alongside DJs John "Jellybean" Benitez, The Latin Rascals and Aldo Marin at around the same time Tony Humphries and Shep Pettibone ruled Kiss FM.

Northcott Productions, established in 1986 with partner Silvio Tancredi, originally provided a platform for electro-geared labels Vanguard, Next Plateau and 25 West Records. However, Musto first gained his reputation for breakbeat mechanisations with Brooklyn DJ Frankie Bones, releasing hit singles "Dangerous On the Dancefloor" and "All I Want Is to Get Away" as precursors to the duo's proto-rave album, **Future Is Ours**. Yet it was Musto's garage-flecked singles for 4th Floor, Nu Groove and Midnight Sun Records which helped to establish his more soul-orientated, long-term ambitions. These were partly fulfilled with his glorious production of Arnold Jarvis' melancholy "Take Some Time Out", one of 1989's finest garage 12"s and one of those perfect sunrise after-hours moments in the haze of Acid House.

Further productions for Pamela Fernandez ("Kickin' In the Beat") and Keith Nunally ("Freedom") were also well received and Musto turned his remixing hand to an abundance of pop stars, bumping up the credibility and club standings of major players including Michael Jackson, Gloria Estefan and Blondie in the process.

In 1994, Musto linked up with Victor Simonelli to form the pop-House collective Colourblind, utilising first the vocals of Barbara Tucker and then Dina Roche, and heralding the cross-over hit, "Nothing Better". In the ensuing period, the pair continued to produce as T.M.V.S with tracks such as "Don't Be Shy" and remixes of Total Eclipse's "Come Together" and Henry's "Only You Will Do".

1993 witnessed the birth of Sub-Urban Records under his North-cott empire. The subsidiary bore classic NYC-style dubs and vocal projections by Victor Simonelli, Sabrina Johnston and Federal Hill. Northcott has also distributed like-minded labels Bassline and Soul-Furic Recordings (home to Urban Blues Project). Following remixes for Tuff Jam and Kim English, in 1998 Musto found himself in the dance charts once again, courtesy of his smoothly produced 12", Next Phase's "Peace of Mind".

◉ Vindallo: The Morning After

x:treme records, 1996

Fine Musto and Simonelli beatmix compilation which includes the skippy "Domything", T.M.V.S's "Don't Be Shy" and Colourblind's garage screamer "Nothing Better" alongside Simonelli's Cloud 9 classic "Do U Want Me".

Muzique Tropique

Having met at Strathclyde University in 1991, Kevin McKay and Andy Carrick set about making music after a succession of nights spent under the spell of Glasgow's Sub Club/Slam DJs Orde Meikle and Stuart McMillan.

Fusing their raw, minimalist rhythms with the expansive soundscapes of jazz, blues and reggae, the duo's ambitious 1994 debut EP, **Prelude to the Storm**, lived up to its title with a selection of blissed-out, bitter-sweet harmonies, especially on the stand-out cut, "Ship-wrecked."

Their second EP (as West Coast Connection) continued the momentum, while the oceanic **Underwater Blues** EP (as 4AM) and the ultra-mellow **Fatal Attraction** EP were also well received. But after only a handful of releases, McKay and Carrick decided it was time to move on, folding the Muzique Tropique label with their swansong, Communication X's "Duality (Parts 1 & 2)".

1997 enhanced their reputation with a smattering of mixes for Andrew Weatherall's Two Lone Swordsmen project, Dubtribe, Omid Nourizadeh and House Of 909. In turn, many of these remixed the pair's original efforts for Muzique Tropique's debut long-player, released on their new and more dancefloor-orientated imprint, Glasgow Underground Records. Perhaps not as fulfilled as early releases such as "Jazz The Sea Turtle" suggested it could be, **Muzique Tropique Collection** (1997) was nonetheless a subtle spectrum of malleable House cuts and likeable meanderings.

The same year, McKay proved himself to be one of Scotland's most inspirational technicians, producing his best release yet – the grinding, bass-heavy "Late Night Jam" – with 16B, under the pseudonym Sixteen Souls, culminating in 1998's **Stranger Girls** album.

After **The Festival** EP for Jus Trax and the well-received **Soul Cruising** EP (both 1997) on Glasgow Underground, 1998 heralded more soothing House projections on "Phazers Set to Funk/Midnight in Atlantis" and a remix of Larry Heard's "I Know That It's You."

◎ Muzique Tropique Collection   Glasgow Underground, 1997

A good collection of the duo's Deep House slates. Although some cuts veer into aimless distraction, others, like the Idjut Boys' funk-fired remix of "Stella Sunday" and 16B's spaced-out take on "Jazz The Sea Turtle", provide the subtle twists and turns of Ambient dance at its best.

⊙ Sixteen Souls: Stranger Girls   Alola, 1998

Nourizadeh and Kevin McKay's mini-LP moulds disco snatches, rumbling bass-lines and vocal tracks into the four-to-the-floor mix and comes up trumps.

Ludovic Navarre (Saint Germain)

U nlike those producers who've plundered disco's back catalogue with abandon in search of inspiration, Ludovic Navarre's releases under his Saint Germain moniker reveal a startling empathy with the deepest traditions of black American music. Producing and engineering a substantial proportion of Eric Morland's Paris-based FNAC and F Communications output until the mid-'90s, Navarre also showed glimpses of warmth and subtlety under his various other guises: creating House, garage, Techno and Ambient as Modus Vivendi, Deepside (**Deepside EP**), DS, Nuages (with label mate Shazz; check the **Blanc** EP, Deep Contest (with DJ Deep; check 1995's "Sexual Behaviour") and Soufflé (**Noveau** EP).

Navarre debuted as St Germain en-Laye in 1993 with the **Mezzotinto** EP. Using snippets of ragtime and southern sleaze alongside his soft grooves, the EP foregrounded his ability to harness a wide-ranging spectrum of musical styles in the mix. The EP also uncharacteristically featured his most upbeat track to date, the samba-fiesta-styled "Soul Salsa Soul".

Under the shortened St Germain banner, Navarre began to attract attention for his series of three **Boulevard** EPs, collected in 1995 as an album of the same title. Drafting in musicians from his government-funded music school to play guitar, piano, flute, percussion and saxophone over his reflective House grooves ("Deep In It") and Afro-American samples (notably a homage to Malcolm X on "Easy to Remember", the Harlem-esque street hustle snatches on "Street Scene" and a scat voice sampled from a 1930s Lightnin' Hopkins cut on "Alabama Blues"), **Boulevard** was a breath of fresh air to clear the stale odour of generic club cuts. Bizarrely, for a white Parisian who still lived with his parents, Navarre's urban, Afro-American influences were also evident on the emotive blues of "Thank U Mum (For Everything You Did)", the hip-hop beats of "Forget It" and the roots-reggae-influenced "Dub Experience II".

⊙ **Boulevard**   F Communications, 1995

Larry Heard once described Navarre's Boulevard EPs as "a combination of what I did, mixed in with Manuel Göttsching and Brian Eno". Sometimes sad but always soulful, Navarre's musical mystery tour through black America's past and present has since taken its place as one of House music's most accomplished albums.

Nervous Records

W hen Nervous Records burst onto the scene in 1991, its presence was first felt through its ingenious line of fashion merchandise. The signature logo (a quirky cartoon character perspiring furiously as a slab of 12" vinyl shaves off the upper portion of his flat-top hairdo) became an instant streetwear icon from its native Manhattan all the way to Japan.

With releases from Roger Sanchez (as Niceguy Soleman), Kenny "Dope" Gonzalez (Swing Kids) and Todd Terry (Latin Kings), the label's initial releases would do much to establish its reputation as a home for the work of many of the US's premier producers. Its discography to date reads like a who's-who of American House music, including Nu Yorican Soul, DJ Pierre (aka Shock Wave), Frankie Feliciano (Groove Asylum), Mood II Swing, Marshall Jefferson and Roy Davis Jr. (Umosia), Erick Morillo and Armand Van Helden (Deep Creed).

In 1993, Nervous was ready to tackle other musical genres, and created a trio of new imprints; by 1998, there would be a total of seven labels under the Nervous banner. Hip-hop sub-label Wreck Records debuted with the Black Moon single "Who Got The Props" (1993), a clarion call to the world that Brooklyn was representin'. The Weeded Records imprint began as a foray into reggae and its first artist, Mad Lion, struck relatively big in America with "Take It Easy" (1993) which highlighted the Lion's distinctive gruff tones, pounding piano and an infectious R&B hook, and sold over 300,000 units. Sorted Records would arrive later in the year to address America's burgeoning rave scene with some of the East Coast's fastest-rising Techno and trance DJs/producers, such as Micro, James Christian and Josh Wink (who, under his Winx moniker, released instant rave anthems like the gimmicky, giggle-driven "Don't Laugh", which went on to sell over 600,000 copies).

However, Nervous Records remained true to its first love, House, and in 1998 released the debut solo albums from Kim English (**Supernatural**), a Chicago soul diva who had already netted three Top 40 singles in the UK, and former Ten City frontman Byron Stingley, whose **The Purist** featured the production talents of Frankie Knuckles, Masters At Work, Basement Boys and Murk.

And as for the clothing? Nervous ended the decade with a new "high-quality" collection aimed at increasing company awareness outside of DJ/trainspotter circles.

◉ Club Nervous – Five Years Of Nervous House   Nervous, 1997

This compilation traces the first five years of their House imprint, from raw, elemental tracks like Niceguy Soleman's "Feel It" to Track & Feel Event's transcendent gospel-House anthem, "Yes He Is".

Network Records

Network Records and label head Neil Rushton may be better known for the pivotal role they played in bringing the sounds of

Detroit Techno to a world-wide audience, but the label has also raised the UK profile of hugely influential American House producers.

Network grew from the success of Kool Kat Records, which had been formed in 1988 by Northern Soul DJ/*Echoes* journalist/Inferno label owner Neil Rushton and jazz-funk DJ Dave Barker. Having stumbled upon Detroit Techno on a visit to the Motor City that year, Rushton returned to compile the first ground-breaking Techno compilation which highlighted works by Derrick May, Juan Atkins and Kevin Saunderson. Rushton would launch Saunderson's Inner City outfit onto the world stage with the release of "Big Fun" and the band would later become central to Network's success.

Network launched soon after with futuristic sleeves and a broader musical range than Kool Kat. The label's first release was Neal Howard's "Indulge" (1990) and Network soon gained commercial success through the chart-friendly rave/pop mechanisations of Altern 8 and KWS. Yet the key role it played was to launch the profiles of US producers like MK (who first picked up attention with 1990's "Somebody New" and "Get It Right" 12"s), Murk (aka Funky Green Dogs & Interceptor), Terence Parker (whose releases had been on imported limited edition before Network issued his singles on the Serious Grooves subsidiary label), and of course Kevin Saunderson's Inner City and Reese Project (check 1994's **Faith, Hope and Clarity**).

In 1993 Network inked a deal with Sony Music and created a new label, Six6, for more underground releases. However, Six6's first release, Glam's "Hell's Party" (1993), became an immediate dancefloor hit. One of Six6's biggest hits came in 1994 with the cleverly masked Sure Is Pure production, "Bells of NY" (recorded under the guise Slo Moshun). Taking its pitch-shifting lead from Lil' Louis' "French Kiss", the single's colossal breakdown, convoluted hip-hop breaks and rave-esque whistle stabs made it a party favourite at clubs across the UK and brought back the welcome sight of pogo-ing to dancefloors like Manchester's LuvDup.

Although at one point Network was acting as something of a focal point for various UK labels – distributing for Bostin', DiY's Strictly4Groovers, Sure Is Pure's Gem, Alan Russell's Hott Records and DJ Greg Fenton's Silver City – the label sadly folded in 1996, shortly before it was due to release Inner City's fourth album, **Hiatus**.

⊙ The Network Collection Passion Music ,1998

The best compendium of Network material available. Includes The Reese Project's "Direct Me", Funky Green Dogs From Outer Space's "Reach For Me", Derrick May's seminal "Strings of Life" and MK's "Get It Right".

Omid Nourizadeh (16B)

W hile one single can make a name legendary in dance music, subsequent producer-led albums have often failed in their inability to expand their horizons beyond the throb of the dancefloor. There were no such problems for London-born technician Omid Nourizadeh (aka 16B), whose **Sounds From Another Room** (1998) lived up to its billing by *Melody Maker* as "contender for album of the year". A breathtaking combination of mood-shifting Ambient and jazz-tinged atmospherics, intricate jacked-up drum patterns and driving, bottomless bass-lines, **Sounds From Another Room** was an incredibly ambitious debut.

With a back catalogue that rubbed up pop-trance alongside jazz-disco, perhaps it wasn't so surprising that relative newcomer Nourizadeh produced such an eclectic album. Ditching his school rock bands in favour of a one-man home studio set-up in 1991, Nourizadeh's career began with a series of deep, jazzy slates, including "Trail of Dreams" and "Voices In the Sky" (both 1996), on his self-financed Alola imprint.

But it wasn't until the summer of that year that his twelfth release, "Secrets", gave any real indication of his potential talent. A subtle, string-laden concoction, made within the space of two days, it drew comparisons with Deep Dish and Chez Damier and set the stage for his first long-player. Nourizadeh also released trance under the guise of ORN and provided diverse remixes for The Cure, Darlesia, Andy Weatherall and Icelandic combo Gus Gus. Testament to his diversity, he continues to record trance under the guise of Phaser and runs the more Techno-oriented Disclosure label.

Indeed, the only generic signpost in much of his work under the 16B banner is the desire to forge escapist, emotionally charged music which often manifests itself in expansive, soothing, semi-Ambient soundscapes. But the one thing that defines him from the wishy-washy, directionless mass of sub-standardists is a cherished sense of House music's inherent rhythm and propulsive groove.

Reflecting his growing popularity in the UK, in 1997 Nourizadeh signed a deal with the HartHouse/Eye Q label and released the spaced-out funk of "Water Ride" and the incessantly percussive "Black Hole". He also worked with like-minded Glaswegian producer Kevin McKay (Muzique Tropique) as Sixteen Souls, releasing the driving singles "On My Mind" and the stunning "Late Night Jam" for Glasgow Underground, culminating in 1998's excellent **Stranger Girls**.

In 1999 the Londoner confirmed his status as one of the UK's freshest talents with the Alola compilation **More Space to Dance** (1999).

⊙ Sounds From Another Room   Eye Q, 1998

An astonishingly ambitious and compelling debut which spans breakbeat, Ambient, Deep House and Detroit Techno without ever becoming pretentious or boring.

Nu Groove Records

Nu Groove was the one label which encompassed the sound of the late '80s/early '90s New York eclectic dance underground.

In so doing, it not only laid the foundations for the more commercially successful Strictly Rhythm and Nervous Records, but more importantly provided a breeding ground for unknown producers Kenny "Dope" Gonzalez, The Basement Boys, Joey Beltram, Bobby Konders, Victor Simonelli and Peter Daou to develop into artists in their own right.

Impossible to categorise, Nu Groove's 107 releases between 1988 and 1992 spanned abstract jazz, dancehall, Deep House and industrial Techno. Based in a nondescript building on the edge of Manhattan's garment district, the label's disregard for publicity was exemplified by spokesperson Judy Russell's nonplussed attitude toward the music press and the non-commerciability of most releases which were accompanied by a host of DJ-styled mixes and instrumental edits.

Ronnie and Rheji Burrell had kicked the imprint into action with its well-received first batch of releases: Tech Trax Inc.'s "Feel The Luv",

K.A.T.O.'S "Booty Dance" and Bas Noir's soothing "My Love Is Magic" (all 1988). Over a third of Nu Groove's output was produced by the Burrell Brothers who recorded under a variety of monikers including Jazz Documents ("Secret Code" (1990)), Utopia Project, NY Housin' Authority and Aphrodisiac ("Song Of

The Siren"(1991)). Ronnie's zenith came in 1990 with K.A.T.O.'s "Disco-Tech", which borrowed heavily from Francine McGee's 1977 disco classic, "Delirium", while Rheji received critical acclaim for the stunning **New Elevators** EP (1991) as NY Housin' Authority. Probably the only common factor pinning many of their releases together was an often minimal and yet overtly soulful structure, with singles often paired down to the simplest rhythms and breaks. Indeed, it's this element of simplicity which has granted longevity.

The label was also home to harder grooves which ranged from Joey Beltram's proto-industrial Techno (check Code 6's "Forgotten Moments" (1990)) to the breakbeats of Musto & Bones' early hardcore mechanics and Lenny Dee's "Looney Tunes" (1988).

But that's only really scratching the surface. Essex-born Joey Negro (aka Dave Lee) slammed his prototype "Do It Believe It" (1990) onto the House map before unleashing a remixed version of the same cut into the UK charts a year later; reggae-House fusionist Bobby Konders cut his teeth with the label, releasing the slow-burning anthem "The Poem" (1991), which heralded the beginnings of a major label trajectory, while Kenny "Dope" Gonzalez previewed his cut-and-paste technique alongside his trademark drum breaks with his **PowerHouse** series of EPs. Victor Simonelli first gained notoriety as Groove Committee with the sleek garage of "I Wanna Know" (1991), as did the Basement Boys under the guise of 33 1/3 Queen. Studio musician Peter Daou both engineered and provided keyboards for much of Nu Groove's output, recording as Vandal ("Laws Of The Chant" (1990)), before becoming a pivotal figure in the success of Tribal Records in the mid-'90s.

Since the label folded in 1992, few have managed to reach the ambitious genre-spanning legacy that Nu Groove left behind or the quality standards it set for underground dance music.

⊙ Nu Groove – Here Comes That Sound Again

Passion Music, 1998

This four-CD set provides an excellent overview of the label's releases, featuring forty tracks that include must-haves like K.A.T.O.'s "Disco-Tech", Vandal's "Unravelled", Aphrodisiac's "Song Of The Siren" and Groove Committee's "I Want To Know".

Nuphonic

Set up at the end of 1994 by David Hill (of Ballistic Brothers notoriety) and Sav Remzi (sometime manager of the Blue Note club in London), Nuphonic has garnered considerable respect and has set the standard for similar independent British labels by highlighting an impressive roster of artists (most notably Faze Action) whilst simultaneously supporting some excellent leftfield material from around Europe (The Money Penny Project) and the US (Joe Claussell's Spiritual Life imprint).

Nuphonic's first release was Faze Action's debut single, "Original Disco Motion" (1995), a silky instrumental track that took its lead from the NY disco era. This was followed by the energetic funk of The Chicago Movement's "Recognise/Percussive Talk" (1995), a heavy, percussion-layered single which appealed to both the underground House and Techno scenes. By the time Blaze's blissfully spaced-out "Moonwalk" (1996) appeared, the London-based label was beginning to create a substantial air of excitement.

Nuphonic's support grew with the release of Faze Action's "In the Trees" (1996), a modern disco-House classic. Utilising the rich sounds of live instrumentation over grooving beats, the emotive cello soaring through the track proved to be a typical example of the releases to follow. Crispin J Glover's superb boogie "Don't Fake It/Breaking Point", Motif's "Let the Madness Begin" and Idjut Boy's Roll Over and Snore (all 1997) highlighted the cream of the talent developing out of London's House scene.

Faze Action consolidated their position as the pivotal act with their debut album, **Plans and Designs** (1997). Encouraged by their success, Nuphonic released three further essential albums: a compilation of Joe Claussell's Spiritual Life material, an album from Ashley Beedle's diverse Black Jazz Chronicles project, **Future Ju Ju** (1998), and the label compendium, **Nuphonic 01** (1998).

The East London-based label have continued to focus upon the more adventurous side of House music, signing new acts such as Fuzz Against Junk and the Fela Kuti-influenced Soul Ascendants, whose singles "Tribute" and "Rise" (both 1998) have offered modern renditions of the funkier side of African music.

◉ Nuphonic 01   Nuphonic, 1998

Apart from the omission of Idjut Boys' dynamic **Roll Over and Snore** EP, this compilation features most of Nuphonic's finest moments to date.

Paul Oakenfold

rguably the most famous, and undeniably the most successful,
DJ Britain has produced, Paul Oakenfold's career spans the
entirety of Acid House. Originally a chef, Oakenfold was first introduced to a set of decks by his friend Trevor Fung at Rumours Wine Bar
in London's Covent Garden. Finding few musical opportunities in London, he moved to New York in the early '80s and began to work as a
courier around Manhattan. During this time he developed a love of the
music played at Larry Levan's Paradise
garage and the nascent hip-hop
scene. Returning to London,
he worked at Polo/Cham-
pion Records and
signed up, amongst
others, Salt N' Pepa,
Jazzy Jeff and the
Fresh Prince and
Raze's "Jack the
Groove".

In 1984, Oak-
enfold spent the
summer DJing in
Ibiza. On his return,
he attempted to
start a club that would
recapture the Balearic
spirit of the island. That
club, Funhouse, was a dismal

failure. Its eclectic music policy (rock, rap and dance records played together) was simply too strange a concept at the time. By 1987 he was running a successful night at a club in Streatham called The Project, playing jazz and soul records. Following his return from Ibiza that year (with Nicky Holloway, Danny Rampling and Johnny Walker), The Project hosted an invite-only "Ibiza Reunion Party". From this, Oakenfold started the legendary Spectrum night at London's Heaven whose inception coincided with the arrival of Ecstasy in Britain. Spectrum – and its equally renowned successors Future, Land Of Oz and Shoom – became the pivotal Acid House clubs and, together with Manchester's Hacienda, were responsible for kicking off the entire scene.

Oakenfold's production duties had begun by 1988, overseeing a range of releases such as Rob Davis' Project Club tracks, "Amnesia" and "Dance With the Devil". However, it was with a series of singles released under the Electra title that Oakenfold, alongside Rob Davis and Steve Osbourne, most effectively captured the blissed-out euphoria of the times. Clubbers were treated to the hypnotic dancefloor experience of "The Future" (1988), the Giorgio Moroder-sampling "Autumn Love" (1989) and a reworking of the Elkin and Nelson track "Jibaro" into a Balearic-dance-rock anthem.

With production partner Steve Osbourne, he remixed the Happy Mondays' shambling "Wrote For Luck" for the dancefloor. Along with Andrew Weatherall's mix of Primal Scream's "Loaded", indie-dance took club music to a whole new audience. In 1990 they produced the Happy Monday's **Pills, Thrills and Bellyaches**, and in 1991 they won the Brit award for Best Producer.

Further high-profile remixes followed (New Order, Massive Attack, The Shamen, Arrested Development and Michael Hutchence), and Oakenfold and Osbourne began trading under the name Perfecto. From this, the duo launched a label of the same name, releasing tracks like "The Lost" by Gonzo and works by Carl Cox, Robert Owens, Gary Clail and Jimi Polo.

In 1993 U2 hired Oakenfold as their tour warm-up DJ for their Zooropa world tour. His production of the stadium rocker "Even Better Than the Real Thing" was also one of the year's dancefloor highlights.

By 1994 East West Records had made Oakenfold their A&R consultant and he used the label to keep Perfecto in the limelight and launch his own recording career with the single "Rise". His DJing visits to Goa in 1995 culminated in the Perfecto Fluoro label, on which he has championed the sound of Goa trance, culminating in an award-winning Essential Mix for Radio 1 and the **Fluoro** album, which mixed trance tracks with Hard House. Singles by Grace ("Not Over Yet"), BT ("Loving You More" and "Blue Skies") and the Oakenfold-alias Virus ("The Sun") also became big club hits.

◉ Perfection   Perfecto/East West, 1995

As you'd expect, it's heavy on the trance with cuts by BT, Grace, Tilt and the Perfecto Allstarz.

187 Lockdown

After releasing a series of multi-generic 12"s under a welter of pseudonyms since the early '90s, producers Danny Harrison and Julian Jonah achieved most commercial recognition under the guise of 187 Lockdown. Like much of their music, this moniker was concocted from an amalgamation: 187 Lockdown is a combination of the US police code for a homicide (187) and American slang for prison (lockdown).

Unlike many of their counterparts, Harrison and Jonah cover the garage spectrum, capable of producing both ten-ton bass-lines and intricate, Todd Edwards-style cuts under guises Nu Birth and Gant as well as 187 Lockdown. One of the most important British production teams to emerge from the 1997 speed garage explosion, they nonetheless remain something of an enigma. While Tuff Jam re-interpreted vocal-led New York garage for a black British audience, RIP introduced the sound of ragga basslines and The Dreem Teem pioneered the sound of "two-step", 187 Lockdown amalgamated these sounds, styles and influences to help take British garage into the mainstream.

Part of the explanation for this rests with their idiosyncratic personalities and shared musical history. Good-time South Londoners with an eye for an opportunity and an ear for a hook, the chemistry between wide-boy Harrison and studio technician Jonah has been evident ever since the duo came together to produce Congress' rave hit "40 Miles" in 1991. Jonah had already achieved notoriety with a series of Deep House outings, releasing 1988's seminal "Jealousy and Lies" before signing to Cooltempo Records as a solo artist.

The pair followed "40 Miles" with more Italo House-style recordings under the moniker of Nush (who scored a massive hit with the handbag House anthem "U Girls"). With their commercial viability established, they formed the Nu Jack label, and set about developing their take on US House with the release of the single "Anytime" (as Nu Birth).

187 Lockdown's debut 12" took them toward the mainstream. "Gunman" (1997) wedded ragga-chat, a neo-Jungle bass-line and genial groove to break into the UK Top 10 and secure a *Top of the Pops* appearance, while their follow-up single, "Sound Bwoy Burial" (as Gant), ensured more success. A mix album, **187 Lockdown Pre-**

sents **Sunday Flavas Volume 1**, further emphasised their relevance and 1998's chart-friendly single, "Kung Fu Fighting", came complete with a Spaghetti Western-style video.

Remixes of Louise, Robbie Williams, Sneaker Pimps and Natural Born Chillers have followed, picking up on the wave of hype that the media's exposure of speed garage engendered. Signed to East West, 187 Lockdown released their debut album, **The World**, at the end of 1998.

⦿ The World   East West, 1998

Never really gels together as an album, but if it's super-heavy bass-lines and crisp drum kicks you're looking for, then it's the best place to find the singles, "Gunman" and "Kung Fu Fighting".

Robert Owens

Robert Owens is unquestionably one of House music's most captivating vocalists and songwriters. From his incredible mid '80s work with Larry Heard as Fingers Inc to his self-produced 1996 single "Ordinary People", Owens has always steered clear of trad-pop optimism in favour of soul-centric, emotive songs which often deal with pain and anguish, but always with reality.

A self-confessed spiritual loner, Owens spent his formative years drifting between his mother's home in Los Angeles and father's in Chicago, where he eventually settled down to work in a steel mill and hospital before taking up DJing and becoming involved with the Windy City's club explosion. His reflective and often melancholy attitude was soon put to good use after an introduction to producer/social security worker

Larry Heard led to Owens providing lyrics for Heard's Fingers Inc project alongside another benefit employee, Ron Wilson. Perhaps too sophisticated for the 1987–88 audience, deep and impassioned vocal masterpieces like "Bring Down the Walls", "I'm Strong", "Bye Bye" and "Slam Dance" never achieved the commercial recognition they deserved.

Moving to New York, Owens worked with producer Frankie Knuckles, which resulted in his most emotionally charged release to date, the sublime "Tears". But even though "Tears" remains one of the genre's defining moments, amazingly it failed to capitalise on its commercial cross-over potential.

The well-received club hit "Visions" preceded the 1990 Def Mix-produced **Rhythms In Me** (1990), but again cross-over success remained out of reach and Owens was dropped from his contract with 4th & Broadway in 1992, even though the interim period had produced such melancholy perfection as his singles "I'll Be Your Friend" (1991) and "As One" (with Bobby Konders).

A move to London in 1992 coincided with his short-term involvement with Freetown Records, for whom he produced the energetic "Gotta Work". The same year, Mr Fingers' **Introduction** album showcased his under-rated gems "Empty", "Dead End Alley" and "On a Corner Called Jazz".

In the ensuing period, he worked as a DJ and set up his own London-based label, Musical Directions. Although the imprint has only released two notable singles to date, both have proved beyond any doubt his credentials one of House music's best vocalists and lyricists. 1995's beautifully haunting "Was I Here Before" was essential, while 1996's Fire Island mixes of his inspirational "Ordinary People" hit the dancefloor head on. In 1998 Owens returned to the club charts again, this time alongside ex-Shamen member Mr.C, with the atmopsheric "A Thing Called Love".

◎ **"Tears"**   ffrr Records Ltd, 1989

With Knuckles on production and Satoshi Tomiee tinkling the ivories,
soul never sounded so good. If you only buy one Robert Owens song,
then make certain it's this. Available on **Classic House Volume 1**.

Pagan Records

Having helped make such an immense success of Tribal
Records in the UK, much was expected of Richard Breeden's
new imprint, Pagan Records, when he established the London-based
label in January 1997.

Whereas Tribal relied almost exclusively on American producers,
Pagan found its own niche in British Deep House, supported through a
strong club network stretching from London (Wiggle/Heart&Soul) to
Leeds (Back2Basics) to Glasgow (Sub Club).

Unlike Breeden's first label, Pagan got off to a slowish start. The ini-
tial batch of 12" releases from the likes of Housey Doingz ("Ride"),
Urban Farmers ("The Hustle"), Discocaine ("Doin' Alrite") and The
Dancer ("I Love What You're Doing") were low key when compared to
those bassbin-shattering debut Tribal releases by Peter Daou, Eric
Kupper and Junior Vasquez.

In fact, it wasn't really until 1998 that the label began to rise to
prominence in the record shops, clubs and international dance market.
With support from influential DJs Ralph Lawson, Elliot Eastwick, Miles
Holloway and Terry Francis, Breeden was able to mature his vision.

London's 16B remixed House of 909's "Main Event", bettering the melancholy original to create a Deep House classic, while Terry Francis' "Dub Town" and House Of 909's debut long-player, **Soul Rebels**, found their way into DJ boxes across the UK, opening up the sounds of Pagan to a wider audience.

1998 found the label increasing both its output and its profile considerably, signing newcomers Swayzak (who produced the well-regarded **Snowboarding in Argentina**) and releasing dancefloor bombs by Charles Webster (aka Presence), Basement Boy Maurice Faulton and House Of 909 (check Cevin Fisher's massive re-versioning of "Beautiful Day"). Tours to Barcelona and America, fronted by DJ Terry Francis, and the release of House Of 909's critically acclaimed **The Children We Were**, took the label global.

A second label compilation, **Pagan Offering** (1998), mixed by the incomparable DJ Derrick Carter, brought more acclaim, welding together oceanic deepness, vocal tracks and angular grooves from the imprint's vaults. Together with the release of Presence's magical **All Systems Gone** (1999), it cemented Pagan's position as one of the UK's most respected and forward-thinking imprints.

O Pagan Offering   Pagan,1998

The Pagan back catalogue mixed to perfection by Chicago's DJ don Derrick Carter.

Pal Joey

Alhough he's remained a relatively unknown figure outside NYC, Long Island's DJ/producer Joey Longo (aka Pal Joey) helped introduce the sound of jazz to House music with a series of irresistible recordings.

Like so many of his counterparts, his musical career began in a New York record store, Vinyl Mania. Working as an intern at a major recording studio gave him the studio engineering prowess to turn his love of hip-hop and House into production skills, debuting with the disco-medley bootleg "Something Special" (1990) which became a favourite with Tony Humphries.

He gained underground notoriety with the jump-up jazz-break style of Earth People's "Dance" (1991) and "Reach Up To Mars" (1991). While recording under a series of bizarre monikers, including House Conductor, Expresso and Dream House (often for his own Loop D' Loop label), it was as Soho that Longo penned his most important 12", 1992's "Hot Music". Incorporating a half-hip-hop, half mid-tempo House groove alongside a repetitive live sax loop, freeform piano hooks and jackin' rhythms, "Hot Music"'s popularity helped pave the way for New York's mid-'90s obsession with jazz-House alongside releases like "Our Mute Horn" (1992) from Masters At Work and the productions of Rheji and Ronald Burrell (with whom Longo collaborated on 1992's vibes excursion "Mother's Day, Father's Day").

While recording as Pal Joey, Longo also provided the first ska-House track, "Jump And Prance" (1990), for Dave Lee's London-based Republic label. Longo's inherent hip-hop sensibilities were more apparent on his production work for KRS-1's **Sex and Violence** (1991), though he also touched base as a remixer, turning out well-regarded re-versionings for The Orb ("Little Fluffy Clouds") and Deee-Lite ("What Is Love" & "E.S.P") (all 1991).

During the late '90s he pushed the jazz-House sound to the fore, most commonly under the guise of CFM (Crazy French Man), with cuts like the sumptuous "I Got Jazz In My Soul" (1994), recorded as Just 4 Groovers, and "Bloo Monday" (1998) for A Man Called Adam's Other Records.

⊙**Soho: "Hot Music"**   Kool Groove Records, 1998

Pal Joey's jazz-House fusion masterpiece from 1992 re-issued with Earth People's marvellous "Dance" as its b-side.

Paper Recordings

T here can be no doubting the significance of Miles Holloway and Elliot Eastwick for British club culture, especially since the inception of their Paper Recordings label. Run with co-owners Ben Davis and Pete Jenkinson, Paper Recordings has charted the more subdued end of the House spectrum, concentrating on "pure" Deep House with elements of funk, jazz and breakbeat thrown in for good measure.

Working hand in hand with Paper has always been Holloway, Eastwick and Simon Brad's Salt City Orchestra, most renowned for being the first and only British act to record for Tribal Records ("Storm"). While Paper Recordings has focused on British House, the label has also released material from Frenchman Erick Rug and Those Norwegians.

If there is one record that stands as the apotheosis of the label's vibe, and style, it's Salt City Orchestra's collaboration with Derrick

Carter, "Got Change For A Twenty?" Existing somewhere between cool garage and the smeared edges of electronica, "Got Change For A Twenty?" was an urban pastoral with a 4am glow similar to the the style of Glasgow Underground. It is a reminder that when British fusion works it's through the charm of atmosphere, hovering on the edges of darkness, rather than through the Americans' sense of raw power.

●Splinter Paper, 1998

First album label sampler from a crew that represents a distinctly British way of making music. Always a pleasure, but rarely earth-shaking.

Paperclip People

While Carl Craig is one of Detroit Techno's most important figures, his work under the guise of Paperclip People, and to a lesser extent as 69, has provided House music with some of its most intriguing and forward-thinking releases.

Paperclip People's storming "Throw" (1994) moulded Techno and House in a startling fusion that impacted across "handbag" and Deep House dancefloors. The centrepoint of the track was Craig's own vocal, a screech that crashed House's most basic trope, "I wanna see your hands up, in the air".

It's this attitude which permeates all of Paperclip People's records. "Steam", the most aqueous of grooves, merged Deep House with light funk on top of Craig's complex drum patterns, while "Slam Dance" moulded samples and beats in such a way that the 4/4 kick drum was almost completely lost. Craig slips into the beat-stream a simplified version of what free jazz drummers called "rhythmic displacement".

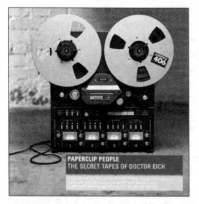

Another example of this was 69's polyrhythmic, and seemingly multi-tempoed, "Jam the Box".

At the most radical edge of Craig's House work is "Country Boy Goes Dub", a tune that does exactly what it says in the title: country guitar vs dub bass-line and breakdown with a beat that is dub-skank, House-funk and breakbeat all at the same time.

O Paperclip People:
The Secret Tapes of Doctor Eich Open/Planet E, 1997

Bewilderingly different from start to finish, Craig's experimental House project is required listening for the open-minded.

Graeme Park

DMC DJ of the year for three years in succession between 1989 and 1992, bespectacled Scot Graeme Park studied sociology and politics at college, worked in a pea factory and then as a tailor before blagging a job buying second-hand vinyl in a Nottingham record shop and reluctantly finding himself stuck behind a pair of decks.

From his newly found position spinning at the city's blues and reggae-dominated Ad-Lib club (later renamed the garage, then Kool Kat) in 1985, Park became one of the first DJs to introduce the UK to the sound of House music. His openly eclectic policy of playing tracks by the likes of New Order and Talking Heads alongside electro and hip-hop cuts by Double Dee & Steinski, Afrika Bambaataa and Rochelle inevitably led to the then radical inclusion of nascent House releases by Steve "Silk" Hurley, Colonel Abrams and Farley "Jackmaster" Funk. While the rest of the Midlands venues were still pre-Kebab, Ritzy-type affairs and most London clubs were style-obsessed shrines to rare groove, Park made his name legendary in the region.

After being asked by DJ Mike Pickering to fill in for his residency at Manchester's Hacienda in July 1988, Park subsequently became resident alongside Pickering at the legendary Nude nights until 1990. Though classics at the club stretched from 808 State's "Pacific State" to Carly Simon's Chic-produced "Why", Park remembers it thus: "We played loads and loads of obscure American House records: songs, basically, with disco bass-lines. It was only really in the North where they were getting played. In London, at clubs like the Trip, it was all Acid, no vocals."

After a short break, he returned to the Hacienda as Saturday night resident until the mid-'90s, playing his seamless mix of mainly vocalled House and garage 12"s to packed dancefloors of dedicated disciples. Though his DJing status has faded in recent years, Park was one of the first British DJs to master the art of long, seamless mastermixes based around the legacies of NYC luminaries Shep Pettibone and Tony Humphries, and is still a popular draw as a guest DJ at venues such as Liverpool's Cream and Birmingham's Miss Monneypenny's, for whom he mixed 1998's **Too Glamorous** compilation.

⊙ Massive #1   AU Records, 1998

Park's mix-tapes became fought after tooth and nail in the mid-'90s and this smooth blend of 1998's best vocal anthems and disco-charged dubs proves why.

Terence Parker

S ince 1988 Terence Parker has emerged from Detroit to establish himself as a consistently influential House producer. Despite the Motor City's urban blight, Parker's music has always remained resolutely optimistic, characterised by his trademark sound of relentless, pounding pianos and blissed-out strings.

It was the emerging electro-disco scene of the mid-'80s, epitomised by the likes of D-Train and Sharon Redd, and heralded by local turntable hero-figure Ken Collier, that turned Parker – initially a hip-hop DJ – onto the endless possibilities of electronica. In 1988 he teamed up with friends Mark Kinchen and Lou Robinson as Separate Minds and gained early success with the raw emotive Techno of "We Need Somebody". But the band soon split, and while MK went on to achieve world-wide solo success, Parker was left high and dry for over three years before finally releasing his debut **TP1** EP in 1992.

He quickly made up for lost time, though, with a succession of well-received singles for both 430 West and Kevin Saunderson's KMS label (most impressively with the sweeping soulful grooves of "Hold On" and the dynamic disco-driven "I Wanna Get 'Cha") under pseudonyms as strange as Disciples of Jovan Blade, Madd Phlavor and Lost Articles.

But it was only with his piano-fuelled 1993 UK club smash "The Question" (under his Seven Grand Housing Authority moniker) that Parker's music crossed over to a wider audience. Built over a sample from Kenny "Dope" Gonzalez's "Axis Project", the track was broken by Tony Humphries at Liverpool's Cream club, and quickly picked up by Olympic Records in the UK.

Since then he has set up his own imprint, Intangible, releasing "I Wanna Go Higher", "Jessica" and "Love's Got Me High", as well as recruiting Kenny Dixon Jr to the fold in 1996 with his excellent "Emotional Content" debut.

In 1996 Parker released his debut album, **Tragedies of a Plastic Soul Junkie**, on Berlin's Studio K7 label. Often accused of diluting the quality of his work across far too many similar productions, here he made brave and often brilliant excursions into evocative, downtempo jazz and soul-drenched soundscapes alongside the more familiar piano-filled territory. The move down a gear was fully realised a year later on his follow-up long-player where only three of the eight tracks featured a four-to-the-floor backbone. Unlike its predecessor, **Detroit After Dark** (1997) smacked of self-indulgence, and was saved only by the inspirational "Once I Was Lost" and the incisive, disco-inflected "You Can Do It" which proved that Parker could still produce incredible, emotional House music.

◉ Seven Grand Housing Authority   Studio K7, 1997

Pounding piano-driven anthems from start to finish; includes the singles "The Question", "Love's Got Me High" and "Jessica".

Philadelphia International

In the mid-'60s Kenny Gamble and Leon Huff's Gamble and Neptune labels were the crosstown rivals to Jesse James' Philadelphia-based Cameo-Parkway labels. After such proto-funk hits as The Fantastic Johnny C's "Boogaloo Down Broadway" (1967) and Cliff Nobles & Co.'s "The Horse" (1968), however, most of James' studio musicians defected to his rivals, thus laying the foundation for the second most successful black-owned label in US history.

Gamble and Neptune had huge hits with the Soul Survivors' "Expressway to Your Heart" (1967) and The Intruders' "Cowboys to Girls" (1968), but Gamble and Huff's most successful records were their productions for former Impressions singer Jerry Butler. "Never Give You Up" (1968) hit the American Top 20 on the strength of an ornate arrangement that would become the hallmark of Gamble and

Huff's Philadelphia International sound, but their biggest hit was the following year's "Only the Strong Survive" which reached #4. The arrangement – soaring strings, clean blues-based guitar, pinpoint instrumental definition, a bass-line lifted from Fontella Bass' "Rescue Me" – and the sermonising vocal would become the Philly International formula when the label was established two years later after Leonard Chess, who distributed Neptune, died.

PI's first record was The Ebonys' "You're the Reason Why" (1971) which became the model for later soft soul records by The Stylistics and The Delfonics, but the label truly established itself with one of the greatest singles of the decade, The O'Jays' "Back Stabbers" (1972). With a luscious arrangement that never destroyed the fierce Latin-tinged groove of bassist Ronnie Baker and drummer Earl Young, "Back Stabbers" was perhaps the best of a series of songs that explored and interrogated the stereotypes of black masculinity in the early '70s. "Back Stabbers" reached #3 on the American chart and its follow-up, "Love Train (1973)", did two better. Both songs were on the stunning **Back Stabbers** (1972) which, along with albums by Sly Stone, Marvin Gaye and Stevie Wonder, began the new market for black albums.

It was a development that dovetailed perfectly with the emergence of a new African-American middle class and Gamble and Huff directed their records directly at this market. Capitalising on new recording technology, Gamble and Huff created lush arrangements at the Sigma Sound Studio that were aimed at the new, hi-tech home stereo systems, just as Motown had arranged their records with the terrible fidelity of the car stereo in mind. The hits didn't stop with The O'Jays: Billy Paul's "Me and Mrs Jones" (1972) and MFSB's (the label's House band) "TSOP (The Sound of Philadelphia)" (1974) both hit #1, while The Three Degrees, Lou Rawls and Harold Melvin & the Blue Notes all broke the Top 5.

While the vocalists got most of the attention, it was MFSB that changed the course of music. On uptempo numbers like "Love Train" and Harold Melvin & the Blue Notes' "The Love I Lost" (1973), Baker, Young, pianist Bobby Martin and guitarist Norman Harris streamlined the groove of funk into a four-square rhythm that was a favourite with the dancers at New York's gay night clubs. The song that epitomised the new disco aesthetic was MFSB's "Love Is the Message" (1974). With melodramatic organs, soaring strings, one of the most propulsive bass-lines ever and a Fender Rhodes riff that would make even Mary Whitehouse squeal with delight, "Love Is the Message" encapsulated the groove, sweeping emotion and seedy underbelly of nightlife so successfully that it still gets played in New York clubs. That and the fact that every garage track ever has stolen from it in one way or another.

Other Philly International underground hits included Teddy Pendergrass' musky "You Can't Hide From Yourself" (1976) which was turned into "You Can't Hide From Your Bud" by DJ Sneak and Dexter Wansel's Afronautic expedition into outer space, **Life on Mars** (1976). Wansel became the label's in-House producer after Baker, Young and Harris left to anchor the House band at the Salsoul label and further define the disco sound. Despite some moderate hits with Jean Carn and the Jones Girls, Wansel was unable to capture the label's early glory and it closed down in the early '80s.

**◉ The Philly Sound: Kenny Gamble,
Leon Huff & the Story of Brotherly Love**   Sony, 1997

Absolutely essential three-disc collection of the best of Philly
International and Gamble & Huff's outside productions.

Phuture

Earl "Spanky" Smith and Herb Jackson were enraptured with the sound cranked out of the underground scene in Chicago and by DJs Frankie Knuckles at the Powerplant and Ron Hardy at the Music Box. When they hooked up with Nathaniel Jones, who went by the name of DJ Pierre, and started a group, a brilliant fluke took place that would have incredible effect.

That fluke involved a bass synth, the Roland TB303. Its unique feature was its ability to pitch-shift tones as they happened, so no note was ever stable for its duration. When Pierre started pushing the modulation all over the place he found the sound which formed the basis of "Acid Tracks" (1987) and, subsequently, the whole Acid movement. Forming these sounds into patterns over a slow, hard pulse, they took a tape to Ron Hardy and asked him to play it. The crowd's initial bemusement gave way to euphoria, and this untitled piece became the talk of the scene. Using Marshall Jefferson as producer, the group went into the studio and turned the tape into a finished article.

Phuture's early association with the legendary Trax label saw them unvalued; European labels didn't license their records, but released them anyway, and they were left in the wilderness. Their time with Strictly Rhythm was perhaps their most stable period, but in those early days they lost Herb Jackson to family life (after "We Are Phuture"), and DJ Pierre to the wild-pitch sound he pioneered on his early Photon Inc. singles, "Generate Power" (1991) and "Everybody Freedom".

These amicable departures led to Damon "Professor Trax" Nelms and Roy Davis Jr. hooking up with Spanky. This team produced its own wild-pitch classic, "Inside Out" (1993). Later DJ Skull, a Chicago Techno producer who put out the brilliant "Graveyard Orches-

earl spanky smith jr
ron dj skull maney
damon proffessor traxx neloms
roy davis jr

phuture303
alpha & omega

tra" on Djax Upbeats, joined the group, and the quartet worked on the album that would let them break away from the legacy of "Acid Tracks". **Alpha and Omega** was finally released on the tiny A1 records, only finding a UK release three years after its 1995 production.

The album didn't stop their personnel problems and Davis and Skull soon left to pursue their own burgeoning solo careers. In 1996 Spanky and Professor Trax were joined by LA Williams and the trio released "Acid Soul" on Djax that year.

⊙ Alpha and Omega   A1/ID&T,1998

Stunning "debut" some ten years after the group's conception. Includes perhaps the most unusual and original release the genre has produced, "Acid Tracks".

Mike Pickering

Although he is the brainchild behind M-People, DJ/producer/scenester Mike Pickering was also one of the first to introduce the sounds of Chicago House to the UK. From his Northern Soul roots, his career has spanned the entirety of the movement the Windy City's jackin' groove inspired.

Pickering began DJing at age 16, joined pop group Quango Quango as saxophonist where he made friends with New Order and positioned himself at the centre of Manchester's new wave rock scene through his role as rep for the band's label, Factory Records. Pickering booked The Smiths for their first Manchester gigs and signed baggy doyens The Happy Mondays and James to the imprint. Later, in his A&R role at Deconstruction Records, he would bring further chart success to acts like Black Box.

But it was as DJ at the Factory-owned Hacienda club that Pickering exerted a decisive influence on the course of House music in the North of England. Resident from 1984 to 1993, he was one of the first English DJs to champion the sound of Chicago's electronic pulse. Indeed, when he arrived to guest at London's Delirium club in 1987, crowds in the capital were so unused to hearing House that he was verbally abused in the DJ box for playing music associated with the gay scene.

From 1988 to 1990 he ran the inspirational Nude nights with DJ Graeme Park; their mix of House, rap, soul and funk was cited as the motivation for local acts like K Klass and DJs like Sasha. Whatever the case, Nude was at the epicentre of the Madchester scene that spawned The Happy Mondays, Stone Roses and Inspiral Carpets, as well as flarewearing, whistle-blowing and air-horn hammering. Once described by *The Face* as "England's most revered DJ", Mike Pickering was one of the main reasons why the Hacienda became such a legendary venue.

Pickering also produced one of the UK's first recognisable House records, "Carino" (1987), and would later provide Deconstruction with nearly all the material for its first label compilation, **North – The Sound Of The Dance Underground** (1988), which proved decisive in spreading the House gospel to a wider audience. He also produced the heavy-duty Acid "Nude Mix" of T.O.T's "What U R" (1991) with Grame Park, a tribute to the duo's famed club night. But having made his name at the forefront of the Acid explosion, Pickering has ensured his place in the musical history books by taking dance music to new commercial heights with his slick pop band, M-People.

Though about as far removed from the raw, energised groove of Chicago House that Pickering had helped push to the fore as a DJ, M-People (Paul Heard: keyboards, Heather Small: vocals, Shovel: percussion) have taken dance into the popular arena since forming in 1991, referencing Pickering's Northern Soul roots and enduring passion for disco along the way. Early singles like "Colour My Life" and "How Can I Love You More?" were aimed directly at the dancefloor, but also paved the way for things to come with their placings in the British Top 40. More chart success followed 1992's **Northern Soul**, a likeable collection of clichéd songs, with the singles, "Excited" and "One Night In Heaven" (1993). Appealing to "handbag" House dancefloors and housewives alike, the band's second album, **Elegant Slumming** (1993), even beat Blur to win the Mercury Music Prize. M-People continued to reference Pickering's club influences with singles like "Movin' On Up" and "Renaissance", the latter named after Geoff Oakes' celebrated Midlands nightspot.

Despite the fact that subsequent M-People albums have too frequently resorted to MOR pop and soul for their inspiration, the band's popular success across mainstream radio, concert halls and charts has arguably opened up new avenues for dance music and for that Pickering must take the ultimate credit.

⊙ Elegant Slumming   Deconstruction, 1993

The slick sound of an upwardly mobile fantasy world hardly makes for essential listening, though it does include the pop-dance favourites "Renaissance" and "Movin' On Up".

DJ Pierre

Nathaniel Jones (aka DJ Pierre) is a man constantly at war with the strict parameters of the House aesthetic. The genre's early moments revolve so much around his ideas that he becomes a symbol of its progress, and its under-rated radicalism.

As a young man who would hit upon the Acid squelch while messing with a Roland TB303, by 1987 Jones had already done enough to kick his name indelibly into the underground's canon. Those early days with Phuture saw Jones explore his own ideas with releases under the name Pierre's Phantasy Club for Trax Records. The excellent "Dream Girls" was a mash of screeching, hard funk mixed with horny daydreaming that created an atmosphere that recurred throughout his work. Behind all the beats was a tint of sexuality, the drone of the erogenous that set it apart from rave's asexuality. Pierre also recorded 1988's anthemic "String Free" (as Phortune), whose relentless, pounding piano prefigured the Italo-House explosion.

After his amicable split from Phuture, Jones went to New York and developed the sound that would become "wild-pitch": the stark noise of Acid House meeting the older principles of funk's horn and vocal cries. This meeting forged a sound full of ghosts that successfully diminished the boundaries between the recognisable and the bewilderingly abstract.

Jones' productions are unashamedly epic, demonstrating that epic dance records are not all sweeping string pads and cod-drum rolls, but come from an ability to move a crowd as one mass, to exhort with a sound that feels like heaven's armies. "Project Blast", a 1994 release on the Strictly Rhythm label, created that form of frenzy, forcing you to funk like a dervish.

"Wild-pitch" began with 1991's "Generate Power" (recorded as Photon Inc.) and its dark groove has resounded across the House community ever since. Even better was the apocalyptic "Everybody Freedom" (1992) which, in its way, was just as powerful as John Coltrane's free jazz epic, **Ascension**. During his prolific career Pierre has also recorded as Audio Clash, Joint Venture and Shock Wave and provided a blueprint for everyone from London's Farley & Heller to New York's DJ Duke, whose **Journey By DJ** mix (1994) is perhaps the definitive "wild-pitch" document. Despite heaps of critical praise, his most recent offering, "Horn Song" (1998), was disappointingly straight-forward.

⊙**Photon Inc: "Generate Power/Mind Bomb"**   Strictly Rhythm, 1991

The early works of Photon Inc. were a new start for House – an intense burst of sound, combining older principles with the mixer's power for fresh noise discoveries. "Generate Power" is where the pitch gets wild for the first time and "Mind Bomb" is an indicator of intent.

Jimi Polo

Chicago-raised producer Jimi Polo is one of those many names in House music's colossal library which probably means absolutely nothing to nearly everyone. However the instantly memorable, driving piano lick from his melodic House slate "Better Days" (1989) has cropped up on a host of commercially successful crossover dance hits ever since, most notably on 1991's happy hardcore anthem "40 Miles".

Polo had sung in gospel choirs as a boy, before becoming a musician in his teens. Though his first studio productions in 1985 heralded the breakthrough club hit "Shake Your Body", the inevitable royalty disputes led Polo to move to the UK where he joined Champion Records in the late '80s. Here he became involved with the nascent rave scene and hooked up with producer Adamski (Adam Tinley), who tinkled the ivories for "Better Days" and dedicated his 1990 **Live and Direct** album to Polo.

Polo's emotive gem "Never Goin' Down" was released in 1992, but with the offer of a major contract from Perfecto Records, further releases "Express Yourself" and **Moods** (1992) inevitably pursued a more traditional soul direction. He has since worked with producer Crispin J Glover and made guest appearances at clubs such as Paul "Trouble" Anderson's The Loft.

⊙ **"Better Days"**   Urban Records, 1989

Adamski's joyous piano hook and Polo's moving song combine to form a timeless slab of dancefloor perfection.

Ian Pooley

U nlike fellow German dance aficionados Sven Vath or Mousse T, Ian Pooley has combined the emotive influences of Detroit technicians Derrick May and Kevin Saunderson with a passion for Chicago's minimalist aesthetic and a love of disco to emerge as the country's most compelling House producer.

Pooley's mission to bridge the divide between the abstractions of Techno and the dancefloor ambition of House began in 1991 when he produced a series of well-regarded singles under the pseudonym Space Cube (with DJ Tonka) for Germany's Force Inc. label. Splitting from DJ Tonka in 1994 proved a good career move and Pooley's first two solo outings, the classic **Twin Gods** EP (1994) and the **Celtic Cross** EP (1995), carved out a more distinctively four-to-the-floor blueprint for his cool grooves to work against. His burgeoning underground reputation was solidified with 1995's bone-shaking "The Chord Memory" single. Produced for John Acquaviva's Definitive Records, the single preceded his eclectic debut album **The Times** (1995), which showcased his disco marginalism and sense of humour which had been evident on previous singles like "Rollerskate Disco" and "Relations Do".

By 1998, Pooley had been signed to Richard Branson's V2 dance label which established him as a new leading light. Rocking as hard on the dancefloor as on the home sound system, his critically lauded album **Meridien** (1998) was packed with intricate melodies and incisive drum patterns which spanned breakbeat soul ("What's Your Number?"), Deep House ("Followed") and angular Techno ("Cold Wait").

⊙ **Meridien**   V2, 1998

Strong melodies and irresistible grooves span downbeat to Deep House. A simplistic, futuristic and eclectic debut that owes more to the legacy of Munich-based disco deity Giorgio Moroder than to Germany's unit-shifting trancers like Sven Vath.

Prelude Records

While disco will probably always be associated in the popular imagination with tight white suits, feathered hair and the Bee Gees, the fact is that disco was just as good, and just as influential, as Kraftwerk. The good stuff was hidden away on small, independent New York labels like Salsoul, West End and Prelude. With mixes and production from three of the most legendary figures in dance music history – Larry Levan, François Kervorkian and Patrick Adams – Prelude was one of the links between disco and House. With the label's ground-breaking exploration of synthesizer technology in the early '80s, Prelude is an unjustly ignored ancestor of electro and Jungle's sub-bass sound.

Prelude was formed in 1977 and attained immediate dancefloor success with Musique's **Keep On Jumpin**' (1977). Produced by Patrick Adams, the album featured two of the most unashamedly propulsive singles ever released: "Keep on Jumpin'" and "In the Bush" which reached the British Top 20 in 1978 on the back of an even more electric François Kervorkian mix. Another (admittedly fairly lame) Adams production managed to dent the British Top 40 the same year, Sine's "Just Let Me Do My Thing", while Saturday Night Band's "Come On Dance, Dance" reached #16. The label's biggest American hit, France Joli's "Come to Me" (1979), proved that Prelude was just as guilty of churning out dross as the major-label charlatans.

Prelude's early releases were all more or less paint-by-numbers disco, but that changed with their last release of 1979, Inner Life's "I'm Caught Up (In a One Night Love Affair)". Produced by Adams and featuring vocals by the incomparable Jocelyn Brown, "I'm Caught Up"'s string-fuelled tale of the victim of a string of one-night stands became an enormous hit at Larry Levan's Paradise Garage where it struck a chord with the hordes of hedonists who assembled there every weekend. Levan, in turn, created one of dance music's most transcendent moments with his 1984 mix of Inner Life's version of "Ain't No Mountain High Enough" and its glorious synth arcs.

Towards the end of 1979 Prelude licensed Martin Circus' disco odyssey "Disco Circus" from a French label and created a club sensation. In its François Kervorkian edit, the track was an outlandish combination of slap bass, umpteen percussionists, handclaps, Moog riffs, he-man guitar solos, tribal chants, roller-rink horn charts, massive electric keyboard hooks, stereo panning, metronomic drumming, neat phasing, pre-Space Invaders sound FX, plunging strings and a barber shop quartet of Temptations and Meters imitators. Needless to say, the record was so fab that people like Carl Craig and Moodyman still play it today in their sets.

It was the advent of drum machines and synthesizers at Prelude that made it the dominant force in New York during the early '80s. A strong feature of both Shep Pettibone's Kiss FM Mastermixes and the radio station's regular programming, a remarkable number of Prelude records reached the American R&B charts purely on the strength of their sales in New York, whose air waves were ruled by Kiss at the time. Underground dance classics like Unlimited Touch's "I Hear Music in the Street" (1980), the kinetic Kervorkian mix of The Strikers' "Body Music" (1981), the proto-sub-bass of Gayle Adams' "Love Fever" (1981), Sharon Redd's "Beat the Street" (1982), Secret Weapon's "Must Be the Music" (1983), LAX's "All My Love" (1983), Tony Humphries' proto-House mix of Visual's "The Music Got Me" (1983) and Bobby Thurston's "Check Out the Groove" (1980) all hit the R&B chart at a time when disco was complete anathema to everyone outside of the Big Apple.

The track that epitomised Prelude's new sound was "D" Train's "You're the One For Me" (1982). With the funkiest synth bass-line in creation, phased handclaps and the greatest keyboard riff ever, "You're the One For Me" defined the sound of '80s funk and dance pop, but was never bettered. "D" Train's piano intro/synth riff blueprint was also used on what was probably the label's biggest hit, Jocelyn Brown's "Somebody Else's Guy" (1984). Following "Somebody Else's Guy", Prelude faded away after the Minneapolis mob of Prince, The Time and Jam & Lewis used the same basic principles to attain superstardom and hip-hop superseded disco as the sound of New York.

⊙ Absolutely... The Very Best of Prelude Records   Deepbeats, 1997

A couple of bad omissions, but still the best available overview of one of the best labels in the history of dance music.

⊙ Prelude Mastermixes Volume 1   Prelude, 1982

Hard to find, but essential, collection of François Kervorkian's mixes for the label. Includes the definitive versions of "In the Bush" and "Body Music".

Prescription Records

Since its earliest 12"s appeared, Prescription Records' roster has included some of the most influential artists in the genre, such as Ron Trent, Chez Damier, Romanthony, Derrick Carter, Roy Davis Jr and Glenn Underground.

Set up in 1993 by producers Ron Trent and Chez Damier to showcase their own and like-minded producers' Deep House slates, Prescription has consistently produced spiritual and timeless grooves. This is largely due to the duo's strict quality control and hands-on involvement (they co-produced every artist released on the label). Early tracks by Noni/D'Pac with Terence FM, "Be My/I Wouldn't", and Chuggles/Nagual, "Thank You/Feel The Rhythm" (both 1993), set an impressive precedent for future releases with their soft, intricate melodies and warm electronic pulses. Chez 'N' Trent's **Prescription Underground** EP fused Techno's angularity and House's rhythm with its distorted synth stabs and startlingly simple structure.

The trend continued in 1994 with the appearance of Abacus' twilight classic, the **Relics** EP. 1995 bore Romanthony's most emotive cut, "The Wanderer": a breathtaking blues-House tear-jerker. While Chez and Ron effortlessly crafted gems like "Come Together" and the **Foot Therapy** EP, other producers from outside the Windy City began to work with the label. Chez Damier and Leeds-based Back2Basics DJ Ralph Lawson produced the Ambient-disco of Chuggles' "Remember Dance", London's Roberto Mello, Zaki Dee and Luke Solomon dedicated "Space and Time/Prescription Every Night" to the label and A Man Called Adam produced a unique rendition of "Que Tal America?" with Larry Heard on the mix.

By this time Chez and Ron had also set up the Prescription offshoot Balance Recordings to focus on fresh talent and more experimental grooves. From its inception in 1994, it too has released a series of acclaimed singles including essentials such as the cutting-edge funk of Circulation's "Emotions Unknown" (1995) and "Memory Extempo" (1996), Frankie Valentine's **Tokyo Offshore** EP, Stacey Pullen's crystalline "Forever Monna" (1996) and Norma Jean Bell's "I Like the Things You Do to Me".

Unfortunately, just as Prescription Records seemed to be peaking, an acrimonious split between Trent and Damier threw the label's future into doubt. Reports suggested that Ron Trent and Larry Heard would join forces to keep the label going, but it remains hard to tell how constructive this partnership really was. Although 1996 bore Confusion

Kiddz's paranoid "Stresskill", Urban Sound Gallery's "The Dance" and Two Tribes' **War Song** EP (featuring Roy Davis Jr), things suddenly went quiet and from 1996 to 1998 Prescription's output almost completely dried up.

Ron Trent has since taken full control at the label, moving to NYC and releasing two imaginative deep instrumental EPs, **Soul Samba Express** and the Confusion Kiddz's **Remember Me** (both 1998). Since then, releases have continued to follow the label's familiar path of spiritual House, and are likely to continue to do so under the watchful eye of Trent.

⊙ The Collected Sounds of
Prescription   Prescription/Slip 'N' Slide, 1996

A good overview of the label which includes Romanthony's "The Wanderer", Ron Trent's "I Feel Rhythm", Abacus' "Come On", Ani's "Love Is the Message" and Heaven & Earth's "Space & Time".

Jamie Principle

O ne of Chicago's most under-valued musicians, Byron Walton (aka Jamie Principle) had originally wanted to be a doctor, but learning to play the drums and clarinet at his local church changed all that. Inspired by both religion and the electronic adventures of David Bowie, Depeche Mode, Human League and, most importantly, Prince, he began recording his own deeply personal songs on tape at home at the turn of the decade. A shy, self-effacing character, Principle's combination of sensous, strong lyrics with haunting, electro-pop keyboard melodies and an innate sense of raw funk produced two of the era's earliest and most inspirational House anthems, "Baby Wants to Ride" and "Your Love". Although these set a precedent for so much of what would follow, Principle's career has never come close to reaching its potential.

Originally Principle had no ambition to see his songs pressed up, and it wasn't until a friend suggested he should take them to Frankie Knuckles to play at the city's Powerplant club in 1984 that they were even heard by a wider audience. In the midst of the New York disco, Philly classics and vocal soul that Knuckles would spin, "Your Love" sounded like it had been beamed down from another planet. Principle's tale of love-torn angst, sung in his typically melancholy, high-register voice, eased over the track's languid bass-line and uplifting synth chords to become the ultimate spiritual anthem at the club. Underpinned by the drum kicks of Knuckles' Roland TR808 machine, it became one of the first recognised "House" recordings to emerge from Chicago. "Your Love"'s devotional overtones were taken to new levels when DJs spliced the single with Martin Luther King's "I Have a Dream" speech to transcend the dancefloor.

"Baby Wants to Ride" proved equally influential for the UK's Acid explosion, and also marked Principle out as a unique songwriter. Opening with a prayer, the ambiguous religious-sexual nature of God's "coming" led into the tale of Principle's encounter with a dominatrix. Just to prove all dance music critics wrong, Principle then added politics to the mix, dismissing America as a "bullshit land" and urging South Africa to set his people free. Like similar messages delivered by Sterling Void ("It's Alright") and Ce Ce Rodgers ("Someday"), Prinicple's tracks captured the spiritualism of the moment in Chicago.

Unfortunately, Principle's recordings never made it onto vinyl until the late '80s. Even when they appeared in 1989, Knuckles took much of the credit for his role in their production. To add insult to injury, when The Source covered "Your Love" in the early '90s they reached #2 in the UK charts.

Following the club success of "Rebels" (1990) in the UK, Principle forged a more commercially orientated partnership with Steve "Silk" Hurley. Though this partnership yielded three emotive singles ("Cold World", "You're All I've Waited 4" and the Italo-House favourite "Date With the Rain"), it culminated in 1991's lacklustre **Midnight Hour** album. A polished production which many felt hardly showcased his strongest assets, the album flopped at the cash register, leaving Principle's career effectively in ruins.

◉ "Your Love/Baby Wants to Ride"   Trax, 1989

Two unique records that set so many of House music's precedents. Though they may now sound slightly dated, Principle's semi-nihilistic vocals, melancholy lyrics and hi-NRG vs electro-pop melodies proved inspirational in both Chicago's musical revolution and England's Acid explosion. Both are available on **The House That Trax Built**.

DJ Q

Paul Flynn (aka DJ Q) has become one of the most compelling producers to have emerged on the scene in recent years, and one whose youth is met by a maturity in approach which sets his records apart from the glut of tracks hitting the market every week. Growing up in the Glasgow district of Cranhill, Flynn's earliest connection with music was the pioneering hip-hop of Public Enemy and Eric B & Rakim, but, as with so many others, it was the initial contact with the sounds emanating from Chicago and Detroit which were to prove pivotal in his development.

In 1992 Flynn heard Derrick May play in Edinburgh, and tracks he played by Lil' Louis, Inner City and others helped invigorate him to use his growing deck skills on a local pirate radio station which led to residency at Industria.

Those experiences inevitably led to production, and after his cuts for Gemini Records (**East End Tracks**), Glasgow Underground (**Porn King** EP) and Go Beat! (**Landing on a Planet Near You** EP), Flynn signed to London-based Filter Records to release possibly his best track thus far, "We Are One". The club-culture poetry of fellow Sub Club acolyte Willie Hall merged into a deep groove, everything fading in and out of focus.

"We Are One" exemplifies the character of Flynn's productions: heavy bass-lines, deeper and further forward in the mix than normal, played against layers of synth and horn sounds. On his debut album, **Face the Music** (1997), this technique is worked through to varying degrees of success. Superficially, it may resemble the approach of modern jazz-funk fusion and has drawn comparisons to Glenn Underground. But where Underground kept the beats streamlined while throwing fat disco licks in your face, Q worked the other way round, grinding you with the bass while the horn and synth stay out of reach, buried in echo.

○ Face the Music   Filter/Dorado, 1997

An assured debut which highlights Flynn's particular taste in full-blooded funk mixed with cool jazz and warm synth stabs. Standouts are the excellent "We Are One" and the manifesto, "Glasgow Jazz".

Danny Rampling

An immensely popular DJ and radio broadcaster, Danny Rampling began spinning in Bermondsey pubs at the age of 18 and soon established himself DJing alongside Kiss FM founder Gordon Mac. A fully paid-up member of the South London soul mafia who regularly played at friend Nicky Holloway's gigs, Rampling soon found his niche with uplifting good-time tunes and was given his own weekly show.

Yet it was a legendary trip to Ibiza in 1987 with soon-to-be Acid House forerunners Paul Oakenfold, Nicky Holloway and funk DJ Johnny Walker which provided the momentum to kick-start his career. Hearing the white island's DJ Alfredo mix up soul, reggae, pop and

early Chicago tracks on the dancefloor of Amnesia, together with the use of Ecstasy at the club, sparked the match that would ignite Rampling's subsequent success.

Returning to London, he and his soon-to-be wife Jenni launched Shoom (said to be named after the sensation felt on the initial rush of Ecstasy) in November 1987 in the Fitness Centre gym near Southwark Bridge, South London. At the time, Danny Rampling's eclectic mix of upbeat pop and dance with Chicago trax by the likes of Marshall Jefferson, Larry Heard and Frankie Knuckles (whose production of the Nightwriters' "Let the Music Use You" was undoubtedly one of Shoom's most celebrated anthems) helped ferment a scene which helped foster the Acid House club explosion.

From 1990 to 1991 Rampling also made his mark as a remixer. His more memorable efforts included a cover of Timmy Thomas' soul standard "Why Can't We Live Together" by Illusion (1990), Hypnotone's "Dream Beam" (1990), The Beloved's "The Sun Rising" (1991) and Love Corporation's "Palatial" (1991). Rampling made his debut as a producer in 1990 with "I Hate Hate", a reworking of the '70s soul ballad with vocalist Steven Eusabe, credited to the Sound of Shoom. At the same time the Ramplings began another hugely influential London club night, this time at Nicky Holloway's Milk Bar venue in Soho. From 1990 until 1992, first Pure Sexy then Glam emerged as the forerunners of all the sex-themed nights that would subsequently dominate UK clubland.

In 1993 Rampling joined the books of Manchester's Deconstruction label, launching a group called the Millionaire Hippies with upbeat singles such as "I Am the Music, Feel Me". Radio One eventually pinched Rampling from Kiss FM in November 1994 as a natural companion to Pete Tong. In 1998 he signed with French label Distance and released the female vocal track "Community of the Spirit".

⊙ Journeys By DJ Volume 3 JDJ,1992

Typically energised and broad musical mix featuring tracks by Cajmere, Martha Wash, Jaydee and Alison Limerick, whose anthemic "Where Love Lives" Rampling helped push into the limelight.

Peter Rauhoffer

Peter Rauhoffer is best known for wrecking dancefloors with his ultra-camp, disco-fired, NYC nightlife-styled pseudonyms, Club 69 and Size Queen. Hallmarked by their propulsive Euro bass-lines and gay themes, Rauhoffer's vocal and tribal tracks have picked up club play since 1991's booty-shaking "Unique" (as Danube Dance).

As Club 69, his implausibly sensual "Let Me Be Your Underwear" (1992) hit the dance charts on both sides of the Atlantic after being a summer cult classic in Ibiza. Harnessing disco's lush harmonics to quirky, wanton lyrics and a pop-dance dynamic, Club 69's **Adults Only** (1995) yielded dancefloor vocal grooves like "Diva", "Sugar Pie Guy" and the MSFB homage "Love Is The Message".

One of the many New York-based DJs/producers to be heavily influenced by the tribal rhythms of Junior Vasquez's Sound Factory club, Rauhoffer's fiercer records as Size Queen included 1996's sharp-tongued, super-drag anthem "Walk" which perfectly encapsulated the city's gay aesthetic. Merging sex-fuelled wit with pounding beats on singles like "Horny" and "The Trick", Size Queen tracks also crossed over to become popular amongst UK DJs like Pete Heller and at clubs like London's Trade. In turn, **Pimps, Pumps and Pushers** (1997) earned him the most media attention he'd had since "Let Me Be Your Underwear". This continued with pumped-up, sleazy re-versionings for Funky Green Dogs ("Fired Up"), Depeche Mode ("It's No Good") and Kevin Aviance ("Din Da Da") which all reached the #1 spot on the *Billboard* club chart. Many of his remixes were collected on **Club 69 (Future Mix)**.

Marking himself out as a diverse talent, Club 69's follow-up album, the garage-pop hybrid **Style** (1997), eschewed any minimalist pretensions in favour of a collection of upbeat, glittering vocal cuts, most effectively on the piano-heavy "Much Better" and the Roland Clark cover "Alright". Alongside Danny Tenaglia, Rauhoffer has carved out the sound of Twisted NYC and

arguably become the one producer who has captured the sound of the Big Apple's gay nightlife scene in the wake of the Sound Factory's demise.

⊙ Pimps, Pumps and Pushers   Twisted, 1997

From the drug reference of "K Hole" to bad-ass grooves of "Horny" and "Music", this is the sound of sleazy downtown Manhattan dancefloors.

Raze

While Washington DC's dance music scene has been dominated in the '90s by Deep Dish, the city's most important contribution to House, Raze's "Break 4 Love" (1988), was the brainchild of producer Vaughan Mason. Mason had previously produced one of the first roller-skating disco grooves, "Bounce Rock Skate Roll" (1980), but he had put that lapse in taste well behind him by the mid-'80s. 1986's simply constructed "Jack the Groove" was one of the first records to employ the word "jack" in its title and its nagging refrain reached the Top 10 in the UK in 1987.

Mason then linked up with vocalist Keith Thompson and, as Raze, produced garage-style club hits like "Let the Music Move U" (1987). It was 1988's monumental "Break 4 Love", though, which assured Mason's name in history. Eventually selling over a million copies worldwide and spawning an infectious slowed-down 4/4 groove for a spectrum of artists to pirate, "Break 4 Love" remains a standout with its addictive piano hook and Thompson's sensual vocals.

Though Mason followed up with "Ready 4 Love" (1989) and New Jersey-style tracks such as "Don't Give Up" (1989) for his own Groove Street label, his only other point of note was 1989's Hip-House classic "Let It Roll", with rapper Doug Lazy.

◉ "Break 4 Love"   Champion Records, 1988

Sensual House music that gets hot and sweaty thanks to Mason's girlfriend. Available on **Classic House Volume 1** (Beechwood Music, 1994).

Relief Records

I n the early days there were just tracks – raw, rough, four-to-the-floor pounding rhythms, eased only by the occasional sample or inspired vocal. But House's progression and diversification meant it had to come full circle in its native Chicago to bring forth a fresh, new generation of producers. Pressing up a seemingly endless supply of incredible, bad-ass, dirty disco-boogie cuts in the mid-'90s, it was first and foremost Relief Records who re-created and re-defined the House that jack built. Formed in 1993 by producer Curtis Jones (aka Cajmere), only 18 months after he had started the already fairly successful, if sporadic, Cajual Records, Relief was originally intended as an outlet for harder, more experimental tech-House tracks.

The insane but brilliant "Preacher Man" (1993), the label's first release from Jones under his Green Velvet guise, set the fierce, cutting-edge tone that would define the majority of its output. A screaming evangelist talking about his adult congregation's sins sequenced over sledgehammer beats and cut-up boogie bass-lines, "Preacher Man" was startlingly original.

Relief attracted a stream of new, like-minded, innovative kids who had no outlets for their music, many of whom now form the backbone of the current Chicago House music scene. A young Gemini was one of the first, releasing the sweeping, soulful grooves of "Klonopin" (1994). Boo Williams followed suit with the underground club smashes "Midnight Express" and "New Beginning" (both 1995), as did Gene Farris and the lesser-known Lester Fitzpatrick with the mesmerising singles "Farris Wheel" and "Frantic Frenzy" (both 1996) respectively.

Perhaps the two greatest talents to step out from the Relief stable were DJ Sneak, a young, Puerto Rican DJ, recruited from his day job behind the counter at Chicago's Gramophone Records, and Glenn

Underground, a spiritual, disco-obsessed studio-head who looked like he'd only just stepped off the set of a '70s blaxploitation flick. With albums **The Blue Funk Files** and **Rice & Beans, Please** (both 1996), DJ Sneak carved up the world's dancefloors with his irresistible, aggressive funk-fuelled instrumentals, and clearly helped inspire acts like Daft Punk and Basement Jaxx with his innovative, excessive use of FX, percussion and vocals sequenced over minimalist beats. On the flipside, Glenn Underground pioneered Relief's disco renaissance with unrelenting samples subtly lifted from Chic and Herb Alpert coupled with ruff rhythms and deep atmospherics.

After 1996 though, the label's influence faded as imitators sprang up everywhere and its once prolific output dwindled. Despite the increased competition and the inevitable development of the artists Relief made famous, the label still found time to electrify House heads the world over with 1997 and 1998 releases from Green Velvet, Sneak & Armand Van Helden and Paul Johnson. Sadly, in 1998 Relief was declared bankrupt, adding its name to the list of seminal Chicago labels that have passed before.

⊙ **Expanding Upon the House That Jack Built**   Relief, 1995

A selection of inspired, bad-ass trax by the leaders of the Chicago nu-skool from the label that re-defined the city's original blueprint.

Justin Robertson

DJ, remixer, producer, songwriter and recording artist, Justin Robertson was born and raised in Buckinghamshire, but his name will forever be associated with the city of Manchester. Robertson began his career as a DJ while studying philosophy at Manchester University, playing parties largely because people judged him the person with the best record collection. Many of Robertson's records were purchases from the city's legendary dance specialist, Eastern Bloc, and once he'd completed his degree, he started working in the shop. A regular at Mike Pickering's nights at the Hacienda, as well as at less salubrious scally raves like Konspiracy and Thunderdome, Robertson was well placed to fully participate in the Acid House boom. Through contacts made at Eastern Bloc, he quickly found himself booked as a regular DJ at Konspiracy and was one of the first wave of DJs to take the ideas of Acieeed pioneers Paul Oakenfold and Danny Rampling to an audience beyond London.

From Konspiracy, Robertson started his own night, Spice, with fellow Eastern Bloc employee Greg Fenton, in 1990. An underground success, Robertson's profile was further raised by his next club, Most Excellent. A forerunner to the eclectic policies of London's Heavenly Social (which itself precipitated the Big Beat boom and clubs like the Big Beat Boutique and Big Kahuna Burger), Most Excellent attracted a faithful crowd, many of whom would later go on to achieve similar fame – Darren Hughes (who cites the club as an inspiration to start Cream), The Chemical Brothers, Noel Gallagher and 808 State. From the first Most Excellent night (a Happy Mondays after-show party) in 1991 until its close in 1993, Robertson showed that Acid House records could be played alongside rock, reggae and ska tunes, and people would still dance.

His next club, the Rebellious Jukebox, saw Robertson pushing his interest in Northern Soul, Studio 1 and Curtis Mayfield to the fore. Though his first remix was undertaken while at Eastern Bloc (Mad Jacks' "Feel The Hit", for Eastern Bloc's Creed operation), his popularity as a remixer grew alongside his demand as a DJ, with bookings

taking him around the country playing alongside Andrew Weatherall, Darren Emerson and Dean Thatcher, and abroad, DJing for Primal Scream. A prolific worker, Robertson's mixes included work for Finitribe ("Forevergreen"), React 2 Rhythm ("Intoxication"), Sugarcubes ("Birthday") and the unfortunate Candy Flip ("Red Hills Road"). In 1993 he was awarded Remixer Of The Year.

Robertson's next step, however, was to record his own music under the moniker Lionrock. His first eponymous single was released on Deconstruction in November 1992 and showcased a heavy reggae influence, before 1993's "Packet Of Peace" – featuring vocals from MC Buzz B – gained him chart success. Further hits followed with "Carnival" (which sampled the MC5) and "Tripwire". Robertson translated Lionrock into a live band (with studio wizard and one-time Simply Red programmer Roger Lyons, MC Buzz B, keyboard player Mandy Wigby and bassist Paddy Steer) and, in 1996, released a debut LP, the Sherlock Holmes-inspired **An Instinct For Detection**, which fused Techno with ragga and ska dynamics.

A second album, **City Delirious**, eventually surfaced in March 1998. The album was less guitar-based and more Techno-powered than the original version which had been mailed out to journalists the year before. It was preceded by his biggest hit to date, the ska-aping "Rude Boy Rock" (1998). Intending it as a soundtrack and tribute to the city of Manchester, Robertson says of **City Delirious**: "I try to make music that's quite descriptive. A lot of dance music is very functional, which is fine, but I wanted to make this album about something. For me, anyway."

⦿ City Delirious   Concrete, 1998

With nods to electro, ska artist Derrick Morgan, John Barry, Duane Eddy, Kraftwerk and Kevin Yost, this is a fine summation of Lionrock's polymorphously perverse influences.

Romanthony

While New Jersey producer Romanthony (aka Anthony Moore) bears a striking resemblance to Prince when he sings and takes his cues from blues, gospel and soul, no one else comes close to capturing his vision of House. His debut album, **Romanworld** (1996), was an acclaimed masterpiece, crammed with invigorating funk basslines, beautiful electronic melodies and compulsive, minimalist grooves. Yet he has never made a public appearance, has only given two phone interviews to date, refuses to even give his telephone number to his record company and remains a complete mystery to almost everyone.

His first track to draw attention appeared on his own Blackmale Records label in 1993. A raw, purposefully under-produced, electric funk groove welded to Moore's extraordinary vocals and female backing harmonies, "Testify" immediately stood out from the glut of processed New Jersey garage cuts. Romanthony confirmed his promise with the quirky "Fall From Grace" (1993) and "Make This Love Right/Now You Want Me" (1993) which proved him capable of both compelling vocal projections and fierce dub workouts. 1994's "Da Change/Hold On" was even more emotive, employing samples of Black Power activists sequenced over live funk and locked rythms. Paying his dues to the influential Tony Humphries, Romanthony

ROMANWORLD | ROMANTHONY

released the frantic disco cut-up "In the Mix (Tribute To Tony Humphries)", and the more solid "Ministry of Love" (both 1994).

1995 marked a shift back to producing more experimental tracks for his Blackmale label, New York's Downtown 161 imprint and Chicago's Prescription Records. While cuts like "Bring You

Up/The Dayz" and "Trust" were well received, arguably he produced his best single for Prescription. "The Wanderer" was perhaps his least dance-floor-friendly release, but its gorgeous blues-inflected melodies, heart-wrenching melancholy lyrics and his vocals have cemented its place as a modern classic.

Despite reports that the perfectionist Romanthony had attempted to halt its release, 1996 saw the release of **Romanworld**, a work of '90s soul that comes closer to matching the genre's true grit and passion than most of what sadly passes for "soulful music".

After a long hiatus, Romanthony's 1998 singles, "Do You Think You Can Love Me", "Up All Night" (released on his new label, World Records) and "Buzz 'N' Da Speaker", although not spectacular by his standards, have confirmed his future as one of House's most gifted producers.

⊙ "The Wanderer" Prescription, 1995

An acoustic guitar-led torch ballad to tear your heart out. The most beautiful song Romanthony has made yet, even if you can't dance to it. Available on **The Collected Sounds of Prescription** (Prescription/Slip 'N' Slide, 1996).

⊙ Romanworld Azuli, 1996

One of House music's most original albums from one of its most original producers. It's all here: the incredible funk bass-lines, the minimalist under-production, the gorgeous cutting guitar riffs, the gospel samples, the Prince-like vocals and the spiritualism.

Ralphi Rosario

Ralphi Rosario first came to prominence as a member of Chicago radio team the Hot Mix Five, who played on Farley "Jackmaster" Funk's show on WBMX 102.7 FM. The Hot Mix Five formed in 1981 with the original line-up of Ralphi Rosario, Steve Hurley, Mickey Oliver, Mario Diaz and Scott Seals (who was later replaced by Edward Crosby and then Julian Perez).

It is this quintet who are largely credited for bringing House music to the citizens of Chicago and their on-air support was instrumental in determining which singles would be a local success (see hits of the era like Jesse Saunders' "On & On 117" or Marshall Jefferson's "Move Your Body"). In 1986, they formed their own Hot Mix Five record label, and Rosario quickly became known for his record, "Puerto Rican Lover", on which he sang his own bilingual lyrics.

But Rosario is, and perhaps always will be, best known for his 1987 anthem, "You Used to Hold Me", which was co-produced by Kenny Jason, released on Hot Mix Five and featured the vocals of Xaviera Gold, who unfortunately would never really be heard from again. He would team up with three other producers that same year to produce another classic House track, 2 Puerto Ricans, a Blackman and a Dominican's "Do It Properly". The 2 Puerto Ricans were David Morales and Ralphi Rosario, the Blackman was Robert Cole and the Dominican, Robert Clivilles. Largely reminiscent of Adonis' 1986 hit "No Way Back", it foreshadowed the type of heavily sample-based records that would emerge from New York City and in the later career of Clivilles and Cole's own C&C Music Factory project.

Ralphi Rosario has laid low since the days of "You Used to Hold Me". In the mid-'90s some of his tracks began to capture the ruling tribal vibe of the times, picking up attention for his tight programming on singles like the **Energy Factor** EP (1994) and **Sexual Factor** EP (1995), both recorded for Stateside label UC Music. Two of the more noticeable 12"s released since then have been 1997's "Take Me Up" and the after-hours vibes of 1998's "Chicago's Most Wanted", released on London's Jus Trax imprint. His remix credits include Deee-Lite, INXS, Pet Shop Boys, The Shamen and Pump Friction (remixing "That Sound", which would bring the King Street label their first *Billboard* dance #1).

1998 saw the release of "Strings of Life" on Nitegrooves, a subsidiary of King Street, which reached #4 on *Billboard*'s National Dance chart. The secret of that single was its b-side, "Funk It", a fierce, New York "bitch"-styled track (banging drums, sharp programming, voice repeating "you better work, baby").

○ "You Used To Hold Me"   Hot Mix Five, 1987

Rosario's signature anthem. No other female vocal track commanded quite as much respect and it has endured through time. Available on **Classic House Volume 1** (Beechwood, 1994).

Erik Rug

Though less well known than most of his Paris-based House contemporaries, DJ and producer Erik Rug has played an equally important role in providing a basis for dance music to flourish in the French capital.

Alongside DJ Laurent Garnier, Rug first brought House music to Paris in 1988. The duo's weekly H²0, based at the city's rock club La Locomotive, was the sole venue where pioneering Chicago cuts by the likes of DJ Pierre, Steve "Silk" Hurley and Marshall Jefferson could be heard. But as well as breaking the hedonistic, jackin' rhythms of Acid House into the notoriously conservative and fashion-obsessed Paris club scene, Rug has also made his presence felt on both radio and vinyl. From 1992 until 1996 he hosted the well-respected Waxgroove show on FG 98.2, until being poached by the biggest underground dance station, Radio Nova 101.5, for their key Saturday night show.

Having played bass with Latin-jazz-fusion band The Mirandas, Rug made his solo debut with 1991's "Black Planet" (under the guise of 2 Frenchmen). Although his series of three **Waxwork** EPs, released on the Toronto Underground label between 1992 and 1995, found their way into many discerning DJs' Deep House sets, it has been his releases under the monikers Dirty Jesus and Daphreefunkateerz that have garnered most attention. Combining his cultivated disco, funk, electro and techno influences, Dirty Jesus' **Cut a Rug** EP and "Don't Fuck With My Shit" (1996–97), recorded for Manchester's Paper Recordings, drew comparisions with the dirty, bottom-heavy vibe administered by Miami's Murk crew. The convoluted breaks and wired FX of his Daphreefunkateerz tracks ("Phree Phresh Phunk" and "1.2.3 Tonz of Phunk") and remixes have also hit hard on a spectrum of dancefloors, but can best be described in Rug's own words, "trash-funk-dub".

With the media frenzy over French House reaching fever pitch in 1997, Rug also provided several exclusive tracks for well-received compilations such as **Sourcelab Volume 3** (check Low Tone Priority's "What About Your Love") and **Future Sound of Paris 1 & 2** (Low Tone Priority's "Take You There" and Dirty Jesus' "Feed Food Theme" respectively). He also mixed Slip 'N' Slide's acclaimed **French Fried Funk** (1997) compilation, and remains one of Paris' premier House DJs alongside fellow old-timers Laurent Garnier and DJ Dimitri.

O **"Cut a Rug/Don't Fuck With My Shit"**

Deep, demented House minimalism from Paris. Available on Splinter (Paper, 1998).

S'Express

T he brainchild of flamboyant, '70s-obsessed DJ Mark Moore, S'Express achieved unprecedented success in the late '80s via a succession of neat Italian House/Europop hits. Moore began DJing at Phillip Salon's Mud Club in 1987, where he played rare groove, funk and hip-hop next to early House records. From there, he went on to DJ at Heaven alongside "Evil" Eddie Richards and Colin Favor.

International success came with the formation of S'Express, and the hits "Theme From S'Express" (their Rose Royce-sampling debut which reached #1 in April, 1988), "Hey, Music Lover" (#6) and the irresistible "Superfly Guy" (#5). With collaborators including core vocalists Linda Love, Michelle Ndrika and Chilo Eribenne, guest vocalists E-Mix and Electribe 101 chanteuse Billy Ray Martin, and rapper Merlin, a debut album for

Rhythm King, **Original Soundtrack** (1989), strengthened Moore's reputation and gave the collective both a club and pop following.

1992's follow-up, **Intercourse**, received a luke-warm reception though, despite the vocals of Sonique Clarke (who herself went on to acclaim as a DJ in the late '90s) on the singles "Nothing To Lose" (1990) and the Bobby Gentry cover "Find 'Em, Fool 'Em, Forget 'Em" (1991). Moore went on to set up his own label, Splish, worked as a remixer (Malcolm McLaren, Erasure, Seal) and set up another label, Stylofication. With his trademark mobile-DJ "telephone" headphones and customised JBL speakers, Moore has continued to DJ his self-confessed style of "annoying repetitive beats" at House clubs like Chuff Chuff, Sign of the Times and Gatecrasher. Moore's reputation as the original "pop star DJ" is undeniable – he even appeared in the BBC comedy series *French & Saunders*. A revised version of "Theme From S'Express", with a harder, faster edge, appeared in 1996 and reached #14 in the UK charts.

⊙ Original Soundtrack   Rhythm King, 1989

Undeniable good-time anthems from start to finish, Moore's disco and funk sensibilities are re-wired for dancefloor devastation on classic cuts like "Theme From S'Express", "Hey Music Lover" and "Superfly Guy". Essential for Afro-wig wearers and air-guitarists the world over.

Salsoul Records

F or all the "kitsch" and "tasteless" rhetoric surrounding disco, much of it was actually expertly crafted, soulful and innovative. While *Saturday Night Fever*, revolving mirror balls and the Bee Gees' high-pitched squeals may be most people's indelible memories of the era, the mid-'70s also heralded the birth of one of the greatest dance music labels of all time, Salsoul Records.

It was Salsoul who released the first commercially available 12", Double Exposure's "Ten Percent" (1976). Mixed by DJ/producer Walter Gibbons, the epic extension of a three-minute album track into a percussive-heavy musical soundscape in excess of nine minutes defined the future possibilities for DJ/club-influenced dance music. Salsoul's consistent support for new production talent – often acting as a filter for new studio/DJ techniques to cross over to vinyl – is evident in nearly all of its single releases, most of which showcase some of the finest mixes from talents like Tom Moulton, Larry Levan, Shep Pettibone, Walter Gibbons and Jim Burgess.

Salsoul's roots lie with early '70s Latin label Mericana Records. Formed and created by brothers Joe, Ken and Stan Cayre in 1973, Mericana released Afro-Filipino musician Joe Baatan's ground-breaking fusion of salsa and soul, "The Bottle" which featured on his ground-breaking album, **Salsoul** (1975). The record's underground club success persuaded Ken Cayre to pursue the blending of Latin/salsa-infused sounds with R&B, forming Salsoul Records (with its trademark rainbow-painted sleeves).

Salsoul's first release, "The Salsoul Hustle" (1975) by the Salsoul Orchestra, only reached number #44 on *Billboard*'s R&B chart, but led to **The Salsoul Orchestra** (1976). Containing gems like "You're Just the Right Size", "Bus Stop" (what would later become "Oooh, I Love It (Love Break)") and "Salsoul Rainbow", the album set the pattern for most of the label's releases. Similar to Philadelphia International's MFSB (and soon to feature many of the same musicians), Salsoul Orchestra's lush string arrangements and seriously funky bass-lines were unfortunately matched by a lack of mainstream commercial recognition.

Some of the label's greatest releases from artists like Loleatta Holloway, First Choice, Double Exposure and The Salsoul Orchestra have

provided the backbone to thousands of House records. Both Steve "Silk" Hurley and Frankie Knuckles forged club classics utilising the bass-line from First Choice's 1977 single, "Let No Man Put Asunder", Black Box hit the UK #1 spot with a wholesale lifting of Loleatta Holloway's "Love Sensation" and in 1997 Bobby D'Ambrosio stormed the clubs with his garage reworking of Inner Life's "Moment of My Life".

Though Salsoul closed its doors in 1985, by 1992 it had started up again, enthused by the world-wide success of House imitators, and subsequently embarked on an ambitious remix project which featured new reworkings like Hurley's mix of Aurra's "Just a Little Love", Tony Humphries' mix of Pressure Point's "Dreaming" and MAW's mix of Double Exposure's "Ten Percent". In England, Northern Soul fanatic/Mastercuts label compiler Ian Dewhirst linked up with the company to re-release a series of Salsoul compilations that helped bring long-overdue attention to the label which played such a central role in moving dance music forward.

◉ Classic Salsoul Volume 1 Mastercuts/Beechwood Music Ltd, 1993

A sublime selection of some of the finest dance songs from the greatest dance music label ever. Just a glance at the mixers – Walter Gibbons, Larry Levan, Tom Moulton, Shep Pettibone – tells its own story. Includes such essentials as First Choice's "Let No Man Put Asunder", Double Exposure's "Ten Percent", Loleatta Holloway's "Love Sensation", Instant Funk's "I Got My Mind Made Up" and Salsoul Orchestra's "Runaway". Every home should have one.

Roger Sanchez

The son of immigrants from the Dominican Republic, Roger Sanchez graduated from New York's High School of Art and Design to study architecture for four years. Although he ditched architecture to pursue DJing full-time, precision lines and solid foundations have rarely left his work.

After playing at clubs like the Tunnel, Sanchez first made his name with his pan-generic club, Ego Trip, which was a platform for his mix of House, disco, reggae and hip-hop. The name also served as the title of his first record in 1990 (released under the moniker Dreamworld), a minimal, after-hours 12" with distinct Techno overtones. Soon after, he used a similar style on the track that would launch both his and Strictly Rhythm's international trajectory. Underground Solution's "Luv Dancin'" (1990) may have sliced its melody straight from Loose Joints' "Is It All Over My Face?", but Sanchez gave the record an even more spaced-out feel with his crisp hi-hats, neat arrangement and subtle fade-outs.

Sanchez continued to produce for Strictly, varying his blueprint from the tribal "Old School House" (as DV8) to Beatboxx's dubby "Keep On Jumpin'". In 1991 he proved his credentials as a vocal producer with dancefloor-filling releases like Aly-Us' "Follow Me", Michael Watford's "Holdin' On" and, most significantly, Kathy Sledge's "Take Me Back to Love", a 12" which showcased a new ambitious and disco-driven style.

Sanchez set up his first label, One Records, in 1991, subsequently releasing singles by himself, Kenny "Dope" Gonzalez, Victor Simonelli and Murk's Oscar G. In 1994, the label released his series of sparse grooves, addictive melodies and killer DJ-tools, **Secret Weapons**. The same year, Sanchez began a second (and more successful) label, Narcotic Records. Narcotic became home to his devastating vocal productions of The Dreem Teem's "Brotherhood of Soul" which brought together Colonel Abrams and Michael Watford, and Kathy Sledge's "Love Is All You Need". A slightly less impressive follow-up, **Secret Weapons Volume 2** (1995), was nonetheless tempered by Sanchez's production work on albums by both Michael Watford and Kathy Sledge, with whom he provided 1996's Stevie Wonder cover, "Another Star".

With repetitive chants that epitomised the tribal groove layered over hypnotic, trance-like melodies, 1996's "Sumba Lumba", recorded as Tribal Infusion, was never likely to venture out from the underground, but it confirmed the S-Man's place as a truly unique technician. Since then Sanchez's productions have become even more varied. While his extensive remix work already included such gems as Incognito's "Givin' It Up" and The Police's "Voices In My Head", 1996 releases like El Mariachi's hugely popular but shamefully cheesy "Cuba" gave him commercial recognition. He has supported Janet Jackson as her tour DJ, as well as touring and recording with producers Junior Sanchez and DJ Sneak (Da Mongoloids). More aggressive drum programming and heavier bass-lines have followed on releases like 1998's storming "Got Funk" (as Funkjunkeez), broadening his appeal across both Deep House and more mainstream dancefloors.

⊙ **S-Man Classics** Harmless Records, 1997

If you only buy one Sanchez album, then make sure it's this one. This is
a must-have for the inclusion of Kathy Sledge's "Another Star",
Incognito's "Givin' It Up", Tribal Infusion's "Sumba Lumba" and, of
course, "Luv Dancin'".

◉ **House Music Movement – Roger Sanchez** Mastertone, 1998

The best representation of Sanchez the DJ: an expertly sequenced
selection of ruff grooves and heavy b-lines courtesy of cuts like "Got
Funk" and "The Potion" as well as S-Man remixes of DJ Sneak, Kings Of
Tomorrow and Sylk 130.

Sasha

Sasha (born Alexander Coe) started his DJing career with warm-
up slots in Manchester in 1989, forging an alternative sound to
the bleepy Techno served up by the majority of DJs. His interpretation
of hard and fast grooves, Italo House, acapellas and mesmerising
bass-lines saw him quickly advance to his first residency at Shelly's in
Stoke. The night etched itself into club folklore and revealed Sasha's
DJ skills to hundreds from around the country every week, leading to a
loyal and devoted following.

A few months later, Sasha's musical ripples had reached London
and he appeared on the cover of *Mixmag* as the first DJ pin-up (the
headline read "Son Of God"). In 1992 he joined the expanding club
empire of Renaissance as their resident alongside John Digweed, a
partnership that would blossom in future years. The move to Renaissance led to widespread popularity, first nationwide, then world-wide,

as he began to boost the reputations of clubs such as Ministry Of Sound and Cream in South America, Asia, Australia and beyond.

Sasha's recording career also began to take off in the early '90s with critically acclaimed remixes for Creative Thieves and Urban Soul. These were soon followed by his own collective called Bmex ("The Barry Manilow Experience"), whose hands-in-the-air, piano-driven "Appolonia" (1992) not only scored huge dancefloor success but helped set the precedent for so many epic and "progressive" House tunes to follow. Soon he was signed to Deconstruction, where he released two suprisingly commerical singles ("Higher Ground" and "To Be As One") that dented the lower reaches of the charts. Sasha left Renaissance in 1995 to concentrate on his recording career and a variety of one-off gigs.

In 1996 he teamed up with sometime collaborator and DJ partner John Digweed to release **Northern Exposure 1**. A mix CD straight from their building DJ set, it was more of a long, moving soundtrack to a club night than the traditional mish-mash of the flavours of the month. The album went on to sell over a quarter of a million records worldwide.

As a result, Sasha and John Digweed were the first ever UK DJs to land a residency at New York's Twilo club beginning in April 1997. A venue that became as much a part of the club legend as the Sound Factory, the duo's distinctively British sound was a breath of fresh air to New York's dance music cognoscenti.

Sasha's reputation as one of the best DJs in the world meant he was now much in demand as a remixer par excellence, and perhaps his most outstanding work of this period was Madonna's "Ray of Light" (1998). Other stars receiving the Sasha treatment have included Pet Shop Boys, Womack & Womack, Seal, Sounds Of Blackness, Orbital and M-People.

Although DJ dates for Sasha in the UK became rare as his other musical commitments increased, he wanted to go back to his musical roots, and started his own underground guerrilla parties under the moniker of Tyrant. These nights, which began in November 1997, enabled him to indulge in his first love, DJing, with spellbinding five-hour sets.

Sasha has also worked extensively with BT (Brian Transeau), most recently on a project for Peter Gabriel's Realworld label. In 1998, BT and Sasha went under the name Two Phat Cunts to record electro with "Ride", a 12" which was caned by the likes of Weatherall and Oakenfold. While continuing to spin around the world, Sasha found time to release a third installment of the **Northern Exposure** series in 1999 as well as a solo album for Deconstruction.

◉ Northern Exposure 1   Ministry Of Sound, 1996

Ambient-inflected soundscapes mixed to perfection by Messrs Sasha and Digweed.

Jesse Saunders

A lthough Jamie Principle was the first Chicago producer to have his House tracks played at the city's most important clubs, it was DJ/producer Jesse Saunders who produced the first recognisable House 12", "On & On 117" (1985). While none of his recordings since have stood the test of time, in 1985 Saunders' collection of raw, synthesised vinyl excursions paved the way for the likes of the greats like Marshall Jefferson, Adonis and DJ Pierre.

A DJ at the Playground club in the early '80s, Saunders was one of the Chicago deck technicians whose sets were characterised by the hip-hop-influenced styles of scratching and cut-and-paste mixing. Like Frankie Knuckles and Ron Hardy, Saunders' spinning looped the heavy kick drum patterns of his Roland TR808 machine over a selection of discofied 12"s. It was a combination of these traits which led to Saunders' monumental "On & On 117", created "live" by looping the Roland's analogue rhythms over a NYC bootleg 12" that amalgamated the dub-charged "Space Invaders" b-line, "Funky Town"'s horns and a chant from Donna Summer's "Bad Girls". Instantly memorable and immensely popular on the dancefloor, the mix soon became Saunders' signature tune, building up a buzz in Chicago as he DJd around the city and on the radio.

A year later, with friend/visionary/entrepreneur Vince Lawrence, Saunders had the foresight, faith and intuition to make the then radical move to press his recording onto vinyl. The pair used the city's only independent pressing plant, called Musical Products, owned by one Larry Sherman. It was the relationship between these two kids from Chicago's South Side and the middle-aged businessman that would eventually result in the creation of House music's most important record label, Trax. Lawrence's musician father had recommended the outlet, and would soon release Euro-synth-influenced recordings by Lawrence and Saunders ("Night Flight", "Dumb Dumb", "I'm the DJ") on his Mitchbal Records.

After gaining the on-air support of radio DJs like Farley "Jackmaster" Funk, "On & On 117" became a huge club hit in Chicago. A second single, "Fantasy", recorded with ex-Ministry singer Rachael Cain (aka Screamin' Rachel), followed. The success of these records persuaded Sherman to become involved, his Precision label releasing further simply constructed singles like "Waiting on My Angel" and "Funk You Up", while Lawrence and Saunders also recorded under pseudonyms Lillian and Bang Orchestra.

Saunders produced Trax's first release, Le Noiz's "Wanna Dance/Certainly", and production work on a variety of other releases (often with Vince Lawrence and producer/DJ Duane Bedford) ensued. Though these tracks may sound incredibly simplistic nowadays, in 1985 they were successful enough to have Saunders looked upon in Chicago as House music's first star.

But just as House's commercial prospects were beginning to be opened up to a British audience, in 1986 Saunders abandoned the four-to-the-floor groove to launch a disastrous R&B project with corporate giant Geffen Records. Not even the golden pop touch of producer Norman Whitfield could help Jesse's Gang, and Saunders has since faded into relative obscurity. He made an attempted comeback in 1998, co-ordinating and producing a compilation album, **Chicago Reunion**. But with poor-taste remixes of classic tracks by the likes of Saunders, Adonis and Tyree, it was largely panned by critics and almost completely ignored by record buyers.

⊙ **"On & On 117"**   JesSay Records, 1985

The first Chicago House record to make it to vinyl. On that basis (only), this is a must for serious house historians.

Shazz

Despite crediting Chicago's Larry Heard and Japan's Ryuchi Sakamoto as his two pivotal influences, it's arguably the geographical setting of New York that has proved the strongest influence on the ex-Gaultier model Shazz. Alongside fellow Parisian Ludovic Navarre, Shazz has carved out the reflective images of Manhattan's alluring mystique on vinyl since first coming to prominence in 1991 with the single "Moonflower".

Switching from the catwalk to the recording studio in 1988, Shazz began to gain recognition in the early '90s, when his deep, subtle soundscapes for F Communications were well received by sections of the British music press. Elegantly crafted singles like Nuages' "Apres Les Larmes", Souffle's Detroit-inflected "Thrill" and excellent "Lost Illusions" (1992) all offered glimpses of an exceptional new talent in the making. Although he produced fast-selling Euro trance under the banner of Aurora Borealis during the same period, Shazz's warm, Ambient productions as Orange gave a better indication of the melodic direction his twist on House music would subsequently take.

It was 1994's **View of Manhattan** EP that marked Shazz out from the crowd. With additional production by label mate Ludovic Navarre, **View of Manhattan**'s crisp, clean angles, stabbing organs and funk-driven bass-lines reflected Shazz's obvious fascination with the Big Apple, while his sharp hi-hats and soothing vocal harmonies evident on the standout track, "Leave Me", suggested he was also capable of producing vocal tracks to match the best from Strictly Rhythm, Nervous or Emotive.

1995's **Back In Manhattan** EP and "Muse Q the Music" (again recorded with Ludovic Navarre) proved the point with the addition of vocalist Derek Bays. The same year Navarre hit the big time, with his well-received **Boulevard** album. Yet Shazz's success hasn't been as quick as initially expected, and a long-awaited album has still to emerge. 1997 witnessed a switch to Chris The French Kiss' Yellow Records, heralding two Latin-percussion-led instrumental 12"s, "El Camino (Parts 1 & 2)", while 1998 produced arguably his best vocal cut to date, "Innerside". Once again, his NYC connections were in evidence with mixes from New Jersey heroes Blaze and "live" House king Joe Claussell backing up Shazz's own expertly constructed versions.

Subtle and evocative, Shazz's music is perhaps the antithesis of most clubs' peak-time playlists. As such, his cultivation needs an album format to give it the sort of commercial and critical justice it deserves.

⊙**View of Manhattan**   F Communications, 1994

The EP which drew noticeable attention to the Frenchman. Its highlight cut, "Leave Me", is available on **La Collection Chapter 2** (F Communications, 1996).

Shep Pettibone

Before he became an associate of Madonna, Shep Pettibone was one of New York's most in-demand mixers during the disco era. His edits were tailor-made for Big Apple dancefloors like the Times Square disco Better Days. More importantly, though, his renowned Kiss FM Mastermixes combined disco's smooth-blending aesthetic with hip-hop's cut 'n' paste jump cuts and the bootleg tapes of these radio sessions that have circulated throughout the global dance community are a crucial influence on DJs and producers everywhere.

One of Pettibone's hallmarks was his use of percussion and subtle effects in his mixes. Pettibone's early mixes like Salsoul Orchestra's bus-stop classic "Love Break (Ooh I Love It)" (1976) and First Choice's proto-garage "Let No Man Put Asunder" (1977) unwrapped the interlocking layers of percussion and looped the Fender Rhodes riffs to create building, surging epics of erotic tension. Triangle chimes, piano tinkles and an elasticated Jocelyn Brown infiltrate his mix of Inner Life's already dense "Moment of My Life" (1982) whose brilliant breakdown was built on a stretched loop of Brown's trademark wailing.

Pettibone's most famous mix, though, was probably Loleatta Holloway's "Love Sensation" (1980) in which the momentum never stopped building and his instrumental drop-out highlighted the pipes of the disco diva to end all disco divas to great effect. Better still was his mix of Latin percussionist Candido's version of Babatunde Olatunji's "Jingo" (1979). With a monster keyboard loop running through the entire track and a gratuitous use of dub effects, Pettibone created an epic of disco excess that still managed to rein in salsa's rhythmic extravagance to fit disco's more regimented boogie framework. His greatest dub excursion, though, was his monumental trance-inducing mix of Sinnamon's "He's Gonna Take You Home (To His House)" (1983) which took the concept of delayed gratification to its limits.

The techniques of Jamaican dub played a large part in his Kiss FM *Mastermixes* which ran from 1981 to 1984 and were instrumental in propagating the cut 'n' paste aesthetic. Beginning at the same time as Mr. Magic's pioneering hip-hop radio show, Pettibone's *Mastermixes* were anything-goes affairs that cut across genres, went deep into the heart of the bass and explored dub's shadow world without ever forsaking disco's propulsive bpms. In defining the sound of early '80s New York, Pettibone's *Mastermixes* would inspire other mix shows, particularly Chicago's *Hot Mix Five* which played a key role in the development of House, and animate the diva passions of Madonna who would go on to work with Pettibone on "Vogue" (1989).

◉ Various Artists: Classic Salsoul Volume 1   Mastercuts, 1993

By all means seek out tapes of his Kiss FM *Mastermixes* which do still exist, but if they prove unattainable grab this collection of Salsoul hits which includes his mixes of "Let No Man Put Asunder", "Jingo", "Love Sensation" and Leroy Burgess' "Heartbreaker".

Victor Simonelli

Perhaps even more so than fellow Brooklynites Todd Terry, Tommy Musto and Kenny "Dope" Gonzalez, Victor Simonelli has found it difficult to shrug off his late '70s NYC musical heritage. The grit, soul and glamour of disco has almost always provided the foundation for his dub and vocal tracks from his early 1990 Brooklyn Funk Essentials cuts for Nu Groove Records through 1993's Inner Life-sampling "Do You Feel Me?" to 1998's Philly-style workout "Another Seven".

Unlike some of his older associates, Simonelli's musical education wasn't a direct product of the Paradise garage or Loft dancefloors, but a result of tuning into the airwaves of 92 WKTU, 106.7 WBLS and 98.7 Kiss FM where DJs Timmy Regisford, Frankie Crocker, Shep Pettibone and mastermixer Tony Humphries' inspirational segues held sway. Graduating from the Big Apple's Centre For Media Arts in 1987, the John Travolta lookalike got a lucky break when he served his apprenticeship at electro-king Arthur Baker's Shakedown Studios, honing his engineering skills on songs by Al Jarreau, The Gipsy Kings and Will Downing.

Early instrumental releases with producer Lenny Dee under the guise of Brooklyn Funk Essentials were smoothly conceived club cuts, but it wasn't until around 1991, when Simonelli moved on to work as an editor for Judy Weinstein's Def Mix production team on tracks like Gwen Guthrie's "Miss My Love", that he made the transition to full-time production and began to dabble with vocals. His uplifting single "Dirty Games", recorded as Groove Committee for the seminal Nu Groove Records, attracted the attention of competing independent label owners and led to Simonelli producing critically acclaimed 12"s for 4th Floor Records, Emotive Records and, most notably, Maxi Records with "Your Love Is Taking Me Over" as SK Projects.

Having established a trademark of long, beat-driven intros welded with upbeat handclaps and disco-fired hooks, in 1992 Simonelli released perhaps his most effective and hypnotic cut, Cloud 9's swooning "Do U Want Me". Produced for friend Tommy Musto's Northcott Records, the track moulded a female disco diva vocal snippet, a pared-down rhythm and flute-led, reflective synth stabbing groove to create an intoxicating track. At the same time, Simonelli released Solution's double-sided, disco-sampling gem "Feels So Right/Givin' It All I Got" on E-Legal Records, and Club Z's emotive, gospel-tinged "I Wanna Be Someone".

On the strength of his growing reputation, Simonelli initiated his own imprint, Bassline Records, in 1993 with "Do You Feel Me" as NY's Finest. With its inspired piano hook and vocal breakdown culled from Inner Life's disco classic "Moment Of My Life", the track became an instant dancefloor filler in clubs on both sides of the Atlantic. Simonelli carried the piano motif over to Groove Committee's vocal monster "You Need Someone", while 1994 saw the similarly veined release of Creative Force's underground vocal garage cuts, 'It's So Good" and "I'm Not the Same" on London's Centrestage imprint. During this same period, Simonelli also turned out the pounding pianos for a glorious remix of Red Light's "Thankful" on Canada's Hi-Bias Records and a gospel-ridden re-versioning of Beat 4 Feet's "Thank You Lord" for Austria's Gig label.

As well as creating Bassline Records' offshoot Big Big Trax, Simonelli consolidated his partnership with DJ/producer Tommy Musto in 1994 when the duo teamed up to form Colourblind, employing first the vocals of Barbara Tucker and then Dina Roche, and releasing the commercially successful crossover hit, "Nothing Better". The pair continued to produce a wealth of fresh work as T.M.V.S., much of which was collected on **Vindaloo: The Morning After** compilation (1996) for London's x:treme records.

Since then, Simonelli has successfully expanded his Bassline and Big Big Trax labels to include notable releases from Jazz N' Groove, Joe Mendelson, Julius Papp and DJ Duke, though many of his own productions have largely failed to capture the same excitement or energy levels of the pre-1996 peak period. Despite that criticism, more recent releases have included Simonelli's well-regarded reunion with Arthur Baker as Blind Truth, Afro-American Coalition's "No More Weeping", Soul Corporation's "Make It Happen", Voices Of Faith's "Clap Your Hands" and Street Player's discofied "Soul Searchin'".

1998 witnessed a move towards a more percussive style with the release of the '70s-snatching "Another Seven" and the conga-led "Latin Impressions Part One" for his new imprint, West Side Records, alongside more traditional vocal cuts like "Nothing Stays The Same". Whether Simonelli can recreate the buzz surrounding his early releases is difficult to predict at this stage, but it looks almost certain that a touch of that disco trademark will be in the mix somewhere.

⊙ **Vindaloo: The Morning After**   x:treme records, 1996

Fine Simonelli & Musto beatmix compilation which includes Cloud 9's dubby classic, "Do You Want Me", Sixth Sense's "Don't You Feel It" and Colourblind's garage belter, "Nothing Better".

Slip 'N' Slide

Created in 1993 as a subsidiary of Hardcore/rave label Kickin' Records, Slip 'N' Slide has established itself as one of the UK's most successful House imprints, though the majority of its output has clearly been centred around the work of American producers.

Slip 'N' Slide's first batch of releases gave no indication of its future direction: Flying/Boys Own extended family members Lofty, Craig Walsh and Clive Wilkie provided dubby instrumentals such as Boomshanka's "Gonna Make You Move" (1993) to complement the more trance-like feel of forgettable cuts by Soundscape, Men Of Faith and Heroes of Another Life.

It was the label's seventh release that signalled a change in direction. At a time when UK clubland was still dominated by Hard House, the 1993 licensing of Roc & Kato's bass-heavy sax-fuelled 10", "Jungle Kisses" (with UK remixes from X Press 2 and Phil Asher and Noel Watson), set the precedent that would make Slip 'N' Slide the stronghold for UK-pressed American Deep House and garage.

Canny licences of garage singles from NYC labels Bottom Line (Vivian Lee's "Music Is So Wonderful" (1994)) and Emotive (Karen Pollack's "You Can't Touch Me" (1994)) were backed up with fresh remixes by the likes of Farley & Heller and Murk, setting the pattern for the label's biggest hit, De' Lacy's "Hideaway" (1995) (licensed from NYC's Easy Street), which was

remixed to devastating effect by Washington's Deep Dish.

Since then, Deep Dish ("DC Depressed" (1995)), Mr Onester (aka African Dreams), 95 North, Rob Rives ("Downtime" (1995)), Kings

Of Tomorrow ("I'm So Grateful" and "Ten Minute High" (1996–7)) and Blaze ("My Beat" (1997)) have all had UK club hits on the imprint. Following Blaze's acclaimed **Basic Blaze** album (1997), Baltimore's well-regarded jazz-House producer Charles Dockins rose to prominence with "Traffic Jam" (1997) and "Journey" (1998). Phil Asher's (aka Restless Soul/ Blak 'N' Spanish) "Mama" was one of 1997's UK House highlights.

Slip 'N' Slide have also played a major role in pushing the sound of jazz onto both British dancefloors and dance charts with their well-rated **Jazz in the House** series of compilations. 1995's **Volume 1** in particular broke the mould by drawing together producers like MAW, Danny Tenaglia, House Of Jazz, King Britt, Rheji Burrell and 95 North.

◉ Jazz in the House   Slip 'N' Slide, 1995

Wonderful collection of jazz-House 12"s from (mainly) American producers. Includes MAW's incredible Miles Davis tribute, "Our Mute Horn", and Danny Tenaglia's Musical Youth-sampling "Harmonica Track".

DJ Sneak

Moving from Puerto Rico to Chicago at just the right time to catch the pioneering *Hot Mix 5* radio show, DJ Sneak discovered America as much through those early jacking beats as through learning to speak English. A decade later, Sneak was on the frontline of Chicago artists reviving the spirit of Acid House during the Windy City's creative renaissance.

Although he divided his early productions between the raw drive of Relief and the melodic madness of Cajual, it is for the Relief tracks that Sneak will be remembered. The attraction of pieces like "Percolate This Track", "Runaway Train" (both 1995) and the **Blue Funk Files** (1996) series is their good-humoured aggression, whacking the brain and body with beats with a benign grin.

1996 saw the simultaneous release of both the **Blue Funk Files** and the **Rice and Beans Please** albums. Dominated by luxuriously ecstatic disco samples and multiple layered, attention-grabbing beats, **Rice and Beans Please** remains one of House music's neglected treasures.

With "You Can't Hide From Your Bud" (1997), a cut-up of Teddy Pendergrass' "You Can't Hide From Yourself", Sneak's disco bombing broke through heavily and the razor beats and huge horn riffs created dancefloor mayhem. Its interplay between the Teddy Pendergrass sample and a hi-hat so processed that it was little more than a stabbing moment of atonal noise ensured that the track was named as one of the tunes of the year in the dance press.

◉ Rice and Beans Please   Cajual, 1996, re-released 1997

Maybe difficult to trace now, but it's a neglected treasure. Disco combines with fascinatingly disruptive beats to scorching effect.

The Stickmen

Producers/DJs Greg Zwarich and Paul Minsoulis (aka The Stickmen) began DJing together in high school in the late '80s, opening a studio and founding Stickmen Records in 1993. Since then, alongside Toronto strongholds like the DNH and 83 West imprints,

Stickmen Records has taken up the torch lit by Fiorucci's Hi-Bias in the early '90s, spawning well-regarded singles by home-grown talents like Paul Jacobs, Klubb Kidz, The People Movers collective (John Acquiviva, David Alvarado, Nick Holder and others), Biotrans and The Stickmen themselves. Remixes by Josh Wink, Richie Hawtin, Derrick Carter and DJ Duke have also helped propel the label to a level of underground notoriety in the States and the UK. The imprint hit big in 1997 with the release of "C Line Woman" by The People Movers, a collective who had first slammed dancefloors with 1993's underrated "Boogaloo".

Favouring a mélange of funky, minimalist grooves and lead-weight bass-lines, The Stickmen have made their mark felt from early single releases like 1993's "Summer of 87/U Love It" to 1996's "Baddest Little Boogie". 1995's **Direct 2 Disk** was a moderate success, though the formula really gelled on 1997's **Afterhours**. While they're never likely to cross over to commercial success with such subtle late-night melodies, The Stickmen have proved popular enough to record for Strictly Rhythm ("Da Real Shit", "The Drug", "Impakt/Tweek In") and Nervous.

The label meanwhile has also served as a distributor for the city's burgeoning independents like Aquarius Recordings, Top Kat Records, Cabinet Records and drum 'n' bass label Placebo Recordings.

⊙ **Afterhours**   Stickmen/Direct 2 Disc, 1997

The best introduction to Zwarich and Minsoulis' late-nite grooves.

Strictly Rhythm

N o other American label is quite like New York's Strictly Rhythm. Not only has it managed to build a reputation as one of the most powerful independent dance music labels in the States, but it has done so while successfully straddling the fine line between underground and mainstream with creative integrity.

Along the way, Strictly Rhythm has stood as a mark of quality across many different sectors of the dance community, claiming rave anthems (Josh Wink's "Higher State Of Consciousness" and Djamin's "Give You") as well as commercial House triumphs (Ultra Naté's "Free" and Planet Soul's "Set U Free"). In a home country that is still largely hostile to dance music, it's one of the few labels to have broken through at all.

Strictly Rhythm owner Mark Finkelstein spent three years at the helm of another dance label, Spring Records. When he started his own company in 1989 he took with him Spring's A&R director, Gladys Pizarro, whose talent led to the signing up of many ground-breaking artists.

Pizarro left Strictly Rhythm in 1991 to help get Nervous Records off the ground, entrusting A&R tasks to the seasoned House producers George Morel and DJ Pierre. She returned a few years later in 1994 when Morel departed to form a new division, Groove On. This was the first of several artist-created imprints to become involved with Strictly, mostly as distributed labels.

Logic's "The Warning" sounded a clarion call for the label in 1990, the first of an enormous string of club hits that shows little sign of slowing. The label's first full-length collection came in the summer of 1991 with **This Is Strictly Rhythm Volume I**. During these early years, producers like Morel, Erick Morillo, Todd Terry, and Little Louie Vega were frequent contributors. Strictly was also home to a side project from the other Master At Work, Kenny "Dope" Gonzalez. Gonzalez masqueraded as The Untouchables and devastated dancefloors in 1992 with simple yet effective tracks like "Dance to the Rhythm". DJ

Pierre has also been an instrumental contributor over the years with his own "Love Izz" and, most importantly, with Roy Davis Jr as Photon Inc. on "Generate Power" (1991).

1994 saw the opening of several new offices for the label in the UK, Netherlands and Argentina. The Erick Morillo-produced Reel II Real became Strictly's most popular act following the release of "I Like to Move It!" which sold over a million copies. The same year also saw the release of huge club anthems such as River Ocean's transcendent "Love & Happiness" and Barbara Tucker's sassy "Deep Inside" and "Beautiful People".

The release of several EPs from then largely unknown producer Armand Van Helden, particularly the unique and devastating "Witch Doktor" (1994), blazed his future path. Less than two years later Van Helden's wickedly ruff

bass-lines and snappy hi-hats would be referenced as a catalyst for a new London genre hybrid, speed garage. Meanwhile, Strictly VP Bari G would sign a project from Florida producer George Acosta called Planet Soul. With a prescient blend of Latin freestyle, hip-hop breaks and energetic House, their debut single, "Set U Free", was a certified gold seller and received large amounts of urban radio play, still rare for a House-orientated label. Planet Soul released the full-length **Energy + Harmony**.

In 1998 Strictly Rhythm focused on developing their artist projects, ruling playlists and dancefloors for most of the year with full-length and single releases from the likes of House grande dame Ultra Naté and Atlanta-based wizards Wamdue Project, who had already provided the label with its most adventurous album yet in **Resource Toolbook Volume I**.

After a decade of operation which has seen the company grow from humble beginnings to one of the most revered independent labels in existence, Strictly Rhythm continues to push itself still further, remaining a vital fixture of dance culture.

⊙ Little Louie Vega: Strictly House Mix Strictly Rhythm, 1994

This is only one of Master Vega's many mix collections, but it's one of the most evocative of his special blend of Nuyorican soul, and offers a vivid snapshot of Strictly proceedings in one of their most vibrant eras. It includes the anthems "Love & Happiness", "Beautiful People" and "I Like to Move It".

Ten City

Taking its lead from '70s soul, Ten City was House music's first band. The trio of Byron Stingley (vocals), Byron Burke (keyboards) and Herb Lawson (guitar) combined R&B with House music's driving dancefloor ambition and Stingley's trademark Sylvester-style falsetto wails to produce some of the genre's most effective singles and live performances.

A chance rehearsal studio meeting in Chicago in 1985 between little known B Rude Inc. members Stingley and Burke with Rise member Herb Lawson led to a unique fusion of sounds and ideas. While Stingley's vocal style drew its influences from Sylvester, Philip Bailey and Eddie Kendricks, Lawson was seduced by the sounds of Pink Floyd and Jimi Hendrix. With the unofficial fourth band member, producer Marshall Jefferson, the trio recorded their first two singles as Ragtime, picking up club play and then press attention for their deeply soulful cuts, "I Can't Stay Away" and "Fix It Man" (1987).

Signed to Atlantic, and a name change to Ten City preceded the following year's monumental "Devotion", which introduced Jefferson's soaring string arrangements and deep melodic rhythms alongside Stingley's incredible high-pitched wail. Its follow-up, "Right Back to You", followed a similar path, but 1989's seminal "That's the Way Love Is" became one of the club anthems of the year, reaching #1 on *Billboard*'s dance chart and storming into the UK Top 10. The astonishing album **Foundation** (1989) was one of House music's first forays into the realms of soul with disco-influenced songs like "Satisfaction" rubbing up lush, Philly-style orchestration against the Windy City's skeletal electronic pulse.

1990's ambitious **State of Mind,** however, couldn't repeat the formula despite spawning the gorgeous hit single "Whatever Makes You Happy". Jefferson's attempt to create a grandiose, Love Unlimited-meets-Vince Montana production found the Chicago Symphony Orchestra in the studio, but the band's introspective lyrics failed to match the standard of their previous records.

After Jefferson departed, **No House Big Enough** (1992) drew Ten City back toward their clubland base and found the band singing about what they had always been best at, love and relationships. With songs produced by David Morales, Kerri Chandler and Smack, the album yielded the sublime "My Piece of Heaven" and the melancholic "All Loved Out".

By 1994 they had moved to Columbia, a switch that would prove disastrous. Although Columbia's press release claimed **Love In a Day** to be another "fresh distillation of esoteric wit, penetrating bass-lines and forceful percussion", there was no hiding the fact that it didn't match either the consistency or creativity levels of their previous output. That said, "Fantasy" reached the *Billboard* dance Top 20.

Acknowledging that they'd taken the formula as far as they wanted to go, the band split in 1994. Although Herb Lawson seems to have disappeared, Byron Stingley has since achieved even greater global commercial success as a solo artist (check 1998's **The Purist**) and Burke has re-emerged with highly rated Deep House cuts under the pseudonyms Komputer Kidz and Visions.

⊙**Foundation**   Atlantic/East West, 1989

With Jefferson at the production helm, this sounds as good today as when released ten years ago. Includes their finest moments, "That's the Way Love Is" and "Devotion".

Danny Tenaglia

D J and producer Danny Tenaglia specialises in music that's aimed directly at the dancefloor: tracks that often begin stripped down to just a groove, with slowly building layers of percussion and writhing bass-lines, perhaps dropping a diva or camp queen vocal into the mix, before erupting into complete mayhem. Unlike Josh Wink's drawn-out snare rolls and colossal breakdowns, Tenaglia's sound stems from a subtle fusion of Chicago's hard-hitting minimalist ethic with his enduring passion for Salsoul's lush orchestration and Latin percussion. There isn't really any better description than his own, it's simply Hard & Soul.

After growing up on a soundtrack of salsa and Sergio Mendes before discovering soul and disco when he heard a mix-tape of DJ Paul Cassella from the Monastery Club in Queens, Tenaglia dropped out of school aged 17 to pursue DJing. He soon landed a gig at his local Roller Palace and later graduated to Manhattan clubs like Stix and Crisco Disco. In 1985, frustrated by a career that wasn't going to emulate that of his hero Larry Levan in a hurry, he took the offer of a residency at an after-hours gay club in Miami, from where his career took off.

While the rest of South Beach's club scene was dancing to Madonna, Rick Astley and Bananarama until 3am, Tenaglia's early morning cocaine-fuelled crowd were open to virtually anything he could throw at them. In just over a year he not only transformed Cheers from a lacklustre nightspot to the centre of the Miami House explosion, but had created the outline for his own DJing style, enticing the crowd with a propulsive mix of early Chi-town House cuts interspersed with slabs

of joyous vocal disco from the vaults of the West End, Salsoul, Prelude and TK Disco labels.

His first production was the sampladelic underground hit "Waiting For a Call" as Deep State, which was signed to Atlantic Records. This was followed by the forgettable Hip-House cut "Everybody Get Down", but it wasn't until his first remix, Seventh Avenue's gorgeous "The Love I Lost" (1988), that the work began to flood in.

Tenaglia was eventually "discovered" when he returned to New York in 1990, becoming a regular DJ at the Sound Factory Bar with Tony Humphries and Little Louie Vega. After surprisingly credible remixes for Right Said Fred, he showcased his own production genius, turning out the novel "Harmonica Track" (1991).

As his name became synonymous with much of NYC's mid-'90s House renaissance, journalists began to label his mix of aggressive, hard-edged grooves and vocals "progressive garage", though Tenaglia came up with a far better description with the title of his 1994 debut album, **Hard & Soul**. Including one of the year's most dynamic singles, "Bottom Heavy", Tenaglia's showcase album foregrounded his eminent production skills as he proved capable of creating slamming instrumentals ("Bottom Heavy" and "Oh No"), solid garage grooves ("Look Ahead"), jazzual cuts like "Yesterday and Today" as well as comical gay anthems like "$ (That's What I Want)".

As his reputation flourished, Tenaglia created two trademark mixes for Tribal Records, **Mix This Pussy** (1994) and **Mix This Pussy 2: Can Your Pussy Do The Dog?** (1995). He continued to churn out remixes for artists including Jamiroquai ("Emergency On Planet Earth"), The Pet Shop Boys, Grace Jones, Frankie Knuckles and countless others (many of which were included on 1997's **Color Me Danny**), and secured an influential residency firstly at Twilo, the club using the old Sound Factory space, and from 1997 onwards at the Tunnel, where his ten-hour sets eventually manifested themselves on vinyl with "Elements".

Having mixed Maxi Records' **Gag Me With a Tune** (1997), 1998 saw his long-awaited follow-up to **Hard & Soul**. **Tourism** carried the torch lit by Inner City with tracks from R&B/pop queen Teena Marie ("Baby, Do You Feel Me?"), newcomer Celeda ("Music Is the Answer") and Chi-town diva Liz Torres ("Turn Me On" and "Do You Remember"). His disco roots were also evident on the cover of Front 242's mid-'80s industrial hit "Headhunter", revealing that the influence of Larry Levan's Paradise Garage remained as strong as ever.

⊙ **Hard & Soul**   Tribal Records/IRS, 1995

House DJ makes great album shock! Tenaglia's debut weds his ultimate bassbin-shattering groove, "Bottom Heavy", to a surprisingly diverse selection of tracks which shift from the groovy garage of "Look Ahead" (a cover of Aquarian Dreams' disco classic) to the inspired Down Tempo breaks of "World of Plenty".

Todd Terry

P erhaps more than any of his early East Coast compatriots, Todd Terry was the producer who really set about changing the parameters of House music in the first post-Chicago wave of the mid-'80s. Combining NYC's then dominant Latin freestyle sound with the Windy City's four-to-the-floor backbone, storming bass-heavy drum kicks and a hip-hop-inspired use and abuse of disco-era samples, Todd Terry makes House music that rarely fails to hit the dancefloor head on.

Growing up in Brooklyn's Coney Island and Brighton Beach neighbourhoods, Terry was inspired by hip-hop to take up DJing with his

first gig coming in 1983. Terry made the move into production in 1986 with his first single, "Alright, Alright". Recorded for Fourth Floor Records, the sample cut-up made little real impact, except for his alias of Masters At Work – a tag he had borrowed from a pair of eager DJs who were to make their mark in years to come. Follow-up single releases – "Bango to the Batmobile", "Weekend" and Royal House's anthemic and irresistible call to the dancefloor, "Can U Party" (all 1988) – were more than just major UK and European club cuts: they served to forge a modern blueprint for much of today's House with their distinctive rapid-fire samples and rugged, raw bass-lines alongside Terry's pounding kick drum loop.

A stream of innovative productions followed under a variety of guises. Classics like Black Riot's "Day in the Life" (1989), Orange Lemon's "Dreams of Santa" and Swan Lake's "In the Name of Love" were all stamped with his trademark catalytic drum kicks and were favourites in the UK's Acid House clubs. He also produced the sample-heavy track albums **To the Batmobile**, **Royal House** and **Kamikaze** (as Black Riot) from 1986 to 1988, followed a few years later by his **Todd Terry Project** album for London's Champion Records, though Terry's best work has always been on 12".

While his early productions had brought a breath of fresh air with their raw energy, a noticeably large proportion of Terry's work after 1990 has simply relied upon past glories to pull in the punters. Despite this laziness, his loyal fans still simply refer to him as "God". Terry can still create carnival mayhem with cuts like CLS's thundering "Can U Feel It" (1992) and Tek 9's "Slam Jam", cause dancefloor devastation with dubs like House Of Gypsies' "Sum Say High", "Samba" and Gypsymen's "I Hear the Music", and make the floor burn with songs like Martha Wash's "Carry On" and "Runaround" (1992), Everything But the Girl's "Missing" (1995 remix) and Jocelyn Brown's "Something's Going On" (1997). Yet all too frequently his remixes have lacked purpose and he has often re-cycled his hi-hats, snares and out-takes again and again (many of which have appeared on his TNT label). Similarly, as a DJ he can be equally perplexing. While few doubt that his technical skills and ability to work the crowd are on a par with his hip-hop heroes of old, Terry has often been accurately accused of solely playing his own tracks, hour after hour, week in, week out.

In 1995 he released the hyper-kinetic **Sound Design: Back From the Dead** EP for the Leeds-based Hard Times label in response to UK producer Grant Nelson's successful sampling of his incredible "Bounce to the Beat" track. 1996's cover of Musique's "Keep On Jumpin'" crashed into the UK Top 10 and became a #1 club track in the States (and a dozen other countries). Similar success followed with the great "Something's Going On" (1997) and the subsequent major-label album, **Ready For a New Day** (1997), which featured contributions from Jocelyn Brown, Shannon and former Peech Boys vocalist Bernard Fowler.

◉ "A Day in the Life" Ministry Of Sound, 1995

If you believe the PR hype, then this was created in just 24 hours. Whatever the case, it's quintessential Todd Terry: a raw mix of brazen beats, driving bass and sinuous samples cut up in a hip-hop stylee.

◉ Royal House: "Can U Party" Warlock, 1988

With its "Can you feel it?" refrain, devastating police sirens and colossal bass-line, this Acid House anthem remains one of the era's most memorable tracks.

Those Norwegians

Though Torbjon Brundtland, Ole Mjos and Rune Lindbaek had worked together for over five years – releasing singles on Djax, Reinforced, Deconstruction and R&S – before forming Those Norwegians, they had produced little of interest to most House fans. Hailing from the northernmost university town on the map, Tromso, Those Norwegians first picked up House attention with their **Kilpisjarvi EP**, produced for Manchester-based Paper Records.

1997's **Kaminsky Park** firmly moved them in a House direction. Album tracks like "L'Hybride Fiasco" summed up their scope: underpinning dirty funk b-lines, haunting melodies and Salsoul-style strings with complex drum patterns while constantly bombarding the mix with obscure oddities and vocal snippets. Cuts such as "Hurdy Burdy" and "38-39-38", on the other hand, proved they could offer a welcome sense of humour in amongst the experimentation. Unlike many retro UK House artists, Those Norwegians haven't just glossed over past glories, but have re-invigorated disco's sense of urgency and style with innovative drum programming, wired sequencing and an incisive ability to harness a cross-spectrum of fantastically weird noises into an ever-propulsive mix.

◉ Kaminsky Park   Paper Records/Pagan USA, 1997

Fun, inventive and addictive. Those Norwegians' debut moulds disco's lush orchestration to a mix of crazed sampling, warped synth stabs and fresh drum programming to make it truly different.

Pete Tong

Pete Tong is one of the most influential figures in British dance music. As host of Radio One's *The Essential Selection* show, Tong's unstinting popularity is a result of a playlist of unashamedly commercial House anthems, his round-up of the country's most popular club nights and his all-important accolade, the "Essential New

Tune", which virtually guarantees cross-over success of a given record. As one of the show's famous jingles has it: "Pete Tong got power".

Tong started DJing in the '70s. As a listener to *Robbie Vincent's Soul Show* on Radio London, his tastes were largely constricted to rare groove and soul/disco (favourites including Crown Heights Affair and Evelyn "Champagne" King). Through promoting club nights as a teenager, he fell in with a group known as the "Kent Soul Mafia" (others included Robbie Vincent, Geoff Young and Chris Hill). By 1981, he was appearing on Radio One as a regular guest of Peter Powell, where he would provide tips on the contemporary dance scene.

When London Records set up in 1983, they appointed him A&R manager. In the same year, Tong began hosting his own show on the independent Kent station Invicta, which in turn led to a stint on Greater London Radio. By 1987 he was hosting a show on London's Capital Radio and in 1991 was poached by Radio One to host *The Essential Selection*. Simultaneously, Tong was continuing to DJ and became a resident at Nicky Holloway's Acid House club, the Trip. When Holloway bought the Milk Bar in Soho, Tong took up residency there, alongside Dave Dorrell, and his reputation as a DJ accelerated overnight.

London Records was amongst the first major record labels to set up a separate dance division: Full Frequency Range Recordings (ffrr) which Tong has run since its inception. ffrr released the first ever House compilation, 1987's **House Sound of Chicago**, as well as House's first cross-over success (Farley "Jackmaster" Funk's "Love Can't Turn Around") and #1 (Steve "Silk" Hurley's "Jack Your Body"). Home to some of House music's landmark anthems (Lil' Louis' "French Kiss", Orbital's "Chime", Frankie Knuckles Presents Satoshi Tomie's "Tears", Richie Rich's "Salsa House", Lisa Marie Experience's "Jumpin'"), ffrr has remained both credibly and commercially successful throughout the '90s. At ffrr Tong has also overseen the development of artists such as Armand Van Helden and Goldie.

◉ ffrr Classics   ffrr/London, 1999

A three-CD collection that spans the label's ten-year history, including classics by Lil' Louis, Orbital, Richie Rich, DSK and Frankie Knuckles.

Trax Records

B uy a Trax record in its black sleeve with Chicago's skyline stencilled in white, and you're buying into one of the great myths of contemporary music. With it comes House music's most glorious moments: Larry Heard, Phuture, Marshall Jefferson, Armando, the birth of Acid House.

At the centre of the history are three men: Jesse Saunders, Vince Lawrence and Larry Sherman; the innovator, the idealist and the steel-edged businessman. Sherman owned a pressing plant, which provided the city with one of its only independently owned outlets of production. Saunders' "On & On 117", the first ever House 12", was the model for the early House ethos: non-musicians riding the freakishness of cheap electronics and abrasive rhythm. The immediate success of "On & On 117" saw Saunders and Lawrence return for repressings. Sherman said he'd look after the business side, and Trax Records was born.

Trax's first release was Saunders' "Wanna Dance" (1985) as Le Noiz, which was shortly followed by "I'm Scared". Four figures emerged who were the real nucleus of Trax. First came Adonis with "No Way Back", then Marshall Jefferson with Sleazy D's "I've Lost Control". These laid the foundation for the mayhem which Larry Heard and Phuture would cause with their Acid masterpieces, "Washing Machine/Can U Feel It" (1986) and "Acid Trax" (1987).

For the next couple of years, Trax would continue to release records of uncompromising minimalism and jackhammer pulses: Marshall Jef-

ferson's "Move Your Body (House Music Anthem)" (1986), Ralphi Rosario's "U Used to Hold Me" (1987), House Master Boys' "House Nation", Laurent X's "Machines". Trax also provided the outlet for the early work of Robert Owens, Lidell Townsend, Fast Eddie, DJ Rush and DJ Skull. But by 1989 the quality was drying up. On top of that was the classic industry tale of exploitation. Sherman's practice was to buy the tracks outright with a minimal contract and little mention of royalties or publishing fees and to license abroad quickly. With Phuture always having licensing problems, Larry Heard unable to get the recognition he deserved, Armando dying young and the inability of Adonis to re-launch his career after virtually inventing the House b-line as we hear it every day, Trax's business practices probably caused the demise of Chicago House. But one thing remains: those black sleeves contain some of the greatest music of our time.

◉ The House That Trax Built   Trax/PRD, 1996

Wall to wall classics, this is an essential collection for anyone with more than a passing interest in modern music.

Ron Trent

R on Trent's impressive career, spanning over ten years, has provided some of the deepest, most soulful House ever made. Apart from producing a ground-breaking EP at the tender age of 16 and running one of the best-loved American House labels, he has continually supported the original roots and ethics of predominantly black dance music both in the past, and into the future.

His first major release was the **Altered States** EP (1990) on Armando's WareHouse label. Made on basic, cheap equipment, its swirling, harsh, metallic rhythms, robo-bass-line and classic Chicago strings connected to produce a brilliant funk groove. In 1991 the EP was re-released on Djax-Up-Beats, with mixes by Carl Craig and Overdose, assuring **Altered States** its legendary status as one of the defining moments in House music's history.

Trent briefly collaborated with Chicago pals Terry Hunter and Aaron Smith as the UBQ Project before he was given the opportunity to develop his own style at ClubHouse Recordings. However, it was his introduction to Chez Damier and the duo's subsequent releases on Kevin Saunderson's KMS imprint which proved the most rewarding for Trent. Their first joint effort, "Never" by Ron & Chez D (featuring Chez on vocals), "O54" (1994) and the classic Witch Doctor track "The Choice", offered both deep, vocal-led songs and rough, hard-edged dubs in an original style. In fact, the heavily echoed organ stabs and gliding beats featured on these EPs became the blueprint for the famed label they launched in late 1993, Prescription Records, on which Trent released many of his most emotive recordings.

While releasing classics on Prescription, he also found time to release the uplifting **A Dark Room and a Feeling** EP on the UK's Subwoofer label and the deeply soulful, late-night vocal tracks, "I'm Your Brother" and "New Day" on Main Street Records, produced with Damier and Maurizio (Basic Channel). In addition, Trent began to gradually develop a collective of like-minded artist and musician friends he could employ to further fulfill his ambition to include more vocalists and live instrumentation. The Urban Sound Gallery became a pseudonym for an increasing number of releases, including 1996's well-rated "The Dance".

Following the departure of Chez Damier from the equation and the subsequent slow-down at Prescription Records, Ron Trent began recording for a new label, Clairaudience, with Anthony Nicholson. Tracks such as USG's sultry vocal-led "African Blues", "Introduce My Love" and Leticia's "Love Will Make It Right" seemed even more focused, using his unique underground sound to produce spiri-

USG Presents African Blues Coconut Jam

tual songs. This hit a creative zenith with 1997's beautiful "N Came U", featuring the vocals of Chicago diva and one-time Prescription publicist D'Bora.

Since then, the influence of African percussive rhythms and early 1980s synthesised effects have become increasingly evident in Trent's work, with releases such as "Soul Samba Express" (1998) drawing comparisons to the records arising from Joe Claussell's Spiritual Life and François Kervorkian's Wave imprints.

⊙ **The Collected Sounds**
of Prescription   Prescription/Slip 'N' Slide, 1996

A good overview of Trent and Damier's hugely influential label. Includes a smattering of his own cuts alongside essentials from Romanthony, Abacus and Stacey Pullen.

⊙ **USG: "N Came U"**   Clairaudience, 1997

One of 1997's best vocal cuts: a soul beauty with D'Bora on the mic and Trent on the controls.

Tribal Records

I n a period when American House was fast losing its way to insipid, washed-out garage, and most of Europe was starting to retreat into Hard-House monotony, it was Tribal Records who merged the two in four-to-the-floor matrimonial bliss and became the one label for any discerning DJ to drop in virtually any set.

Inspired by the burgeoning "progressive" sound of New York's diverse club scene, it was a young assistant at I.R.S's press office who picked Tribal off the ground and put it firmly on the musical map. Under Rob Di Stefano's direction, Tribal America's first 12", "Are You Satisfied" (1993), wasn't far short of a revelation. Produced by Danny Tenaglia and long-standing keyboardist Peter Daou, its raw African drums, driving percussion and pleading, sleazy vocals (sung by Daou's wife, Vanessa) encapsulated the fierce hedonistic vibe of the now-legendary Sound Factory club.

The Daous' second single, "Give Myself to You", followed, and a UK outlet opened up to cater for the label's growing underground status in Europe. However, it was Murk's bottom-heavy groove behind Liberty City's "If You Really Love Somebody" (1994) that really set the ball rolling. Months later and Junior Vasquez's ultimate drag-queen bitch-anthem, "Get Your Hands Off My Man" (1994), had given the label its first sizeable critical and commercial success.

With Tenaglia acting as a part-time A&R scout, The Underground Sound Of Lisbon signed up, releasing their disturbingly hypnotic debut single, "So Get Up", to an astonished reaction in clubs across the Atlantic. Tribal America recruited Def Mix supremo Eric Kupper and the increasingly impressive Washington duo, Deep Dish, to the roster, pressing up K-Scope's "The Theme" and Prana's wonderful "The Dream".

Tenaglia even found time to follow up one of 1994's biggest underground smashes, "Bottom Heavy", with an excellent debut album, **Hard & Soul**, in early 1995. Sadly though, despite the massive underground critical success and a string of fairly impressive albums the label had achieved in its short existence, Tribal was quickly put to the sword when EMI bought out parent company I.R.S. in 1996. The music's popularity hasn't waned though (Stefano has since set up the similar Twisted Records, releasing new albums by Danny Tenaglia and Peter Rauhoffer), and 1998 saw the release of Tribal Records' best anthology to date through Pagan Records.

⊙ Chronology – The Very Best Of Tribal
United Kingdom   Pagan, 1998

Some of House music's finest moments captured on a double CD. From Danny Tenaglia's "Bottom Heavy" to Deep Dish's "The Dream" and Junior Vasquez's "Get Your Hands Off My Man", virtually every track is a winner.

Tuff Jam

For Matt "Jam" Lamont and Karl "Tuff Enuff" Brown the early part of 1997 would be the start of a career trajectory that would rise dramatically over the next couple of years. Though relatively unknown outside London, Tuff Jam's pivotal DJing slots, perfectly timed 12" releases and professional attitudes would have them namechecked time and time again alongside The Dreem Teem as the figureheads of what the media dubbed "Speed garage", an association that Lamont and Brown would later be keen to break from.

Before he started spinning records, Lamont had been a draughtsman in the building trade. Brown, on the other hand, had already tasted brief pop success with rap act Double Trouble, who scored a chart hit with 1989's "Street Tuff".

Both established their DJing credentials by pitching up American garage 12"s at important small pubs and clubs in and around South London, the most famous being Happy Days at Southwark Bridge Arches and the Frog & Nightgown on the Old Kent Road. Lamont would also champion new developments at the scene's true spiritual home, Twice As Nice, a weekly club held at the Coliseum in Vauxhall.

In 1995, the pair released "Experience" on Fifty First Recordings, under the name Ultymate. Although not their first release (they had already put out **Tuff Jam Vol 1** on New York Sound Clash), the single's beefed-up drums, sharpened hi-hats, deep bass-lines, cut 'n' paste vocal samples and swinging tempo laid down the blueprint for much of the new underground UK garage sound.

Clearly influenced by American producer Todd Edwards' dynamics, further singles, "The History of House" (as Unda-vybe) and "Set It Off" (as Tuff&Jam), solidified their burgeoning reputation. As the scene exploded into the limelight and onto commercial radio in 1997, Tuff

Jam were carried along on the wave of media hysteria. While they hardly indulged in the trademark neo-Jungle bass-line antics of their counterparts like RIP, 187 Lockdown and The Dreem Teem, the duo were still cast in the same net and hailed as speed garage leaders. Angry at the misconception, they deliberately distanced themselves as far as possible from what they regarded as a media slur, pointing out to anyone that would listen that their music was, in fact, "underground UK garage".

Meanwhile their records were appealing to dancefloors on both sides of the Atlantic. They quickly became in demand as guest DJs, importantly spreading their vibe in and around London, the Midlands, Scotland, and across Europe. Their 1997 co-production with Catch, TJR's irresistible "Just Gets Better", reached #28 in the UK national charts. To consolidate their position, they established their own label, Unda-Vybe Music (UVM).

But it was to be on the remix circuit that Tuff Jam crossed over to the mainstream. 1998 found them remixing Rosie Gaines, Brand New Heavies, En Vogue, Soul II Soul, Tina Moore, Usher and Ce Ce Peniston. Some of these were to be found on their mix albums, **Underground Frequencies Volumes 1 & 2** (1997–98).

In 1998, their profile reached new levels when they landed a much-coveted Saturday night show on London's Kiss FM. Some months later, signed to XL Records, they released their first single for over a year, "Need Good Love". While the speed garage media frenzy was simply another passing phase consigned to dance music's history books, the career path paved by Brown and Lamont has ensured that Tuff Jam will be around for some time to come yet.

⊙ Sunday Service   Interstate, 1997

Mixed by Lamont, this was one of the first albums to capture the emerging London garage scene in its infancy. An excellent example of the way British DJs took to "pitching up" American garage cuts to combine them with the releases by new British talent like Grant Nelson and Joey Mustaphia.

Tyree

One of DJ International's most prolific artists, Tyree will forever be remembered as one of the producers who spearheaded the often uneasy musical merging of hip-hop and House. Tagged "Hip-House" by the man pulling the strings, DJ International owner/producer/DJ Rocky Jones, the genre has since spawned a multitude of dancefloor screamers from infectious Italo-House classics like D'Rail's "Bring It On Down" to 1998's remix of Run DMC's "It's Like That".

A teenage prodigy, Tyree Cooper had hooked up with Jesse Saunders and Marshall Jefferson at Chicago parties led by Farley "Jackmaster" Funk in the mid-'80s, reputedly borrowing Jefferson's 808 drum machine to construct his first batch of demos. An initial spate of under-produced instrumental tracks including "Lonely (No More)" and "Rock the Discotech" made little mark, but 1988's "Acid Over" became an epochal cut in UK clubland and an instant classic at Paul Oakenfold's Spectrum club. Moulding the Roland 303's angular bleeps to a caustic, minimally constructed groove, "Acid Over" remains Tyree's most effective, and certainly most durable, release to date.

His move toward Hip-House came at the suggestion of label owner Jones. Having already mixed much of the label's output, Tyree's "Turn Up the Bass" (1988) defined the genre with its bounding bass-line, simple piano hook and Tyree's trademark 909 roll segued with rapper Kool Rock Steady's instantly forgettable lyrics.

Tyree's Got a Brand New House (1988) continued the momentum and even stretched out to include a b-boy-styled rival shoutdown with the anti-Todd Terry message "T's Revenge". But along with the weaker propositions, **Nation of Hip House** (1989) and **The Time Iz Now** (1990), it sounds dated.

With disputes and label problems mounting, DJ International closed up shop in 1991. Tyree has since reverted to producing a series of raw instrumental tech-House cuts, including his **Soul Revival** series, and runs the little-known Supadupa Records.

⊙ **Tyree's Got a Brand New House**   DJ International, 1988

While not a great album, it does include Tyree's two tracks of note: "Acid Over" and "Turn Up the Bass".

Ultra Naté

A former trainee psychotherapist, in 1997 Ultra Naté finally achieved the commercial success she'd threatened since first coming to prominence eight years earlier. Yet despite being one of House music's strongest singers, Naté has still to escape from the clichéd persona of "disco diva" which has stuck with her.

Spotted at a local club by producers The Basement Boys, Baltimore-raised Naté was sprung from obscurity and inked a deal with WEA after singing backing vocals for Monie Love and producing a raw, but ambitious, demo with the then Basement trio of Jay Steinhour, Teddy Douglas and Tommy Davis.

Her 1989 debut single, "It's Over Now", may have been virtually ignored off the dancefloor in the States, but with its joyous piano hook and raw vocal performance, it became an instant club success in the UK, where it even entered the lower recesses of the Top 40. With the Basement Boys' raw and minimal production technique, Naté followed up this release with a trio of well-received emotive dancefloor gems – "Scandal", "Deeper Love" and "Rejoicing", the third of which became a dancefloor filler in 1992 when accompanied by Leftfield and Deee-Lite remixes. Naté's debut long-player, **Blue Notes in the Basement** (1991), remains a captivatingly moody, jazz-laden affair. Nonetheless, at a time when dance albums were still regarded as something of a joke, it passed by largely unnoticed outside of her small fan base.

1993's **One Woman's Insanity** may boast a witty, self-deprecating title and production in parts by Nellee Hooper, but it was ultimately dis-

appointing, featuring a number of smooth but insipid Down Tempo and R&B cuts. Her witty lyricism continued though with the title track poking fun at the diva category with which she's been unfairly associated. Gutsy vocal performances were also still in evidence on the garage-by-numbers "Joy" and rather better "How Long", which when released and remixed as a single provided the basis for Farley & Heller's club and chart hit "Ultra Flava" in 1995.

Regardless of its better moments, the album was a commercial flop and in the hiatus that followed Naté returned to Baltimore and business school for a time, before being plucked from her studies by Strictly Rhythm Records to record the fierce gay anthem "10,000 Screaming Faggots" for New York's Gay Pride festival in 1996, and the upbeat follow-up, "Party Girl", for King St Records soon after.

A year later, Naté escaped from her contract with the Basement Boys and returned shaven-haired and hyped-up with her biggest cut since "It's Over Now", the aptly titled "Free" (1997). Mood II Swing's reflective guitar hooks, incessant beats and lush production welded with Ultra's expansive vocal range and widely appealing singalong lyrics not only made the tune top of every DJs playlist, but also made her an international pop star across Europe, reaching the #1 spot in Italy and Spain.

However, that didn't stop most UK critics from panning **Situation Critical** (1998), despite the fact that two more singles released from the album, "Found a Cure" and "Release the Pressure", had dancefloors shaking across the world and further strengthened her future career as a pop-House starlet.

◉ Blue Notes in the Basement   WEA, 1991

Naté may have called her debut an "experimental album", but the minimal Basement Boys production, off keys and raw jazzy melodies gel with Ultra's reflective lyrics to make it arguably her best.

Urban Blues Project

Powerful vocal anthems stretching from Michael Procter's "Deliver Me" (1995) to Jay Williams' "Testify" (1997) have cast Miami's Urban Blues Project (a mask for the collaborative work of producers Marc Pomeroy and Brian Tappert) into the limelight. Eschewing the organ-plodding rut and instantly forgettable lyrics so many of New Jersey's garage bods have continued to deliver in the '90s, UBP's songs have appealed across both garage and House dancefloors.

Following a move to Florida in 1990, New Jersey-born Tappert began to attract attention for his productions with R&B vocalist and keyboard player Roy Grant, recording vocal singles like "Do Ya" (1993) under the Jazz-N-Groove moniker for Miami's E-SA label and producing Mone's Deep Dish-style 12"s "Never Gonna Be the Same" and "Movin'" (both 1994) for Victor Simonelli's Bassline Records.

Sound engineer Marc Pomeroy, who had just finished producing an album for Nile Rodgers' Ear Candy imprint when he met Tappert and Grant, began to add mixes and keyboards to tracks around the same period, recording jazzy instrumentals under the guises of Native Rhythms ("Ya-Hey") and RMA ("Past and Present").

Urban Blues Project's debut, 1995's "Deliver Me", featuring Michael Procter, quickly became both the tune of that year's Miami Music Festival and one of the year's most memorable vocal propositions. Killer piano hooks and propulsive melodies were applied in equal measure to 1996's "Your Heaven (I Can Feel It)", recorded with diva Pearl Mae. Michael Procter's "Love Don't Live" (1996), a slightly more predictable rant, was equally successful on the dancefloor and licensed to A&M Records in the UK. 1997's "Testify" (with vocalist Jay Williams), Michael Procter's "Fall Down" and The Thompson Project's "Messin' With My

Mind" (1998), featuring the Teddy Pendergrass-like vocals of Gary L, have confirmed UBP as the one of the best vocal production teams in the business.

Having already released their UBP singles on their own Soul-Furic Recordings label, subsidiaries Soulfuric Trax and Soulfuric Deep have released deep late-nite grooves from Pomeroy and Tappert like 1997's "U.N.I" by Soul Searcher and 1998's "The Re-Vibe Experience".

⊙ **"Deliver Me"**   Hott Records, 1995

Tune of the 1995 Miami Music Festival and the one which established UBP's credentials.

Armand Van Helden

While Chicago's Adonis almost single-handedly created the House b-line with his string of early Trax classics, Armand Van Helden's radical mid-'90s remixes of Tori Amos, CJ Bolland and Sneaker Pimps have established him as the undisputed "King Of The Bass-line". Further still, his unique combination of Jungle's teasing beats, intricate breakdowns and bass-heavy oscillations with House music's 4/4 rhythm more or less founded speed garage.

Van Helden came to prominence as one of NYC's premier Hard House specialists. A b-boy at heart, Helden's move toward House was geared by both an open admiration for Todd Terry's aggressive cut-and-paste dynamics and a passion for the late '80s Hip-House of the Jungle Brothers, Tyree and Fast Eddie. After spending his childhood at army bases in Holland, Italy and Turkey before settling in Boston, it was Hip-House's mix and match ethos that provided the basis for his

tough, sample-heavy early cuts with the city's X-Mix Productions outfit that first drew attention his way. By 1992 he had become both promoter and DJ for the after-hours Loft club and made his solo debut with NYC's Nervous Records, "Stay On My Mind/The Anthem" (recorded under the Deep Creed moniker).

Van Helden moved to Strictly Rhythm soon after and steadily built up a solid fan base amongst both American and English DJs with a set of single releases that filtered Techno, trance, disco and tribal alongside the mandatory tuff beats. Sultans of Swing's "Move It To The Left", Circle Children's "Indonesia" and "Mamba Mamba" (all 1993) betrayed a tribal vibe scuffed with b-boy posturing, while 1994's massive Witchdoktor EP, a fiercer and darker proposition, made its mark on dancefloors both sides of the Atlantic. The aptly named Hardhead's "New York Express" (1995), an accomplished example of sampling which his hero Todd Terry would be proud of, Mole People's "Break Night" (1995) and Da Mongloids' insistently funky "Spark Da Meth" (1995) solidified his burgeoning reputation as the city's freshest Hard-House producer. But it was his "Pyschic Bounty Killaz" (1996) track, recorded with DJ Sneak for Chicago's Relief Records, which prefigured his rise to international notoriety with its fresh combination of Jungle bass-lines and House beats.

A huge fan of Ibiza Records and the "jump-up" Jungle style popularised by London DJs like Aphrodite, Hype and Rap, Van Helden pioneered a unique melding of their urgent dancefloor aesthetic with his mix-desk wizardry to create a new musical fusion alongside the works of New Jersey's Todd Edwards, later tagged "speed garage" by UK journalists and taken onward by London protagonists like Tuff Jam and The Dreem Teem. Van Helden's 1996 reworking of Tori Amos' "Professional Widow" was the single which truly made his name. With the singer's "It's gotta be big" vocal strung out across 12"s of phat bassline, mangled hi-hats and perfectly timed phase-outs, the single not only established Van Helden as a worthy commercial proposition (#2 in UK), but also helped once again to re-define the parameters of dance music. His ensuing remixes of the Sneaker Pimps ("Spin Spin Sugar"), CJ Bolland ("Sugar Is Sweeter"), Ace Of Base ("Living In Danger") and Nu Yorican Soul ("It's Alright, I Feel It!") – alongside his self-produced "Funk Phenomena" rub – pushed the formula onto virtually every dancefloor across the UK and US. Van Helden's full foray into the realms of drum 'n' bass, a mysterious 1997 white-label single release simply entitled "Ain't Armand" (utilising the vocals of Monica's "Ain't Nobody"), was less well received.

An album, collecting together all of Van Helden's classics for Strictly Rhythm and some of his early remixes, was released in 1997. This was his swansong to the NYC stable though; he soon signed exclusively to Polygram dance subsidiary ffrr. This new deal saw him return to his b-boy roots with his debut album, **Sampleslayer – Enter The Meat Market**. An elemental hip-hop party set packed with bravado beats and sample-heavy breaks, the album received mixed reviews. The beginning of 1999 saw him return to destroying House dancefloors with the UK #1 single "You Don't Know Me" and **2 Future 4 U** was one of the year's best dance albums, affirming Van Helden's position as a superstar.

◎ Greatest Hits   Strictly Rhythm, 1997

All the fierce mid-'90s instrumental cuts from the NYC stronghold are here – "Witchdoktor", "Zulu", "Break da 80's" and "NY Express"– making it the best introduction to Van Helden's work.

◎ Tori Amos: Professional Widow   East West, 1996

Gut-wrenching bass-line and colossal breakdown combine to make an irresistible dancefloor proposition. Alongside his mix of the Sneaker Pimps' "Spin Spin Sugar", this was the record that paved the way for "speed garage" and made Van Helden world-famous.

Junior Vasquez

Fired up by New York's thriving gay disco scene of the late '70s, Donald Gregory Jerome Pattern (soon to be known as Junior Vasquez) began spending his days serving DJs from behind the counter at Downstairs Records and his nights on the energy-infused dancefloor at Larry Levan's Paradise Garage. In the early '80s, he made the move into DJing himself, playing at trendy Manhattan House parties, becoming friends with artist Keith Haring, and hanging out with producers Arthur Baker and Shep Pettibone in the studio. It wasn't until he opened his Baseline club in the wake of the closing of the Paradise Garage, though, that things really started to take off. Building up a loyal, largely black and Latino gay following, in 1989 he went on to hold court in a wareHouse – which he would subsequently dub the Sound Factory – situated in Manhattan's West Side.

Over the next six years, bringing back the notion that one DJ should play all night, Vasquez's fourteen-hour sets broke tracks in the same way Levan and Tony Humphries had done years earlier. His pas-

sion for East Coast hip-hop's raw bass-lines, sparse beats and breaks transferred itself to a penchant for semi-minimalist, percussive and often aggressive House tracks, creating a sound that journalists, producers and labels would dub "Tribal House". Inventive and unique, Vasquez's three-turntable sets took the dedicated crowd of voguers, dancers and club kids upward and onward as the night progressed, dropping in Sade, Ambient and "Looney Tunes" cartoon cuts alongside amplified sirens and technical trickery to break up the monotony and add a sense of both style and humour. Testament to his influence, at one stage *New York Magazine* modestly pronounced him "the World's Greatest DJ....Messiah Of Dance", DJ Duke and Angel Moraes both made tribute records to his club and major labels cried out for a Vasquez remix in a vain attempt to gain credibility for pop stars stretching from Cyndi Lauper to David Bowie.

However, Vasquez's early records proved he was a far better DJ than producer. Debuting under the persona of Ellis Dee, early '90s cuts like "Work This Pussy", "I Wanna" and the subtle "Cum On U Can Get It" hardly registered off his own turntables and were later collected on the instantly forgettable album, **Just Like a Queen**.

1993's throbbing remix of Pascal Bongo Massive's "Pere Cochon" was an acknowledged improvement though, harnessing what would become his recognisable tribal drum pattern. In 1994 he took the formula to its creative extreme, turning out a stunning percussive mix of Lectroluv's "Dream Drums" for Eightball Records. However, with the exception of the thundering trannie anthem "Get Your Hands Off My Man", most of Vasquez's cuts from 1994 to 1996 never inspired the same way that his Sound Factory sets did. All of his twisting, sexually charged cuts weren't created for anywhere else but his own club and must rank as part of the reason for its success. "X" was about a group of Sound Factory voguers called House Of Extravaganza, while "Get Your Hands Off My Man" was an angry drag queen diatribe about the girls who "stole" the bisexual boys.

Although at one point UK club owners were reputedly prepared to pay up to £10,000 for an exclusive Vasquez set, he has been unable to translate his DJing successfully overseas. Since the demise of the Sound Factory, Vasquez seems to have found it hard to re-capture the vibe which made the New York club so legendary.

Performances at London's Ministry Of Sound and Liverpool's Cream were received with comparative indifference and Juniorverse, the massive event at London Arena where he was scheduled to play in 1996, was cancelled. Vasquez has struggled to forge a new base in NYC as well. He was lured to spin at the Tunnel in 1995, later at Peter Gatien's Palladium club and back to the old Sound Factory space, Twilo, amidst a well-publicised bust up with former resident Danny Tenaglia.

⊙ "Get Your Hands Off My Man"   Tribal Records, 1994

Vasquez's bad-ass trannie anthem still sounds incredible when played as God intended – from the bowels of a fierce club sound system.

⊙ FSNY – Future Sound of New York   Ministry Of Sound, 1995

At the height of the Sound Factory's reputation, the Ministry had the marketing savvy to release a mix by Vasquez which features his best productions and the progressive garage sound he helped inspire.

Johnny Vicious

Alongside Danny Tenaglia, DJ Duke and Junior Vasquez, ex-metal head/producer/DJ Johnny Vicious helped re-define the sound of disco during the mid-'90s and thus re-established NYC's significance in the ever-shifting House equation. Given a free rein over Salsoul's back catalogue, the self-confessed sample-head conspired to bring his rock background to the doorstep of disco's most famous label, earning himself a reputation through a series of radical 12" remixes that spawned the moniker "punk-disco".

Vicious began DJing in New Jersey aged 19, subsequently holding court at the Palladium club and working as a studio technician before making a life-changing visit to Junior Vasquez's Sound Factory. The minimalist, steel-edged sounds of Tribal House which so often eminated from Vasquez's turntables have had a clear influence on Vicious' stripped-down production style, but it was a lucky break that changed the course of his career. While DJing in Asbury Park, New Jersey, Vicious was lucky enough to meet the owner of Double J/Salsoul Records, Jack Cayre, and after successfully turning his hand to remixing one of the label's famed acapellas, was given a free run of the legendary imprint's back catalogue.

Using the old 2.5" masters, Vicious made his mark with his energised, punctured cut-ups of classic vocal acapellas, the most popular of which was Loleatta Holloway's "Stand Up" (1994). Coupling the disco queen's vocals from her 1976 ballad "Dreaming" with a militant, stripped-down groove and agressive Techno-styled melodies, the track became a favourite in NYC and with British DJs like Terry Farley when licensed to the Network Records subsidiary, Six6. Based around one of Philadelphia International's greatest hits, 1994's JV vs MFSB's "TSOP (The Sound Of Philadelphia)" was also a major dancefloor sensation.

As proprieter of Vicious Muzik, Vicious also produced massive club cuts of his own making, cutting through dancefloors with his extreme Hard-House 12"s, "Frozen Bass" and "Liquid Bass" (both 1994). Girl's "Activator" and a wired remix of Deee-Lite's "Bring Me Your Love" served to further solidify his burgeoning mid-'90s reputation.

Though things have slowed down a little since then, Vicious has continued to produce well-regarded and sometimes inventive soundclashes based on similar principles. While less than thrilling grooves like Houztown's "Robots/Danger" have disappointed, cuts like Noise Maker's "Moments" – a dirty, building remake of Art Of Noise's "Moments in Love" – have shown glimpses of his potential. In 1997, Vicious was to be found once again cutting up Salsoul greats, tempering his previous extremes with more conventionally tough, filtered mixes of Loleatta Holloway's "Hit & Run" and First Choice's "Let No Man Put Asunder".

⊙ **Loleatta Holloway: "Stand Up"**   Vicious Muzik/Network, 1994

A fierce, punctuated cut-up of the Salsoul standard that led to the sub-sub-genre, "punk-disco".

Wamdue Kids

Despite the name, the Wamdue Kids (short for "What I'm Gonna Do") is strictly a one-man affair. Atlanta-born producer Chris

Brann may well have hooked up with like-minded DJs Deep C and X-Press to complete the line-up in 1994, but the stream of predominantly ethereal and spaced-out grooves which have emanated from their Deep South refuge have nearly all had only his name on the production credits.

Brann's career effectively began with the release of the stunning four-track **Wamdue Kids** EP (1995) for Atlanta's tiny indie label, Bahari Records. The emotive piano hook and impassioned spoken-word of "This Is What I Live For" and the soothing jazz-flavoured "In My Soul" marked him out as a talent of startlingly creative ability.

After a few more well-regarded releases, Brann's trickling pianos, warm strings and rolling grooves were brought to the attention of Strictly Rhythm's Gladys Pizarro via his productions for vocalist Ira Levi, and an album was commissioned. Brann's debut, **Resource Toolbook Volume 1** (1996), was an accomplished and eclectic masterpiece that expanded his serene four-to-the-floor vision across innovative Down Tempo, Ambient and drum 'n' bass landscapes. The Wamdue Kids then released the equally excellent **These Branching Moments** for Peacefrog Records in 1996. Perhaps less all-encompassing than Brann's debut, this album's warm and reflective House-based melodies nonetheless still veered close to Deep House perfection.

A willingness to experiment was again evident on the 1996 Techno-slanted **Deep Dreams** EP and the haunting **Ocean Between Us** EP. However, the diversification toward aggressive drum and piercing bass workouts yielded a comparatively texture-less compilation album, **Wamdue Works** (1996), for Berlin's Studio K7 label.

Remarkably, since then, as Brann's reputation spiralled across Europe, much of his work lost its once seemingly effortless emotion. While 1997's excellent **Studies in Form** EP and **Smuthullet** EP proved Brann was still more than capable of moments of genius, album releases **Club Fall** (1997) and **Program Yourself** (1998) were disappointing

because they gave precedence to commercial concerns at the expense of quality.

Then again, Brann's 1998 remix of Naked Music NYC's "It's Love" and his self-produced **Cascades of Colour** EP (1998) for NiteGrooves have proved two of his most mesmerising outings yet even though they both failed to make a noticeable impact on either the dancefloor or the charts.

⊙ **Wamdue Project: Resource Toolbook Volume 1**   Strictly Rhythm, 1996

Brann's first album remains his creative highpoint and one of the dance debut's of the '90s.

Michael Watford

While Robert Owens is *the* voice of Deep House and Byron Stingley remains the ultimate falsetto of '90s disco, it is Michael Watford who has captured the guts and soul of garage. Though born in the Deep South, Watford will be forever associated with New Jersey, his home both geographically and spiritually.

Having joined the gospel group The Disciples Of Truth aged only five years old, Watford's church-trained larynx first graced a four-to-the-floor backbone as a backing vocalist on various Smack team productions. These went largely unnoticed though, and he first rose to prominence with the deep and dub-inflected Roger Sanchez collaboration "Holdin' On" (1991). He then signed to East West Records after building up a club following in NYC thanks in part to the S-Man's influential Ego Trip nights and his growing stature with Strictly Rhythm.

While the lyrics never strained the imagination, Watford's gutsy, gospel-driven voice resonated over the sequential, R&B-styled "Luv-4-2" and the sparser rhythms of 1994's towering gospel-House 12" "Michael's Prayer". In fact, so individual and powerful was his voice on such singles that journalists such as *DJ Magazine*'s Phil Cheeseman would question why Watford didn't take his inherent talents to the R&B payroll in the States and earn himself some real cash. He didn't and the formula finally produced two club classics with 1994's piano-driven

"So Into You", mixed by Bobby D'Ambrosio and Smack, and the MAW production of "My Love".

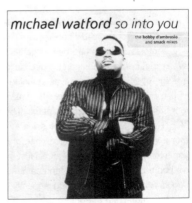

After a series of hot and sweaty live performances at Little Louie Vega's Sound Factory Bar sessions and Paul "Trouble" Anderson's Loft club, Watford achieved more limited success with the Farley

& Heller-produced "Love Changeover" and somewhat flaccid "Come Together" singles, released on the Leeds-based Hard Times imprint.

Subsequent excursions for London's Azuli Records, the 12"s "I'm Coming Home" and "You Got It", fared better, the latter becoming a firm favourite with South London's champagne-guzzling crew when remixed by "speed garage" dons Tuff Jam. In 1998 Watford returned from a lenghty hiatus, again with a distinctly UK-garage-flavoured single, "As Always".

⊙ Michael Watford East West, 1994

This is the cheapest way to pick up his three essential singles, "So Into You", "Holdin' On" and "Michael's Prayer".

Way Out West

The backgrounds of DJs/studio musicians Nick Warren and Jody Wisternoff ensured whatever they produced would be of considerable interest. Warren had been a gamekeeper at Gary Glitter's Sussex estate, before handing in his deerstalker and heading to Bristol at the age of 21. By 1990 he was spinning at the city's first real Acid House club Vision, playing tracks he'd made in his kitchen on a simple four-track mixer with an eclectic range of breaks and *Bladerunner* samples. He later DJd alongside Massive Attack on their first American tour a year later. Wisternoff, born and bred in the outskirts of Bristol some ten years after Warren, got his first musical break aged 14, when his home-produced hip-hop tape came to the attention of local producers Smith & Mighty. He subsequently began to work with DJ Die, now an integral part of Roni Size's drum 'n' bass collective, Reprazent,

and the pair went on to produce a series of highly acclaimed Hardcore EPs on the indie label Earth Records.

The duo's first collaborative effort, 1994's "Paradise" (as Sublove), went largely unnoticed, but served as a raw prototype for Way Out West's trademark mélange of lush, epic soundscapes and energised breakbeats. A few singles down the line and Warren's Balearic/House roots combined with Wisternoff's use of Hardcore's intense drum patterns and sub-heavy bass-lines to produce their first two singles as Way Out West, "Shoot" and "Montana". With an influence from '90s melodic German trance by artists such as Sven Vath, Cosmic Baby and Jam & Spoon, the 4/4, 135 bpm beats and slowed-down, half-speed melodies made their tracks immediate club favourites across the UK with big-budget DJs like Paul Oakenfold, Pete Tong and Sasha.

Way Out West's second single release on Deconstruction, 1995's cross-over pop-dance hybrid "The Gift", proved the band's most popular to date. Swiping its vocal pattern from Joanna Law's "The First Time Ever I Saw Your Face", "The Gift"'s appearance on a TV advert brought the duo into the limelight.

1995's JFK-sampling "Domination" and perhaps their finest track, "Ajare", followed a similar pattern, while their cinematic re-versioning of Subliminal Cuts' (aka Patrick Prins) "Le Sol et Voleil" (1995) has become a clubland anthem with its building strings and piano breakdown. 1997's self-titled debut album harnessed Prodigy-style Big Beat ("Drive By" and "King Of Pop") alongside the singles, despite never making quite the commercial impact initially expected. While the duo have released little of note since, Warren has continued to DJ across the world, producing several live mix compilations including 1998's **Nick Warren 008 Brazil** for the Global Underground series, while Wisternoff has kept up a residency at Bristol's Lakota club.

⊙ **Way Out West**   Deconstruction, 1997

Expertly produced pop-House debut which shines in its superior moments of breakbeat-ridden trance.

Andrew Weatherall

Born in April 1963, Andrew Weatherall witnessed the '70s punk explosion from the sleepy town of Windsor on the outskirts of London and seemed to connect with all the energy and imagery associated with the scene. As a huge fan of Bowie and The Clash, it is little surprise that Weatherall's music has consistently been characterised by both style and substance.

In 1986 Weatherall joined up with mates Terry Farley and Steve Hall and started the *Boys Own* fanzine. Now legendary, the mag acerbically recorded all that was hot and all that was not about music, football and related capers. In 1988 Weatherall found himself with a regular spot at Danny Rampling's seminal club, Shoom. Over the next few years, an often unshaven and long-haired Weatherall, sporting Sam Walker-style knitted jumpers and old Levis, could be witnessed causing dancefloor mayhem across the capital with his eclectic mixes which would freely cross Italian piano monsters with cut-and-paste indie and dub break-downs.

In 1989, he found himself in the studio working alongside man of the moment Paul Oakenfold on the remix of Happy Mondays' "Hallelu-jah", adding an even slinkier groove to the Manchester band's junk-rock workout. Shortly afterwards, Weatherall took on his first solo remix for Primal Scream, reworking their tortured rock ballad "I'm Los-ing More Than I'll Ever Have" and turning it into the classic "Loaded". Kicking off with Peter Fonda asking, "What is is that you want to do? We wanna be free, to do what we wanna do", the track emerges with familiar Soul II Soul beats, Stones-influenced guitars, retro organs and Bobby Gillespie's almost whispered, spoken-word vocals. The remix's effective simplicity led to commercial success and a partnership was forged which would ultimately produce an album of timeless beauty, Primal Scream's **Screamadelica** (1991).

Further indie reconstructions followed with his epochal reworking of My Bloody Valentine's "Soon" (1990). The standout track from MBV's **Glider** EP, it was created by sampling Westbam's "Alarm Clock" and adding a heavy rumbling bass-line to create an absolute corker that was still getting played four years later by The Chemical Brothers.

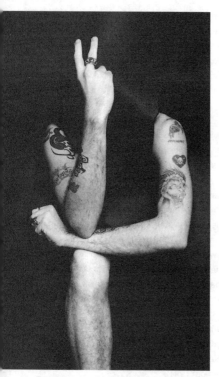

Weatherall captured the moment of Britain's dance explosion brilliantly with his stunning remix of Flowered Up's "Weekender". Perfectly capturing the highs and lows of Saturday E-scapism, Weatherall reworked the track into a twenty-minute epic.

With Scottish group Dove, Weatherall produced a series of sublime singles which culminated in the band's lauded 1993 album, **Morning Dove White**. With partners Jagz Kooner and Gary Burns, Weatherall changed directions and established the swashbuckling Sabres of Paradise label. Despite taking the label's name from the b-side to Hayzee Fantayzee's mid-'80s single, "John Wayne Is Big Leggy", Weatherall's music was becoming increasingly dark and uncomfortable to many ears. Interviews at the time suggested that he was tired of the superficiality of the highs and lows of Ecstasy club culture, which explained his move to the fiercer sounds of Hard House and minimalist dub. His new outlook was fully manifested on the **Sabresonic** album (1993) which included the awesome "Smokebelch".

The follow-up album, **Haunted Dancehall** (1994), was a similar experiment in excessive dub matter. Although slightly disjointed, the varied textures made for better listening. The first single, "The Theme" (1994), was a *Mission Impossible*-style track updated for the smoke-filled '90s, while the follow-up, "Wilmot" (1994), sampled the trumpet sound from Wilmot Houdini & the Night Owls, while taking the bpms all the way down to 84 in this electro-skank work-out. Feeling he was losing the vibe and that the Sabres material was no longer sufficiently cutting-edge, Weatherall closed the label. Once again, as the nation was becoming tuned in to his work, the party host pulled the plug. The other Sabres members, Kooner and Burns, hooked up with Dean Thatcher to add further talent to his Aloof project.

Taking a slightly lower profile, Weatherall's contribution to the **Cut the Crap** compilation (1996) indicated that his love of dub had certainly not waned and reports filtered back of increasing interest in more avant-garde jazz artists as he found little within the traditional rock world to fuel his interest. However, he felt the time was right to start a new label. Emissions Audio Output was split into three parts to accommodate the diversity of its output: Lo-fi, Static, Echoic. Artists on the label included Conemelt, Blue and Deanne Day, with Weatherall recording in partnership with Keith Tenniswood under the name Two Lone Swordsmen, releasing the warped dub-House album **Fifth Mission**. Certainly a smokers' favourite, stand-out tracks included "Rico's Hell", the only track to break into a canter, and "Beacon Block", which moved from gently serene to devilishly psychotic. The follow-up album, **Stockwell Steppas** (1997), had a similarly deep and menacing sound, as did 1998's **Stay Down**.

◉ Primal Scream: Screamadelica   Creation, 1991

A glorious merging of mind and soul. Includes the essential singles "Loaded", "Higher Than the Sun" and "Come Together".

◉ Back2Basics: Cut The Crap   Back2Basics, 1995

Weatherall's mixed CD (compiled for the Leeds Back2Basics club) fuses his menacing Two Lone Swordsmen output with the dub-heavy vibe of Attica Blues and Skylab.

Charles Webster

While DiY may be the Midlands' most famous dance music acolytes, few British producers have made breathtaking Deep House as consistently as Nottingham-based Charles Webster. In a career which began in the mid-'80s with UK breakdance posse The Rock City Crew, he has since recorded well over sixty tracks for labels including his own Love From San Francisco and Remote, as well as Emotive, R&S, Global Cuts, Time and Pagan. That he has never achieved the notoriety of fellow UK innovators Basement Jaxx or Muzique Tropique is partly down to the fact that he has as yet been unable to release an album that would give him both the publicity and scope his work clearly deserves.

Webster moved to Nottingham in 1984, having studied photography at art school and jammed as a keyboard player with various electro-punk bands. After his long since forgotten, raw electro cut "Mile High Club" on his own indie label Aalto Records, Webster graduated to work with early tech-House bods T Cut F. It was as a sound engineer for Network Records' Techno subsidiary, Kool Kat Records, that Webster came into contact with Detroit's Belleville Three of Derrick May, Juan Atkins and Kevin Saunderson, who he admits influenced both the depth and the quality of his own future productions. Indeed, much of his work has crossed the boundaries between House's rhythmic and soulful sensibilities and Techno's angular structures.

Becoming in-House engineer at Nottingham's Squaredance studios he honed output by Brit-Techno acts including Nightmares On Wax and Unique 3. But it wasn't until the turn of the decade that his engineering and production skills began to have a noticeable impact upon British House music. Although his own recordings with producer Dave Thompson as SINE were reasonably well received, it was behind the mixing desks at Thompson's Time Records imprint and DiY's Strictly 4 Groovers label where Webster's touch proved most effective. In 1993, disillusioned with his lack of progress and the state of UK House in general, Webster moved to the warmer and potentially more hospitable climes of San Francisco.

Ditching the Midlands proved a good move. From his West Coast refuge, he formed the Love From San Francisco label with fellow ex-DiY crew members Steve Gray and Damien O'Grady, picking up acclaim for the sublime "Want Me (Like Water)" under his Furry Phreaks moniker. Though the label's output has been tiny – only six releases since its 1993 inception – quality control has been indisputable ever since Webster's debut release under his Presence banner, "My Baby". Arguably his most compelling guise, Presence's deep and groovy sound has since been highlighted on 1995's exceptional "White Powder" and the sax-driven **Florida Fantasy** EP, the chilled grooves of 1996's **Unreleased Stuff Volumes 1 & 2** and one of the best vocal singles of 1997, "Better Day".

Webster has proved able to switch from his deep mode to uplifting piano stormers like 1994's **Happy Trax Volume 6** for Mad Mike's Underground Resistance imprint and Natural's "Switch" for Rey-D Records. He has also turned his hand to rump-shaking, bass-heavy monsters like Hot Lizard's "The Theme" for Pacific Records and Metro Dance's "The Andor Voyage" for Music Man.

Returning to Nottingham in 1995, he achieved wider club success a year later with Furry Phreaks' spacious "Soothe". But the momentum failed to continue and he has gone back underground, starting the Remote label to House essential 12"s like Presence's "Gettin' Lifted" and Symetrics' "Live For Love". With releases on Chicago imprint Guidance, and a project signed to XL Records, Webster's long wait for recognition may be over.

⊙ **"Better Day"**   Pagan Records, 1997

Rated by some critics as the top House single of 1997, Webster's best vocal cut proves why he deserves to be whispered in the same breath as producers like Ron Trent, Chez Damier and Roy Davis Jr.

West End Records

Like their competitors, Prelude, West End Records defined the
sound of disco after it went underground in the face of record-
burning rallies and "Disco Sucks" t-shirts. The label's production techniques and remixes were often directed at the dancefloor of Larry
Levan's legendary Paradise Garage which was one of the venues
where disco mutated into House. With their minimal feel and maximal
groove, the productions of Nick Martinelli & David Todd and Kenton
Nix and mixes by Larry Levan and Walter Gibbons were the direct precursors of House records by the likes of Larry Heard, Blaze and DJ
Pierre.

West End started off in the late '70s with fairly standard disco
tracks like Michelle's "Can't You Feel It" (1977) that filled the floors at
such New York nightspots as the Loft and Odyssey 2000. The label hit
its stride with Walter Gibbons' remarkable remix of Bettye Lavette's
"Doin' the Best That I Can" (1978) which, despite the "dub-House-
disco" dilettantism of labels like Guerilla and Basic Channel, remains
dance music's most effective exploration of the spectral shadows cast
by Jamaican dub's space invaders.

Another early West End classic was Billy Nichols' "Give Your Body
Up to the Music" (1979) whose piano line is the source of nearly all of
the keyboard riffs of the early Chicago House records. The best part of
the record, though, was the breakdown where "Copacabana" Latin
percussion and a "Boogie Oogie Oogie" bass-line fused to produce
three minutes of disco bliss. Proto-House keyboards and the skipping
hi-hats of garage were ushered in in Taana Gardner's "Work That
Body" (1979) which could easily find a place in Terry Farley's record
box today.

Seven more bpm and nobody would have batted an eyelash if Danny Rampling had dropped Loose Joints' "Is It All Over My Face" (1980) at Shoom. One of the great Arthur Russell's many House ancestors, "Is It All Over My Face" was a masterpiece of compressed dynamics and rhythmic minimalism that inspired numerous House producers, particularly Roger Sanchez who pilfered it for his own "Luv Dancin'". While "Is It All Over My Face" was a cult hit in New York, West End's most famous record practically started a stampede at the city's record stores. Sporting a nifty Larry Levan mix, brilliant production by Kenton Nix and one of the most famous bass-lines in the history of dance music (check out Ini Kamoze's "Hot Stepper" or Treacherous Three's "Heartbeat" or...), Taana Gardner's "Heartbeat" (1981) sold 100,000 copies during its first week of release in the Big Apple alone.

With a mighty Shep Pettibone dub that made the most of a killer synth line, Stone's "Time" (1981) was another huge hit for West End and the shrill vocals seemed to pave the way for Madonna. The label's hot streak continued with more proto-House courtesy of Sparque's "Let's Go Dancing" (1981), the dubby boogie of Martinelli/Todd's mix of Brenda Taylor's "You Can't Have Your Cake and Eat It Too" (1982), Mahogany's "Ride on the Rhythm" (1982) and the eternal "Do It to the Music" by Raw Silk (1982), whose "music's hypnotising" line has been sampled seemingly hundreds of times.

Again, just like Prelude, West End's best moments were behind it by 1983 when lacklustre records by the Shirley-Lites ("Heat You Up (Melt You Down)") and Sybil Thomas ("Rescue Me") were all the label seemed to be able to produce. West End's swansong was probably Barbara Mason's "Another Man" (1983). The song itself was a pretty tawdry answer song to her '60s classic "She's Got the Papers (I've Got the Man)", where the man she stole turned out to be gay, but the production, especially a sub-bass riff that hip-hop crews like EPMD would kill for, was a landmark of '80s funk and would be borrowed by electro-funkateers like World Class Wrecking Cru a couple of years later. With this record, as with Prelude's release of Jocelyn Brown's "Somebody Else's Guy", West End seemed to sow the seeds of its own demise.

⦿ Various Artists: The West End Story Volumes 1 and 2   Unidisc, 1992

They don't always use the best mixes, but these two volumes are the best overviews of West End available. Volumes 3 and 4 are a series of diminishing returns.

Wildchild

Though Roger McKenzie (aka Wildchild) tragically passed away in 1996, in the short time he'd been producing he had already left an indelible mark on the UK House scene. Having relocated to Brighton in 1990 from his native Southampton, McKenzie became a fixture on the South Coast's rave scene with his cut-and-paste virtuosity behind the turntables.

It was these technical skills that also marked his move into production with a series of steel-edged, sample-heavy House 12"s for Brighton's Loaded label. McKenzie's debut, the **Wildtrax EP** (1992), sold around 5,000 copies, and the tag "British Todd Terry" did no harm at all to McKenzie's reputation. "Bitch" and "Bad Boy Soundclash" (both 1992) followed on Eric Powell's estimable Bush Records. 1993's **Wildtrax Volume 2** sealed the momentum with the brassic, hip-hop-styled "Jump To My Beat" becoming a club monster. Perhaps more surprisingly, these tracks also became popular in the States, especially in NYC, where Hard-House fetishism had become all the rage thanks to the popularity of Junior Vasquez's Sound Factory and the breed of new record labels like Power Music, Tribal and Relief.

As a result of his popularity, in 1994 McKenzie made the move to Brooklyn to set up Dark Black Recordings. He subsequently became

one of the only British artists at that time to record for respected US labels, releasing energised instrumentals for Groove On (Jimbalaya's "Have a Good Time"), Strictly Rhythm and Vibe.

Originally released in 1995 (peaking at #11 in the UK charts), McKenzie's most effective single achieved the most commercial success after his death. With its unstoppable rapped refrain, "Back once again with the renegade master/Beat boy damager with the ill behaviour", superfly bass-line and funky guitar riff, "Renegade Master" sent crowds wild, becoming a massive club hit at both House and Big Beat nights and reaching #2 in UK charts in 1998.

⊙ The Wildchild Experience –
The Best Of Wildtrax   Loaded Records, 1995

From the steel-edged, pumping grooves of "Bring It Down" to the cut-and-paste dynamics of "Keep It Going" and deeper melodies of "Meet the Pressure", hip-hop's energised aesthetic is forever present. Also includes the enduring order to dance, "Jump To My Beat".

⊙ "Renegade Master"   Polydor, 1998

Cheeky, cheesy, and irresistible.

Boo Williams

E xemplifying the hard, insistent, minimal sound of Chicago's Relief label, Boo Williams was one of the figureheads of the Windy City's mid-'90s revival. His "Midnight Express" (1995) 12" was a minimal funk workout of note. An underground club smash, the single was followed by the equally pumping, stripped-down sound of "A New Beginning". Both tracks have stood the test of time to become revered classics with DJs like London's Terry Farley. Williams' work on flat-mate Glenn Underground's **Parables of SJU** in 1996 also garnered him notable respect amongst Deep House lovers with the album marking a shift towards a "live", jazz-based sound from collaborators Underground, Williams, Brian Harden and Timothy Jaz.

Williams' 1997 debut album for Relief, **Home Town Chicago**, was somewhat luke-warm, however. The addictive melodies and analogue funk were still present on cuts like "Lazy Mood" and "Devil Music", but many felt other tracks simply sounded like a mélange of overly simple synth-hooks and 909 drum patterns. Since Relief closed down in March 1998, Williams has been involved in numerous productions, most notably for Chicago's Guidance label, but none have lived up to his one glistening moment, "Midnight Express".

⊙ **The Future Sound Of Chicago**   Ministry Of Sound,1995

Sublime compilation of the Cajual/Relief story up to the heady days of 1995. Mixed by Cajmere and DJ Sneak, it includes Boo Williams' steaming "Midnight Express" alongside essentials from Gemini, Green Velvet and Glenn Underground.

Josh Wink

I n an age of "faceless Techno bollocks", Philadelphia's Josh Wink injected a sharp dose of personality into the DJ-producer blueprint. With his long white dreads, healthy lifestyle (he's a drug-free, vegetarian fitness buff) and pioneering sound, he was always going to stand out from the crowd.

He had first shown signs of greatness as a teenager, spinning eclectic sets at various bars and parties in Philly after being weaned on the likes of Run DMC and Depeche Mode by liberal parents. By 1990 he had recorded his first tune, "Tribal Confusion", as E-Culture with fellow Philly man King Britt, a partnership which flourished as remix outfit Winking (Cover Girls, Datura, Rozalla, 4 Hero) and later came to fruition with the formation of their Ovum Recordings imprint in 1994.

His biggest impact on the dancefloor was to help re-popularise the Roland TB303, the machine that produced the infamous Acid squelch, with 1995's "Higher State of Consciousness" – a raging, abrasive breakbeat monster that looped a succession of mad, Acid riffs into a frenzied howl of screaming bleeps and pure white noise. It somehow connected with mainstream audiences and was topping charts all over Europe in 1995.

Wink followed up this success with more 303-inspired moves, most notably "Don't Laugh" (which featured a synthesised maniacal cackle from Wink) and "I Am Ready" (reworked to dancefloor-devastating effect by Dutch Acid-Techno wizard DJ Misjah). However, he came a bit unstuck with his debut album, 1996's **Left Above the Clouds**.

Although it featured the aforementioned singles, the rest of the material comprised studio meandering, "humorous" interludes and, erm, poetry. It echoed the "concept albums" of yesteryear and was panned by many critics.

Maybe as a result of this backlash, Wink retreated from the media spotlight for nearly two years. Cutting down on his DJ dates and working hard on developing the standing of Ovum Recordings, he set about fashioning a more mature and streamlined follow-up album, **HearHear** (1998). With a more freeform and mellow first half, building to his trademark minimal Techno bangers, **HearHear** answered Wink's critics in fine style.

⊙ **"Higher State Of Consciousness"**   Strictly Rhythm, 1995

A primeval howl into the electronic wilderness, this is the definitive Acid breakbeat workout.

Yoshitoshi Recordings

Yoshitoshi Recordings is part of a three-label triad owned and operated by Maryland-based House producers Ali "Dubfire" Sharizina and Sharam Tayebi, better known as Deep Dish. As DJs who had both lost regular gigs over a refusal to comply with what they called "the infestation of cheese" dominating clubs and radio, Deep Dish were determined to see their sonic visions realised. Even if it meant finding their initial successes on the other side of the Atlantic.

Their first imprint, Deep Dish Recordings, was formed in 1992 with a co-production called "A Feeling" under the Moods moniker, but it was the next two releases, from an old school mate of Sharizina's from

Washington DC that would help garner the label its earliest recognition. Brian Transeau (later known as BT) joined forces with Deep Dish to co-produce "The Moment Of Truth" (1993) and have them remix "Relativity". Both are vital points in tracing the history of the American progressive House/trance continuum.

Yoshitoshi launched in 1994 with Submarine's self-titled single, followed by the hip-hop-oriented Middle East Recordings, which completed the triad. It is Yoshitoshi that has emerged as the flagship, consistently sharpening its sound to the delight of DJs and dancefloors world-wide. By their fifth release, "Give Me Luv" by Alcatraz, Yoshitoshi had a certified club hit in the UK.

After an introduction from New York garage DJ/producer Danny Tenaglia, Yoshitoshi created an alliance with Tribal America/Tribal UK at the end of 1994. This brought further exposure of the Yoshitoshi sound in the UK over the next year with a string of Deep Dish-helmed singles for Tribal like "The Dream" (by Deep Dish Presents Prana), "Wear The Hat", "Up In This House" (as NYDC) and "Sexy Dance" (Deep Dish Presents Quench D.C.) (all 1995).

Yoshitoshi released a full-length compilation through Tribal in 1996 called **In House We Trust** which was mixed by Dubfire and Sharam.

Tribal went out of business in 1996, but a working relationship with Tribal founders Rob DiStefano and Mark Davenport was rekindled two years later after the pair had established a new label, Twisted. Twisted released two volumes of **One Nation Under House**, a collection comprised of Yoshitoshi singles, in 1998.

Throughout the course of the label's history the focus has been on nurturing and developing new artists, deflecting the spotlight away from themselves. They have stuck by artists such as Mysterious People, Kings Of Tomorrow, Joystick and Chiapet for several years now, adding newer talents like German producer Heiko Laux and Los Angeles-based Eddie Amador, who scored one of the label's biggest anthems with the nostalgic and elegant "House Music" (1998).

⊙ One Nation Under House Vols. 1 & 2   Twisted, 1998

While Yoshitoshi will probably always remain primarily a vinyl-lover's label, they are still thoughtful enough to round up CD collections every so often. If pressed for choice pick up **Volume 1**, with essential cuts like Eddie Amador's "House Music" and Heiko Laux's "Dedicated To All Believers" .

Kevin Yost

E merging from the isolated backwaters of Pennsylvania, Kevin Yost has become one of House's most musically adept producers since releasing his 1996 **Unprotected Sax** EP on Chicago's Guidance Records. With the emphasis firmly rooted in a "live" sound, Yost has so far pushed his polished jazz-inflected, ultra-percussive sound on a series of instrumental 12"s that have successfully steered clear of the well-worn sample ethic.

While the acclaimed **Unprotected Sax** may have set the stage with its wayward sax cut, "So Far Away", and the chilled vibes of "Amor Unico", Yost exceeded all expectations with his follow-up, the **Night Of a Thousand Drums** EP (1996). Recorded for the New Jersey-based I Records (home to cut-up king Todd Edwards), the EP's standout track, "One Starry Night", remains his finest moment. A timeless piece of crisp, late-night deepness, the record left both jazz aficionados like Giles Peterson and House heads like Little Louie Vega and Justin Robertson completely spellbound by such an accomplished production.

Yost's passion for freeform jazz and live instruments which had been evident on the xylophone-led "Hip On You" (1996) became more apparent on his **Plastic Jazz** EP (1997), where his innovative use of samples, raw instrumentation and driving rhythm confirmed his place alongside Deep House mainstays such as Glenn Underground. The **Dawn Approaches** EP (1997) followed a similar path on "Round 'Bout Midnight" and "Unpredictable U", but the sirens, flute hook and funk-driven bass-line of "Spring Again" made this EP perhaps his most dancefloor-friendly release.

Yost's 1997 **Thesticksandstones EP** for I Records again featured his trademark tinkling ivories and sweet guitar licks on "On My Way" but veered into harder, more conventional, stabbing organ sounds on the disappointing "Hypnotic Progressions" cuts. Thankfully, he steered straight back to his best for "The Things We Do" on the **Fourth Avenue Project** EP.

His mixing talents haven't gone unnoticed by other labels eager to benefit from his production skills, and in 1998 he remixed both Josh Wink and Shazz. The same year also found him mixing **In Motion Volume 2** for Distance Records, ensuring his widening popularity.

◉ **"One Starry Night"**   I Records, 1997

A phenomenal slice of smooth, Latin-tinged Deep House that's so simple it's timeless. Available on **Copamundial Muzique** (Guidance, 1998).

◉ **"2 Wrongs Making It Right"**   Guidance Records, 1997

One of Guidance Records' best releases to date. Available alongside his "So Far Away" cut on **Hi Fidelity House Imprint Two** (Guidance Records, 1998).

Stay in touch with us!

ROUGHNEWS is Rough Guides' free newsletter.
In three issues a year we give you news, travel issues, music reviews, readers' letters and the latest dispatches from authors on the road.

I would like to receive ROUGH*NEWS*: please put me on your free mailing list.

NAME . . . .

ADDRESS . . . .

Please clip or photocopy and send to: Rough Guides, 1 Mercer Street, London WC2H 9QJ, England

or Rough Guides, 375 Hudson Street, New York, NY 10014, USA.

ROUGH GUIDES: Travel

ROUGH GUIDES: Mini Guides, Travel Specials and Phrasebooks

MINI GUIDES
Antigua
Bangkok
Barbados
Big Island of Hawaii
Boston
Brussels
Budapest
Dublin
Edinburgh
Florence
Honolulu
Lisbon
London Restaurants
Madrid
Maui
Melbourne
New Orleans
St Lucia

Seattle
Sydney
Tokyo
Toronto

TRAVEL SPECIALS
First-Time Asia
First-Time Europe
More Women Travel

PHRASEBOOKS
Czech
Dutch
Egyptian Arabic
European
French

German
Greek
Hindi & Urdu
Hungarian
Indonesian
Italian
Japanese
Mandarin
 Chinese
Mexican
 Spanish
Polish
Portuguese
Russian
Spanish
Swahili
Thai
Turkish
Vietnamese

AVAILABLE AT ALL GOOD BOOKSHOPS

ROUGH GUIDES:
Reference and Music CDs

REFERENCE
Classical Music
Classical:
   100 Essential CDs
Drum'n'bass
House Music

World Music:
   100 Essential CDs
English Football
European Football
Internet
Millennium

ROUGH GUIDE
   MUSIC CDs
Music of the Andes
Australian
   Aboriginal
Brazilian Music
Cajun & Zydeco
Classic Jazz
Music of Colombia
Cuban Music
Eastern Europe
Music of Egypt
English Roots
   Music
Flamenco
India & Pakistan
Irish Music
Music of Japan
Kenya & Tanzania
Native American
North African
Music of Portugal

Jazz
Music USA
Opera
Opera:
   100 Essential CDs
Reggae
Rock
Rock:
   100 Essential CDs
Techno
World Music

Reggae
Salsa
Scottish Music
South African
   Music
Music of Spain
Tango
Tex-Mex
West African Music
World Music
World Music Vol 2
Music of Zimbabwe

AVAILABLE AT ALL GOOD BOOKSHOPS